THE

FLEETS OF THE WORLD.

THE

FLEETS OF THE WORLD.

THE GALLEY PERIOD.

BY

FOXHALL A. PARKER,

COMMODORE U. S. NAVY,

AUTHOR OF

"FLEET TACTICS UNDER STEAM," "THE HOWITZER AFLOAT," &c.

"In the long days and nights of sailing, given over, it is likely, to his own thoughts and the unfathomable dialogue with the ever-moaning brine; not the worst High School a man could have, and indeed infinitely preferable to the most that are going even now, for a high and deep young soul."—CARLYLE.

NEW YORK:

D. VAN NOSTRAND, PUBLISHER,

23 MURRAY ST. AND 27 WARREN ST.

1876.

TO

HIS BROTHER SEAMEN

OF EVERY CLIME,

THIS VOLUME

IS DEDICATED.

BY

THE AUTHOR.

CONTENTS.

ILLUSTRATIONS.

PREFACE.

While the great land battles of the world have been described by the ablest historians and the most eloquent orators, while military chieftains have ever been attended through life by enthusiastic admirers, who have recorded their every action, and each word that has fallen from their lips, thus ensuring the transmission of their fame to remotest posterity, great sea fights, upon whose issue has not unfrequently hung the fate of Empires and of States, have received from history and oratory, alike, but a passing notice, while the principal actors in many of them have sunk into such oblivion with the tomb, that their very names are unknown to us. Therefore, in preparing this volume for publication, the author had it in view to give some account of the fleets which from time to time have made their appearance upon the deep, together with a sketch of the gallant men who organized and fought them—a laborious and, perhaps, a thankless task, but one which seemed imposed upon him by his profession.

In furtherance of this view, he read, and carefully collated, the various, and too often conflicting, statements of all the authorities upon the subjects of which he treats, that he was enabled to get hold of, using his judgment, as a seaman, as to their special and relative value; and being careful not to follow in the track of those who have unscrupulously sacrificed *truth* to the *picturesque.*

In treating of the Norsemen, however, he was compelled, in order to give a connected account of their spirited and sanguinary engagements, to fill up many blanks in the relations of Snorro Sturleson and others; but being mindful, in so doing, to adhere rigidly to the Norse mode of fighting, and to introduce no episode not in strict accordance with the character, manners, superstitions and religious observances of the Norse people, he confidently believes he here presents to the public the most correct *marine* picture of Scandinavia yet drawn.

Should the author be encouraged to persevere in his undertaking, he will be enabled, in future volumes, to take his readers over more certain ground. Together they will visit Van Tromp and De Ruyter in the British Channel, Blake at Santa Cruz, Rodney in the Antilles, and Suffren off Trincomalee; and later, from the quarter-deck of the Victory, behold the magnificent fleet led by Nelson, as it "sweeps through the deep," on its way to Trafalgar, where the mighty hero fell.

Finally, leaving the Eastern Hemisphere, they will see, passing before them in regular succession, those famous sea-captains whose deeds of daring have emblazoned the naval annals of the United States.

THE FLEETS OF THE WORLD.

THE GALLEY PERIOD.

CHINA.

HORACE, in one of his Odes, celebrates, or rather inveighs against the sublime hardihood of the man who first invaded the dominion of Neptune in a frail bark, rudely constructed by unskilful hands. The invective of the poet, if we may believe the annals of the Chinese, must surely have fallen upon the head of some unfortunate Chinaman, long after his body had been consigned to an earthy or a watery grave; and it is much to be regretted that the name of this "ancient mariner," whose "breast and ribs were brass,"[1] with a live-oak backing, has not been handed down to us, either by the historian or the Roman lyrist; nor shall we ever know, in all probability,—for neither the American nor the European constructors will be likely to tell us,—whether or not his exhumed frame served as a model for our modern iron-clads. All that we can conjecture with any degree of certainty is, that the poor fellow, like the seaman of the present day, fared badly, during his life, on "hard tack," greasy pork and "salt junk," and was quickly forgotten when he died. Certain it is, however, that the art of navigation died not with him; for his countrymen, possessing a knowledge of the properties of the magnet,[2] long before its use was understood by the other nations of the earth, were enabled by it to extend their commerce at a very remote period along the

2

coast of Hindostan, and across the Arabian Sea, even to the Persian Gulf.

With an eye painted on the bows of their cruisers, to inculcate, most probably, the necessity of watchfulness, and their compasses, rudders and cables adorned with stripes of red cloth—the color red being sacred to some one of their marine divinities—they ventured boldly to sea, in the full faith that their watchful pilots and well-trained seamen, whom they not inaptly denominated "eyes and ears," would guide them safely to the "haven where they would be." In fine weather all the crew worshipped, morning and evening, before the shrine of the *Queen of Heaven*—the sailor's patron saint; but, when storms arose, and the whole fury of the Wind Spirit was upon them, they burnt gilt paper, and made other offerings to the *devil*, whose wrath they desired to appease; it being their doctrine that fair winds came direct from Heaven, while foul ones received their life-destroying mission from Satan himself! That this *devil-worship* has descended to our own times, I myself was a witness, in the year 1850, at Singapore.

Thus, with the assistance of the gentleman in black, the Chinese were getting along very comfortably; and they would, no doubt, have soon made their name known and respected in the four quarters of the globe, but for one of their emperors,—a narrow minded old fellow,—who, fearing lest his subjects, in their intercourse with foreign nations, might imbibe notions dangerous to the State and his dynasty, and subversive of his freedom in the cutting off of heads, issued an edict forbidding them to cruise outside of the sea of China, and directing that his vessels (which are said to have been greatly superior to the modern *junk*) should be so altered as to make them resemble, in shape, one of his royal slippers. This entirely put a stop to distant navigation, as it had the effect of rendering the vessels somewhat unmanageable, and made it quite impossible for them to make headway against contrary winds. Notwithstanding this, however, the edict is worthy of the seaman's commendation, since, by it, for the first and only time in the world's history, he was placed upon the same footing with his brethren of the land. Nevertheless, it gave the *coup de grace* to any further maritime enterprise on the part of the Chinese, whose foreign commerce dates its decline from the very moment of its promulgation, while their Navy, at the present day, serves for little else than to transport troops from one sea-port to another of the "Flowery Kingdom;" this duty being occasionally enlivened by a brush with the pirates who infest every part of their coast, in which the *pirates* usually come off *victorious.* Thus have the mighty fallen!

EGYPT.

Next come the Egyptians; of whose fleets and early voyages, however, we know very little.

Guided by the stars or the compass, tradition represents them as crossing the Indian Ocean and driving a brisk trade with India, whence they carried home pearls and other rare gems, together with spices, and "precious cloths" most elaborately embroidered. Their paintings and sculptures represent their vessels generally as of fair models and propelled by both oars and sails; and Jal, in his *Archéologie Navale*, gives it as his opinion that their war-galleys, in the time of Rhamses IV., differed but little from those built by the Grecians, a thousand years later, and used by them during the Peloponnesian war. One of the *bas-reliefs* at Thebes represents a naval victory gained by the Egyptians over the Indians, about 1400 B. C. The fleet of the former, drawn up in the form of a crescent, seems to be endeavoring to surround that of the latter, which, with oars boarded and sails furled, is calmly awaiting its approach. A lion's head (made of iron or other metal), securely fastened to the prow of each Egyptian galley, shows that *ramming* was then, as now, one of the expedients resorted to for the destruction of an enemy. This *bas-relief* would seem to confirm the statement of Herodotus that the Egyptian men-of-war were manned by soldiers; for the rowers are here represented with quilted bonnets, while the dress and arms of the other men correspond exactly with those of the army. The length of their war-galleys is supposed to have been about one hundred and twenty feet; their breadth, sixteen. Archers were stationed on their raised poops and forecastles, and slingers wherever they could advantageously use their weapons, while the pike, spear, javelin, battle-axe, pole-axe and falchion were kept conveniently at hand for the boarders. A wooden bulwark, rising considerably above the deck, afforded protection to the oarsmen from all missiles not coming vertically toward them; but, to ward off death from the exposed combatants, the bronze helmet, the coat of mail and the great wooden shield[3] covered with tough bull's hide were relied on. The planks, ribs and knees of the Egyptian vessels were of the acacia, but their masts were most probably made of the tall Syrian fir, numberless ship-loads of which were annually imported into Egypt. An immense piece of timber placed on the kelson and extending quite across the bottom of the vessel, served as the step of the mast, which was still further secured by stays and shrouds, and lashed, at the foot, to a stout knee rising to some height in front of it. Their yards were large, subtending a square sail which it is believed was reefed[4] according to the fashion prevailing in our day. In ships of war they always remained aloft, but in merchantmen were lowered to the deck when the sails were furled. Such was the durability of the acacia, such the skill of the Egyptian shipwrights, that a number of Egyptian vessels, two hundred years old, were cruising in the Gulf of Persia, if we may believe the Greeks, at the time of Alexander the Great.

To Isis the Egyptians attribute the honor of having taught men the use of sails; and Tacitus says the Suevians of Germany worshipped her "under the figure of a sailing ship, the symbolic representation of the goddess." According to Wilkinson, many of the Egyptian noblemen's pleasure boats were adorned with linen sails, "richly colored and embroidered with fanciful devices." Purple sails were used by members of the royal household alone; and it was because Cleopatra was queen of Egypt that her galley carried purple sails at the battle of Actium, and not, as is erroneously supposed, because they were the distinguishing mark of an admiral's vessel. In steering their crafts, the Egyptians made use of sweeps or long oars, confined by a strap to an iron pin on the quarter, or working in a groove at the stern, just as we see large lighters steered at the present day. Some of their river boats are represented with a sweep on each quarter. For anchors they used large stones.

PHŒNICIA.

Near Egypt, and in constant communication with it, was the province of Phœnicia, stretching, in length, along the Mediterranean, one hundred and twenty miles, but in breadth not averaging more than three. Its chief cities Tyre and Sidon are frequently mentioned in the Scriptures, and it is to a colony of the latter, which Josiah, fourteen hundred and fifty years before the Christian era, calls "the great Sidon," that the former owes its origin. Tyre, however, soon eclipsed the parent city in wealth and commercial enterprise, and sending forth its redundant population to other shores, it founded Byzantium, Thebes, Carthage and Cadiz. Tyrean galleys, carrying on their prows the brazen image of a cock, the emblem of vigilance, now penetrated to the remotest seas, and about B. C. 1000, when Tyre had attained the summit of power, so absolute was its rule upon the deep that "a Tyrian sea became a proverbial expression for a sea whose navigation was prohibited to all but those who claimed the ownership thereof."

In the year 610 B. C., the Phœnicians, who had then become subject to Egypt, undertook the circumnavigation of

Africa, by order of their sovereign, who was anxious to ascertain the exact form of that country. An account of their voyage is found in Herodotus, whose quaint and concise narrative, I shall give in his own words: "This discovery was first made by Necos, the Egyptian king, who, on desisting from the canal which he had begun between the Nile and the Arabian Gulf, sent to sea a number of ships manned by Phœnicians with orders to make for the Pillars of Hercules, and return to Egypt through them and by the Mediterranean. The Phœnicians took their departure from Egypt by way of the Egyptian Sea, and so sailed into the Southern Ocean. When autumn came, they went ashore, wherever they might happen to be, and having sown a tract of land with corn waited until the grain was fit to cut. Having reaped it, they again set sail; and thus it came to pass that two whole years went by, and it was not till the third year that they passed the Pillars of Hercules, and made good their voyage home. On their return, they declared (I, for my part, do not believe them, but perhaps others may) that, in sailing round Libya, they had the sun upon their right hand. In this way was the extent of Libya first discovered."

About two centuries after their voyage around Africa, the Phœnicians, stretching boldly into the North Atlantic, reached the British Isles, to which they gave the name of the Cassiterrides, or land of tin; "and it is remarkable," says Wilkinson, "that the word *Kassiteros*, used by Homer to designate tin, is the same as the Arabic name *Kasdeer*, by which that metal is still known in the East. It is also called *Kastira* in Sanscrit." As tin was used as an alloy in Egypt and Phœnicia, long before the traders of the latter visited Britain, it is supposed to have been originally imported into those countries from India and Spain; but so anxious were the Phœnicians to confine the knowledge of the rich mines of Cornwall to their own people that a Tyrian vessel bound to Britain, and closely followed by a Roman galley, actually ran upon the hidden rocks off the Scilly Islands, its master preferring to suffer shipwreck with his pursuer rather than to betray the secret of his country's prosperity.

Of Tyre, in the height of her grandeur—when "her wise men were her pilots, and all the ships of the sea were in her harbor"—we have a magnificent picture in the twenty-seventh chapter of Ezekiel the prophet who, with a pen of fire, describes her riches and her pride. Well, then, might "all that handle the oar, all the mariners of the deep," lament for her, with a loud and bitter lamentation when she fell, and cry with one voice: "What city was like Tyrus, like the destroyed in the midst of the sea." Razed to the ground by Nebuchadnezzar, after resisting the whole Babylonian power for thirteen years, "until every head was bald and every shoulder peeled," she rose from her ashes, and again asserted her supremacy on the Mediterranean. Two and a half centuries later, however, she surrendered, after an heroic defense, to the military and naval forces of "the mighty murderer," Alexander the Great, and was utterly blotted out from the list of nations; those of her inhabitants who escaped the sword being sold into slavery.

Aye, Tyre is dead, but the fame of her mariners will *never* die! for their hardihood and daring in rounding the Cape of Storms and in crossing the dread Bay of Biscay are not less worthy of the admiration of mankind, taking into consideration the age in which they lived, than is the exalted courage shown by Magellan and his men, when, reduced to the necessity of eating the strips of hide with which the rigging of their vessel was covered, they still resolutely persevered in their circumnavigation of the globe.

THE GREEKS AND PERSIANS. AN ACCOUNT OF THEIR WAR GALLEYS AND MERCHANTMEN AND OF CERTAIN FAMOUS SHIPS OF ANTIQUITY.

From the Phœnicians the Persians and the Greeks learned the art of constructing and manœuvring the war galleys with which they afterward engaged in that struggle for the mastery of the Ægean Sea which ended so unfortunately for the former; a correct understanding of which cannot be arrived at without a description of their vessels, which I shall here endeavor to give with as much exactness as the meagre accounts and the imperfect representations of them which have come down to our day will permit. They were built of various kinds of wood, but ordinarily of oak or fir, which the Greeks were careful to cut between the 15th and 23rd day of the moon's age, since they firmly believed, according to many of their writers, that wood cut at any other time was unfit for ship building, "it being sure to rot within a year." Whether or not the Persians entertained any such notion, it is impossible for us to find out. The keel being laid, and continued in a curved line up the front, so as to form the stem, served as a foundation for the floor timbers, whose lower ends were let into it and kept in place by the keelson. Next came the futtocks and the upper timbers; and thus the frame, or carcass, as it was called, being complete, the vessel was ready for her outside planking, which was secured to the frame by large iron nails or bolts, clinched on the inside. Alongside the kelson, and near the centre of the hold, was the well where all the bilge-water settled, and was pumped out, as often as was found necessary, by the crew. The space between the kelson and the lower beams, which served to support the deck where the rowers sat, was used for the stowage of provisions, rigging, etc., etc.; and, although it must have been of very limited dimensions in the "long ships," or men-of-war of light draught, whose greatest breadth of beam was not over one eighth of their length, while their lower row-ports are believed to have been but three above the level of the water, yet it no doubt afforded ample room for a people, who, coasting along the shore, obtained their supplies every few days from whatever port they happened to be in. Some of their men-of-war were single-decked, with a high bulwark, some of two decks, and some even of three;

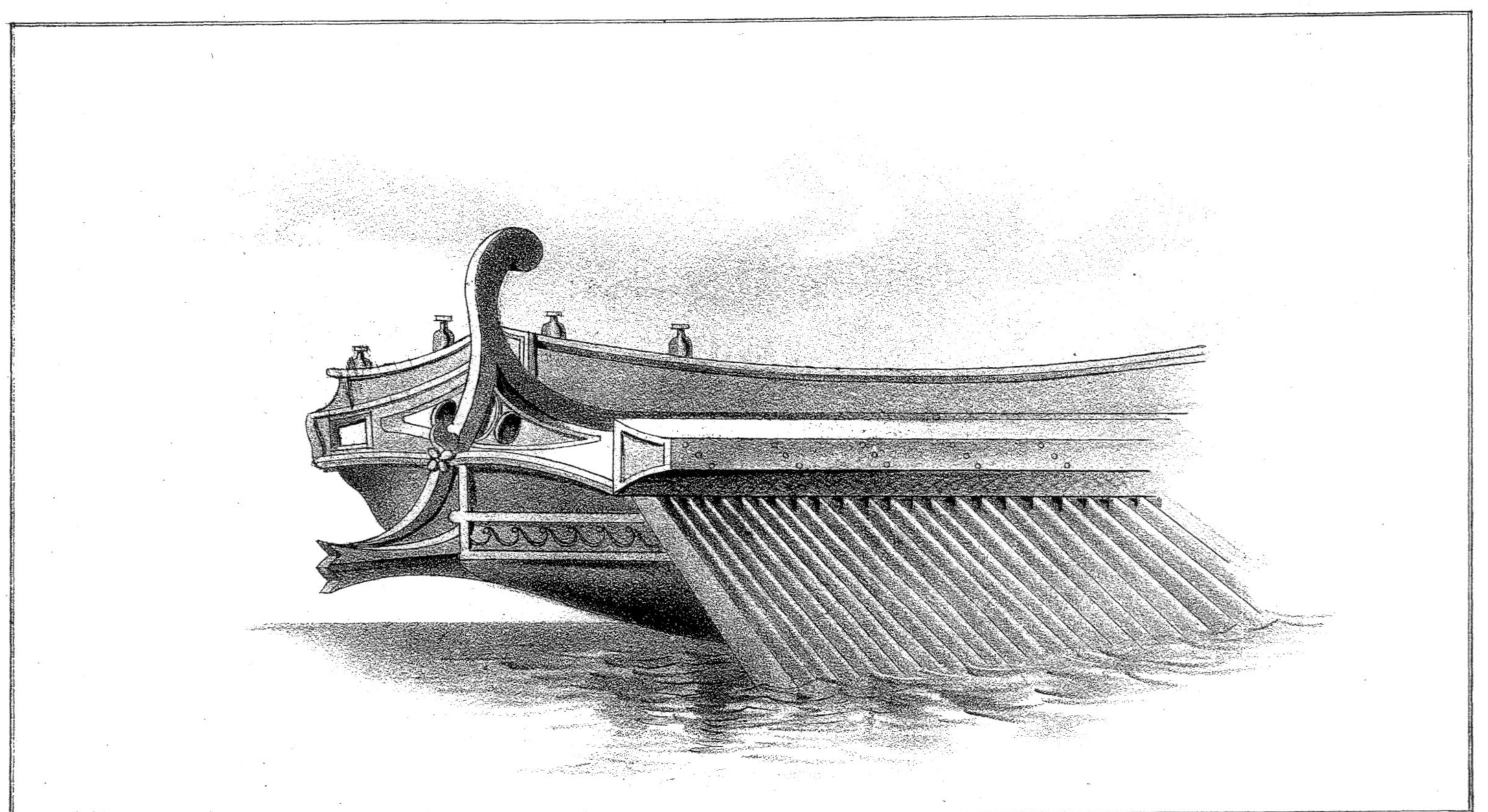

PLATE I

ALBERT ROSS. LIEUT. U.S.N.

AN ANCIENT GALLEY.

but, to suppose that there were more than three tiers of oars, *one above the other*, is absurd. It is possible, and indeed highly probable, that there may have been, in addition to these, long sweeps on the poops and forecastles to assist in turning a vessel round; but the treatises written by scholars, learned in everything except the subject which they have given their opinion upon, to show how any number of oars might have been pulled by placing the benches of the rowers in diagonal ranks one above the other, like a flight of stairs, have only served to convince their readers of their entire misconception of the true meaning of Greek and Latin sea-terms. The force of men on each oar must, of course, have varied with the size of the oar, and this been regulated, in a great degree by its height above the water. In bad weather the lower oars were undoubtedly taken in, and their ports closed. By some antiquaries it has been asserted, that the opening for the oars was continuous throughout the whole length of the vessel; but that the row-ports were separate, is sufficiently proved by the name given to them by the Romans of *columbaria*, or pigeon-holes. The beak was of hard wood, covered with brass, and placed low down, so as to pierce an enemy near the water-line. It was of every conceivable form, and sometimes divided into three sharp prongs, which the Greeks significantly called *teeth*. The masts were of pitch pine, and the sails both square and lateral. Many of the galleys which served as flag-ships carried flame-colored sails; and Alcibiades, who affected regal state, is said by some authors to have entered the harbor of Athens, upon his triumphant return from Byzantium, in a gilded galley with purple sails, and, although Plutarch denies this, it is probably true, since it is quite in accord with the character of the man. The anchors were first of stone, depending entirely upon their weight to keep them on the bottom; next of hollow wood filled with lead, and finally of iron, having arms at their lower ends, curved like a hook; to which indeed they owe the name they still retain,—the Greek word *ancuros* signifying hooked.

Diodorus Siculus relates that a Phœnician merchant captain, having loaded his vessel with silver, in Sicily, until her rail was near the water's edge, extracted the lead from his anchors, and refilled them with the more valuable metal. As a proof that stones were originally used as anchors in Greece, as well as in Egypt, we have the testimony of Aman, a distinguished Greek historian, born at Nicomedia, in Bythinia, about A. D. 100, who says he was shown in a Grecian temple an iron anchor which the priests declared had belonged to the Argo, but which he knew, from its close resemblance to the anchors used in his time, must have been made at a much later period than that assigned to the Argonautic expedition. In an out-of-the-way corner of the temple, however, he afterward espied the crumbling fragments of a stone anchor which he supposes to have been that of Jason's vessel.

Such, in general, were the "long ships" of the ancients, commonly known as galleys, which ploughed the waters of the Mediterranean for three thousand years. Painted with a variety of colors, their nationality was sometimes known, not only by the flags which drooped from their flag-staffs, but also from the images placed on their prows, representing the bird, beast or reptile sacred to the tutelary god or goddess of the country to which they belonged. The conflicting accounts of their speed render it impossible to affirm positively what it really was; but it would seem that under the most favorable circumstances, using oars alone, they could not make more than 100 miles in twenty-four hours though for a *spurt*, as in ramming for instance, they could be forced through the water at the rate of seven knots an hour. According to reliable data, it took a single-decked galley, one hundred and thirty-five feet long, with fifty-two oars, a quarter of an hour to describe the full arc of a circle in turning.

The merchantmen, or "round ships," differed from the galleys in being much shorter and broader. They were flat-floored, drawing but little water, and depending rather upon their sails than upon their oars for making a voyage, they slipped out of port with a fair wind and ran for the nearest anchorage the moment it hauled ahead, since they were but indifferent sailers with the wind forward of the beam. In accompanying a naval armament as transports, they were usually taken in tow by the galleys. Of their internal economy, their neatness and discipline, we get an excellent idea from the admirable description left us by Xenophon.[6] "I remember," said Ischomacus to Socrates, " I once went aboard a Phœnician ship, where I observed the best example of good order I had ever met with; and especially was it surprising to observe the vast number of implements which were necessary for the management of such a small vessel. What numbers of oars and ship-hooks were there for taking the ship in and out of port! What numbers of cables and hawsers for securing her in dock. With how many engines of war was she armed for her defence! What a vast quantity of provisions were there for the sustenance and support of the sailors! And, beside all these, the cargo of the ship was of great bulk, and so rich that the very freight of it was enough to satisfy the captain and his people for their voyage; and it was stowed so neatly that a far larger space on shore would not have contained one-half the articles of which it was composed. Here I took notice that the good order and disposition of everything was so strictly observed that, notwithstanding the great variety of materials the ship contained, there was not anything on board which the sailors could not find in an instant; nor was the captain himself less acquainted with these particulars than his men: he was as ready in them as a man of learning would be to know the letters that compose the name Socrates, and how they stand in that name. Nor did he only know the proper places for everything on board his ship; but while he stood upon the deck he was considering with himself what things might be wanting in this voyage, what things wanted repair, and what length of time his provisions and necessaries would last; for, as he observed to me, it is no proper time when a storm comes upon us, to have the required implements to seek for, or to find them out of repair; for the gods are never favorable to those who are negligent or lazy; and it is their goodness that they do not destroy us when we are diligent."[7]

As to the immense ships mentioned by Diodorus Siculus, Athenæus, Plutarch and others, it is safe to conclude that like the giants of old, they existed only in imagination; since the description given to us of their prows, beaks and rudders, and of the vast number of men required to move them, itself clearly demonstrates that they were *impossible vessels, having no affinity for salt water.*

The particular description of one of these, taken from Athenæus, which Burchett gives us in his "Complete History of the Most Remarkable Transactions at Sea," is so entertaining, however, that we cannot forbear transcribing it for the benefit of such of our readers as may delight in the marvellous: "We should be wanting to the subject we are treating of," says he, "as well as to the respect due to the memory of that great master of the Mechanicks, Archimedes, should we omit giving an account of the famous ship said to have been built by him for Hieron, King of Syracuse, which we cannot better do than in this place. It was so extraordinary a piece of workmanship, that one Moschion wrote a particular treatise concerning the same, the substance whereof Athenæus has preserved to us in the fifth book of his *Deipnosophistæ.* For the building of this ship (he tells us) there was cut down on the mountain Ætna so much timber as would have made sixty ordinary gallies; beside which, the wood for tree-nails, ribs and knees, was procured from other parts of Sicily, and from Italy; and materials for cordage were fetched from Spain and the river Rhodanus, as were other necessaries from various places. King Hieron, having hired a number of shipwrights and other workmen for the service, placed Archias, a Corinthian architect, over them, but all under the supreme direction of Archimedes, and exhorting them diligently to carry on the work, he to encourage them thereto, would be whole days present at their labors.

"The number of men employed was three hundred master-workmen, besides their servants, who in six months time built the ship up to half of its designed height, and as the several parts were finished they covered them with sheet-lead, to preserve them from the weather. When it was brought thus forward, Hieron gave directions for removing it into the sea, and that the rest of the work should be perfected afloat; but how to get this vast pile into the water they knew not, till Archimedes invented the engine called the *helix*, by which, with the assistance of very few hands, he drew the ship into the sea; where, in six months more, she was entirely completed, and driven full of large nails of brass, many of ten pound weight, and others of fifteen, which were let into the timbers by large auger-holes, to rivet them well together, and covered on the outside with pitched cloths, over which were nailed plates of lead.

"The ship had twenty tire of oars, and three decks; to the lowest whereof, next the hold, there was a descent by several pair of stairs. The middle-deck had on each side of it fifteen apartments for dining, each furnished with four couches, such as they used to lie on at their meals; and on the same deck was also the place for the accommodation for the mariners, whereon were fifteen couches, and three large chambers for men and their wives, each having three beds, next which was the kitchen for the poop, the floors of all which were paved with mosaick work, wherein was represented the whole story of the *Iliad;* and suitable to so rich a floor was the workmanship of the ceiling and door to each apartment. On the upper deck was a place for exercise, and a fine walk, wherein were several garden-plots, furnished with plants of all kinds, which were watered by leaden pipes laid to them from a great receptacle of fresh water; where were also several arbors of ivy, and vines set in hogsheads of earth, whose roots were watered in like manner as the plants. Next to these was an apartment devoted to the pleasures of love, the pavement whereof was of agate, and other the richest stones that were to be found in Sicily. The roof was of cyprus-wood, and the doors of ivory, and the wood of the almug-tree. It had three beds in it, and was richly adorned with pictures, statues, and drinking vessels of exquisite workmanship. Adjoining to this was a room for retirement and conversation, which was furnished with five couches, and wainscoted with box, with doors of the same wood ; within this there was a library, and in the ceiling thereof a fine clock, made in imitation of the great dial of Syracuse; as also a bagnio, with three cisterns of brass, and a bath which held forty gallons, adorned with the gems called tauromenites. There were also a great number of cabins for the marine soldiers, together with twenty stables for horses, ten on each side of the deck, with good accommodation for the horsemen and grooms. In the forecastle was the receptacle for fresh water, made of planks, well lined with cloth and pitch, which held two hundred and fifty-three hogsheads; and near that was a well, lined with sheet-lead, which being kept full of sea-water, nourished great numbers of fish. From the ship's sides there jutted out,at a proper distance from each other, several beams, whereon were made places for keeping wood, as also ovens, kitchens, mills, and other necessary offices; each of which beams was supported on the outside by a carved image nine feet high; and the whole ship was very handsomely painted.

"It was also furnished with eight wooden towers, two in the forecastle, two in the poop, and the rest in the midships; from each of which there jutted out two beams, whereon was raised a breast-work, full of loop-holes, from whence an enemy might be annoyed with stones. Each tower was full of those and other missive weapons, and constantly guarded by four soldiers, completely armed, with two archers. On this upper deck there was also raised a stage, with a breast-work round it, whereon was placed a machine invented by Archimedes, which would fling stones of three hundred pound weight, and darts of eighteen feet long, to the distance of a hundred and twenty paces; round which machine was hung, by chains of brass, a kind of curtains, composed of large cables, for its security. The ship was furnished with three masts, and each of them with two engines for throwing stones, from whence also large iron hooks and dolphins of lead were to be flung into an enemy's ship. It was also fortified with an iron palissade all round, to prevent an enemy's boarding, and had grappling irons in readiness in all quarters wherewith to seize and bring to such hostile vessels as it might be engaged with.

"Sixty soldiers, completely armed, kept continual guard on each side of the ship, and as many at each of the masts, and their respective engines. Their round-tops were of brass, wherein was constant watch kept by three men in the main-top, and two in each of the others; to whom, in case of action, stones were to be conveyed in baskets by the help of certain tackle for that purpose, and they were to be supplied with darts and arrows by boys appointed to that service. The fore and mizen masts were without difficulty procured in Sicily; but a main mast of proper dimensions was hard to be got, till at length one was found in the mountains of Britain, which was brought down to the sea by Phileas, an engineer of Tauromenium. The ship was furnished with four anchors of wood and eight of iron. And tho' it was of so vast a depth, its pump, by a device of Archimedes, was managed by one man. She was at first called the Syracuse; but, when Hieron thought fit to send her to Ptolemy, he named her the Alexandria. She had several tenders to accompany her, one whereof was a galley called the Cercurus, and the rest fisher-boats, and other small vessels. Her whole company consisted of an immense multitude, there being in the forecastle alone six hundred seamen, always in readiness to execute such orders as should be given; and the power of punishing all faults and misdemeanors done on board her was committed to the captain, master, and master's mates, who gave sentence according to the laws of Syracuse. There were put on board her sixty thousand bushels of corn, ten thousand barrels of salt-fish, twenty thousand barrels of flesh, and as many bales of goods and necessaries, besides all the provisions for her company. But at length Hieron, finding that all his harbors were either very dangerous for a ship of so vast a burthen. or else not capable at all to receive her (as 'tis reasonable to believe not any of them were), he came to a resolution of presenting her to Ptolemy, King of Egypt, as hath been before observed, to whom she was accordingly sent, being towed in safety to Alexandria. This Ptolemy, surnamed Philopator, was, as Athenæus also tells us, already possessed of two ships of extraordinary dimensions of his own building,—one of which had forty tire of oars, and was four hundred and twenty feet in length, and in breadth fifty-seven ; its height from the keel to the bulkhead of the forecastle was seventy-two feet, and to the poop-lanthorn seventy-nine and a half. When the king made an experiment of her sailing, she carried above four thousand rowers, four hundred seamen, and two thousand eight hundred and fifty marine soldiers, besides a great number of other people between decks, with a vast quantity of provisions."

MINOS, KING OF CRETE, CLEARS THE GRECIAN SEAS OF PIRATES.

Minos, mentioned by Homer as a Phœnician adventurer, chosen by the Cretans to rule over them, seems to have been the first of the Grecian princes who had a naval armament sufficiently powerful to put down the pirates, who, previous to and during the first years of his reign, infested the Grecian Seas to such an extent as to stop commerce, and even to force the inhabitants along the shores to destroy their habitations and retire inland; so that nothing was to be seen on approaching the Grecian coast, but a piratical village, or a poor fisherman's hut. No sooner had piracy been suppressed, however, by the wise Phœnician, than the Greeks turned their attention to maritime affairs, and, building seaboard towns and cities, soon acquired wealth, and, as a natural consequence, power. Among the most important of their commercial towns was Corinth, which, situated on the Isthmus between the Saronic and Corinthian gulfs, soon became the centre of trade, not only between Asia and Europe, but for Greece itself, since "formerly the Grecians, both within and without Peloponnesus, more accustomed to land than sea, could have no traffic with one another, without passing through its territory." To it Thucydides gives the honor of having built the first Grecian men-of-war, and he says further, that Aminocles, a Corinthian ship-carpenter, built four of these vessels for the Samians. "The oldest sea-fight," he adds, "was that of the Corinthians against the Corcyreans;" but as he goes on to state that until the Greeks began to prepare for the threatened invasion of the Persians their vessels were without decks, it is evident that this was a small affair, as was indeed every other naval engagement, recorded by history or tradition, up to the time of that great battle, which we shall now endeavor to describe, wherein republican valor opposed an effectual barrier to the further advance of the forces of the Persian king.

WAR BETWEEN GREECE AND PERSIA. GREAT SEA-FIGHT OFF SALAMIS.

In the four hundred and eightieth year before Christ, Xerxes, the youthful monarch of Persia, commenced his march from Asia into Europe, for the purpose of revenging upon the Greeks the death of those Persians who, ten years previously, had fallen on the plains of Marathon. Seven years, according to Herodotus, had been consumed in preparing for this undertaking, and all the resources of the Persian Empire, both by land and sea, were brought into requisition, to ensure its successful termination. The various nations composing the vast army of the Eastern despot, were seven days and nights in passing over the bridge of boats at the Hellespont; and as they deployed before their leader on the Thracian side of the Strait, preceded by ten thousand Persians carrying garlands on their heads, seemed more like frantic Bacchanals than stern warriors bent upon encountering the resolute soldiers of Greece.

The fleet which accompanied this unwieldy army was composed of twelve hundred and seven vessels, without including the transports, and carried two hundred and forty-one thousand four hundred men. It was divided into three grand divisions, each of which was commanded by a Persian of the highest rank, while the reserve, consisting of the Dorian and Carian triremes, one hundred strong, was intrusted to the care of the celebrated Artemisia, Queen of Halicarnassus; the Admiral-in-Chief being no less a personage than Ariabignes, a son of the great Darius, and half-brother of the present king.

Like the army, this immense fleet left Asia with great pomp; and it steered for Greece in the full assurance of complete success. Skirting along the coasts of Thrace, Macedon and Thessaly, after days of tiresome rowing, and nights spent in anxious watching, its van division came in sight of three Grecian guard vessels, stationed off the island of Sciathus, about twenty miles north-east of Artemisium in Eubœa, where the main body of the Grecian fleet lay at anchor. Leaving their look-out vessels to fall into the enemy's hands, the Greeks now retired from Artemisium to Chalcis, with a view of holding the Euripus, that narrow channel which runs between Eubœa and the mainland, while the Persians pressed forward to Artemisium, where they offered up the bravest of their Greek captives a sacrifice to their gods. But fortunately for the Greeks, as we learn from Herodotus, Boreas, the Northwind, tired of the dreary life he was leading in the frozen regions about the Pole, had moved down into Attica, ages before this, where he saw, fell in love with, and married Orithya, the daughter of an Athenian named Erectheus. Orithya, who, by this marriage, had become immortal, was very beautiful, and, like all the Grecian women a great coquette, and she now, with many tears and supplications, implored her husband to go to the relief of her distressed countrymen, promising, if he did so, to be a model wife to him in the future, and threatening if he did not, to petition Jove for a divorce, and pass the remainder of her days with his rival and bitter opponent, Auster, the South wind, whom, he well knew, all the Grecian women adored. Upon this, Boreas, who loved his wife dearly, became fearfully angry, and, summoning Pluto and all the Furies to his aid, he raised such a dreadful storm as had never before been known to rage upon the coasts of Greece.

> "The wind blew as t'wad blaun its last,
> The rattling shou'rs rose on the blast;
> The speedy gleams the darkness swallowed,
> Loud, deep and lang the thunders bellowed—
> That night a child might understand
> The Deil had business on his hand."

And when day dawned the rocky beach of Euboea was strewn with wrecks, while four hundred Persian galleys had actually gone to the bottom, some foundering in the open sea and others at their anchors.

Encouraged by this the Grecian fleet advanced once more to Artemisium, while the Persians entered the Pagasæan Gulf, about ten miles distant, to repair damages.

Confronting each other thus, neither party could long remain inactive, and in the course of as many days, three battles had been fought, without any decisive result, when news reached the Grecian commander-in-chief, Eurybiades, a Spartan, that through the neglect of the Phocian guard, posted on the summit of Anopœa, Leonidas had been surrounded, and that the vast Persian host, leaving the dead bodies of *the immortal three hundred* in their rear, was even then carrying fire and sword into Phocis and Bœotia. Such evil intelligence could not long be concealed from the fleet, and no sooner was it generally disseminated, than officers and men were alike clamorous for a retreat, which, being resolved upon, was effected in excellent order, the Corinthians on the left leading, as the column was to move in that direction, and the Athenians, who were anchored on the extreme right, nearest to the enemy, getting under way last, and bringing up the rear. They continued their flight to Salamis, unmolested by the Persians, who were content with moving forward as far as Histea and Artemisium, and taking military possession of the important island of Eubœa. Three days did the subjects of the "Great King" remain idle in the bay of Artemisium; but on the fourth they weighed anchor, and shaping their course along the shores of Locris and Bœotia, passed, on the fifth day, through the Euripus, and, on the seventh, came to anchor off Phalerum, in Attica, where they made a connection with the left wing of their army, and again found themselves face to face with the Grecian fleet; whereupon Eurybiades assembled his divisional and squadron commanders on board his vessel, and, pointing out to them the Persian fleet, informed them that a bearer of despatches had just reached him with the sad news of the taking of Athens by the Persian army: "Thus, O commanders!" said he, "their land and sea forces have made a complete junction, and it remains for us to decide what course we shall pursue in this emergency."

An excited conference now took place, where all, with the exception of Themistocles, the Athenian admiral, advocated an immediate retreat to the isthmus of Corinth, and in this humor the council of war broke up, the great officers of which it was composed repairing to their respective flag ships, fully intent on carrying out their designs.

But, fortunately for civilization, literature and art, there was one man in the Athenian fleet—a former teacher of rhetoric at Athens, noted for his "strong common sense"—

who seems to have been a brave fellow, and to have perfectly comprehended the situation. His name was [8]Mnesiphilus, and when Themistocles returned to his vessel, he met him at the gangway, with the anxious inquiry,—"What is the determination of the council?" "To retreat instantly," said Themistocles. "Then," replied Mnesiphilus, "Greece is lost; for if the confederate fleet once disperses, no human power can bring it together again: each division, each squadron, yea, each vessel of it, will repair to the state to which it belongs, and all, by detachments, eventually fall into the enemy's hands. Can nothing be done to avert such a calamity? Cannot you persuade Eurybiades to re-convene the council?"

Moved by the earnestness of his captain, Themistocles again took his seat in his barge, and ordered the officer of it to convey him to the galley of Eurybiades, where another conference was held, which would have resulted like the former, but for Themistocles, who, supported by the commander-in-chief, rose and spoke as follows: "O Grecians! whither, and to what end would you fly? Defeated everywhere on land, the fate of your countrymen depends solely on their fleet, which has been put afloat at so great an expense, and, except in numbers, is in every respect superior to that of the *barbarians*. In these straits your flanks will be protected by the land, while Ariabignes cannot detach any portion of his force to sail around Salamis and attack our rear, lest getting wind of his design, we should fall upon such detachment with our whole strength, and destroy it utterly, before the rest of the Persian fleet could come to its support. At the isthmus of Corinth you will have no such advantage, for—" "Themistocles!" here interrupted Adimantus, the Corinthian admiral, "those who in the public games rise up before their time are beaten with many stripes!" "True, admiral," was the calm reply; "but those who refuse to take part in the contest cannot win the crown." "It ill becomes you," retorted Adimantus,—"you who have no home, to attempt to dictate terms to us!" "Corinthian!"

exclaimed Themistocles, now justly moved to anger, "What you say is as false as it is ungenerous! While Athens possesses two hundred war-galleys, which constitute more than half of the united forces of all Greece, she cannot be without a home, since brave men may live at sea as well as on the land. What I desire to impress upon all here present is, the stubborn fact that in this strait all the advantage is with us, while at the isthmus, on the contrary, it will be entirely with our enemies, who, taking advantage of their numerical superiority, will not fail to attack us simultaneously in front, flank and rear, thus ensuring our utter destruction, and making of every free-born Greek a Persian slave! This is so clear to my mind that, unless you decide to fight where you are, I shall immediately take on board of the vessels I command, all the Athenian women and children they can accommodate, and, abandoning the Confederacy forever, sail directly for the southern coast of Italy, where Athens has already founded a colony."

Moved more by the threat contained in the last words of the great Athenian than by the force of his arguments, sound as they were, the allied commanders now resolved to give battle where they were, and commenced making preparations accordingly.

At Phalerum, on the other hand, Xerxes had called together his Great Lords, and Wise Counsellors, to consider the expediency of attacking the Grecian fleet without delay; and, as he spoke first in the assembly, declaring himself in favor of this project, his words produced a marvellous unanimity of sentiment among its members, all of whom, without exception, voted with their Imperial Master, whispering one to another, as they did so, that his speech was *golden* and its arguments *orient pearls*.

At this moment, however, a beautiful woman entered the council-chamber, and, sweeping proudly by the crowd of crouching slaves who surrounded the king, stood erect, and with flashing eyes, before him.

"What is your opinion, Queen Artemisia?" asked Xerxes, as he half rose from his throne to receive her.

"By the shade of your father, the great Darius, I call upon you, O King!" she replied, "to abandon your rash design! On land you have, thus far, been victorious, and you will continue to be so, so long as your fleet remains intact, to keep open your communications with Asia, whence reinforcements and provisions in abundance are hourly arriving; but one great defeat at sea must insure your ruin; for you will then not only have to contend with the whole power of the Greeks, who, animated by their victory, will rise to a man to oppose you, but also with gnawing hunger, that worst of all enemies, which causes the friend to forsake his friend, the husband his wife, the mother to abandon her children! Assailed by its pangs, your troops will commence a disorderly retreat to their native land, and every foot of their march will be enriched by the carcasses of those who perish by the way! Believe me, O King; you have everything to lose and nothing to gain by a naval combat. Be wise, then, and remain inactive; and you will shortly find the Greeks dispersing of their own accord, since they have but a few days' provisions on board their vessels, and cannot obtain supplies from the island of Salamis—and thus, by their own act, you will remain master of the Grecian seas!"

Xerxes now rose, and although he complimented the queen upon her discourse, broke up the assembly, with the sullen resolve to be guided alone by his own rash judgment. He therefore gave orders to Ariabignes to get ready for action, and to prepare a seat for his sovereign on some high cliff overlooking Salamis, whence the whole sea of battle could be discerned.

And now all was bustle and activity in both fleets; Cimon, the son of the celebrated Miltiades, with all the principal young men of Athens, reinforcing the Greeks, while to each Persian vessel were added thirty veteran soldiers, well skilled in the use of the javelin and the bow.

Such was the condition of affairs when Themistocles, fearing that unless an engagement was brought on within twenty-four hours, some of the Grecian commanders would withdraw from the Confederacy, sent one of his slaves, a Persian named Sikinnos, who acted as tutor to his children, to say to Xerxes that his master was anxious to desert to the Persians, and therefore informed him that grave dissensions had arisen among the Grecian admirals, who would soon be under way with their comrades for their respective States, and that such another opportunity would, in all probability, never again be offered to him of capturing the combined naval forces of Greece. The vain monarch easily falling into the snare laid for him by the wily Athenian, issued an edict declaring that the Greeks were about to fly, and assuring his commanders that their heads would pay the forfeit should a single one of the Grecian vessels escape them.

Then night spread her sable mantle over the sea, and under its cover the little island of Psyttaleia, lying between Salamis and the mainland was taken possession of by a large body of Persian archers, and an Egyptian squadron dispatched to cruise off Nisæa in Megaris, for the purpose of intercepting the retreat of the Greeks in that direction; and, this being done, Ariabignes drew out the rest of his force in order of battle, in the form of a semicircle, and after giving strict orders to the captains of his galleys to keep underway all night lest any of the Grecians should endeavor to steal by them and make off, he waited anxiously for the morrow.

In the meantime, Aristides, the Just, who, returning from banishment, and protected by the darkness, had passed in a small boat, unchallenged, along the whole Persian line, gave notice to Eurybiades of what he had seen, thus enabling that commander to form his plan of battle with a full knowledge of the disposition of his enemy; and when day dawned the barbarians discovered, to their dismay, that, instead of being scattered in flight, as they had expected to find it, the Grecian fleet, vastly inferior to them in numbers, but their superior in everything else, was drawn up at a little distance in battle array, with the Athenians on the right and the Spartans on the left, opposed respectively, to the Phœnicians and the Ionians, who formed the extremes of their own advanced line, while the intrepid Artemisia with her Dorians led their reserve.

A light breeze sprang up and the sun rose in all its Eastern splendor, whereupon the Persians, both on sea and land, prostrated themselves—an impressive spectacle! for the fleet consisted of not less than a thousand vessels, carrying a quarter of a million of men, while all the adjacent shores, as far as the eye could reach, were lined with an innumerable multitude of soldiers and camp-followers anxious to witness the impending struggle. On their side the Greeks offered up sacrifices to all the gods, and poured out a special libation to Zeus, the Protector, and to Poseidon, Ruler of the Seas.

Just as these religious ceremonies were concluded, a Grecian trireme, which a few days before had been despatched to Ægina, was descried returning, hotly pursued by the enemy. An Athenian trireme, commanded by Ameinas, a brother of the poet Æschylus, dashed forward to her assistance. At this Eurybiades, seeing that all things were ready, and that the ardor of his captains could no longer be restrained, made the usual* signal to engage, by displaying above the deck of his vessel a gilded shield. The Grecian trumpets now sounded the advance, when the right wing moved forward in admirable order, followed instantly by the whole line—all sweeping toward the barbarians, and all, with one accord, bending to their oars and loudly chanting their battle cry, *O, sons of Hellenes, forward, free your country.* The Athenians were first engaged, next the Æginetans, and soon after the battle became general, with this advantage on the part of the Greeks that their vessels were in rapid motion when they came in contact with the Persian fleet, which at this critical moment was just beginning to move forward.

* For ancient and modern methods of signalling, see a very able article by Capt. S. B. Luce, U.S.N., in Johnson's Cyclopædia.

Thus a great many of the Persians were sunk at the first onset, and a gap made in their line, which although quickly filled by vessels coming up from the rear, produced for a while the most terrible confusion. Then Ariamenes, the admiral commanding the left wing, seeing that it was necessary to encourage his people by some brilliant exploit, bore down at full speed upon the flagship of Themistocles, with the intention of carrying it by boarding. A desperate hand to hand conflict ensued, which threatened at one time to end disastrously to the Greeks; but many Athenian captains hurrying up to the aid of their leader, the magnificent galley of Ariamenes was sunk by repeated shocks from the brazen beaks of their vessels, and the brave admiral himself slain and his body thrown overboard from the prow of the trireme he had hoped to capture. At this moment, too, a rumor ran along the lines that the great Ariabignes, whom all the Asiatics revered for his father Darius's sake, had fallen, pierced with a javelin; whereupon the barbarians groaned aloud, while the Greeks sent up a shout of triumph and derision. Still the battle was maintained by the Persians with great fury until the Athenians, having passed through the Phœnician line, and pulling strong with their starboard and backing their port oars, turned short round and fell upon their left flank and rear, when a universal panic seized them and they fled in disorder, with the exception of the Dorians, who, led by their glorious queen, fought with great valor, in the vain hope of restoring order where all was irrecoverably lost. At length, however, observing that the fugitives were not to be rallied, and that the whole sea was strewn with "wrecks" and the "floating corpses" of her friends, Artemisia reluctantly gave the signal to retreat. As she was making off in her own galley, she found herself closely pursued by Ameinas, whereupon she ran at full speed into a Lycian trireme, whose commander had behaved like a coward in the action, and sunk it instantly.

When the Greek saw this he concluded that the galley he had been following was either one of the Confederate fleet or one that had deserted to it, and gave up the pursuit; and before he discovered his mistake the heroic woman had escaped. Thus Ameinas, the Pallenian, lost the reward of ten thousand drachmas offered by the Athenians for her capture; but he afterward obtained, by the unbiassed suffrages of his countrymen, what was no doubt infinitely more prized by him, the honor of being mentioned as one of "the three valiants" who had most distinguished themselves in the battle; his companions in glory being Polycritus of Ægina, and Eumenes, the Anagyrasian.

The victory being complete, Aristides put himself at the head of a large body of Athenians, and landing on Psyttaleia, slew the Persians there, under the very eye of their sovereign, who, with all his immense army around him, could not render them the slightest assistance. Then the mighty lord of so many nations and such countless myriads of slaves rose from his seat, and rending his royal robes, burst into a flood of tears. Well might some one of his followers have applied to him at this instant, the bitter speech addressed two thousand years later, by the fiery mother of Boabdil to her weeping son, "You do well to cry like a woman for what you could not defend like a man." Thus ended the great battle of Salamis, which decided the fate of Greece.

Of the many accounts of it written by contemporary historians, that of the poet Æschylus, in his "Tragedy of the Persians," is doubtless the best. As the poet bore a part, too, in the action he so vividly describes, it seems but meet that he should be heard in relation to it. I therefore, subjoin the following extracts from his work,[9] which will serve to fill up any details I may have omitted. They occur in that part of the tragedy where a Persian messenger is supposed to be giving to Atossa, the mother of Xerxes, an account of this dread disaster to the Persian arms. Surrounded by the elders who formed the chief Council of State of the Empire, and who bore the honorable title of "The Faithful," the queen mother listened with fear and trembling to the messenger, whose sad tale was frequently interrupted by cries of woe and lamentation :

Mess.—The author of the mischief, O, my mistress,
Was some foul fiend or Power on evil bent;
For lo ! a Hellene from the Athenian host
Came to thy son, to Xerxes, and spake thus,
That should the shadow of the dark night come,
The Hellenes would not wait him, but would leap
Into their rowers' benches, here and there,
And save their lives in secret, hasty flight.
And he forthwith, this hearing, knowing not
The Hellene's guile, nor yet the god's great envy,
Gives this command to all his admirals,
Soon as the son should cease to burn the earth
With his bright rays, and darkness thick invade
The firmament of Heaven, to set their ships
In three-fold lines, to hinder all escape,
And guard the billowy straits, and others place
In circuit round about the isle of Aias:
For if the Hellenes 'scaped an evil doom,
And found a way of secret, hasty flight,
It was ordained that all should lose their heads.
Such things he spake from soul o'er wrought with pride,
For he knew not what fate the gods would send ;
And they, in no disorder, but obeying,
Then made their supper ready, and each sailor
Fastened his oar around true-fitting thole ;
And when the sunlight vanished, and the night
Had come, then each man, master of an oar,
Went to his ship, and all men bearing arms,
And rank encouraged rank in vessel long;
And so they sail, as 'twas appointed each,
And all night long the captains of the fleet
Kept their men working, rowing to and fro;
Night then came on, and the Hellenic host
In nowise sought to take to secret flight,
And when day, bright to look upon with white steeds,
O'er spread the earth, then rose from the Hellenes
Loud chant of cry of battle, and forthwith
Echo gave answer from each island rock,
And terror then on all the Persians fell,
Of fond hopes disappointed. Not in flight

The Hellenes then their solemn pæans sang;
But with brave spirit hasting on to battle,

With martial sound the trumpet fired those ranks:
And straight with sweep of oars that flew through foam,
They smote the loud waves at the boatswain's call;
And swiftly all were manifest to sight.
Then first their right wing moved in order meet;
Next the whole line its forward course began,
And all at once we heard a mighty shout,—
"O sons of Hellenes, forward, free your country;
Free, too, your wives, your children, and the shrines
Built to your fathers' Gods, and holy tombs
Your ancestors now rest in. Now the fight
Is for our all." And on our side indeed
Arose, in answer, din of Persian speech,
And time to wait was over: ship on ship
Dashed its bronze-pointed beak, and first a barque
Of Hellas did the encounter fierce begin,
And from Phœnician vessel crashes off
Her carved prow. And each against his neighbor
Steers his own ship: and first the mighty flood
Of Persian host held out. But when the ships
Were crowded in the straits, nor could they give
Help to each other, they with mutual shocks,
With beaks of bronze went crushing each the other,
Shivering their rowers' benches. And the ships
Of Hellas, with manœuvring not unskilful,
Charged circling round them. And the hulls of ships
Floated capsized, nor could the sea be seen,
Filled, as it was, with wrecks and carcasses;
And all the shores and rocks were full of corpses.
And every ship was wildly rowed in flight,
All that composed the Persian armament..
And they, as men spear tunnies, or a haul
Of other fishes, with the shafts of oars,
Or spars of wrecks went smiting, cleaving down;
And bitter groans and wailings overspread
The wide sea-waves, till eye of swarthy night
Bade it all cease: and for the mass of ills,
Not, though my tale should run for ten full days,
Could I in full recount them. Be assured

That never yet so great a multitude
Died in a single day as died in this.
* * * * * * * *
The captains of the vessels that were left,
With a fair wind, but not in fair array,
Took flight.

Chorus. And now the land of Asia mourneth sore,
Left desolate of men,
'Twas Xerxes led them forth, woe! woe!
'Twas Xerxes lost them all, woe! woe!
'Twas Xerxes who with evil counsels sped
Their course in sea-born barks.
Why was Dareios erst so free from harm,
First bowman of the state,
The leader whom the men of Susa loved;

While those who fought as soldiers or at sea,
These ships, dark-hulled, well-rowed,
Their own ships bore them on, woe! woe!
Their own ships lost them all, woe! woe!
Their own ships, in disastrous onset urged,
And by Ionian hands?
The King himself, we learn, but hardly 'scapes
Through Thrake's wide-spread steppes,
And paths o'er which the tempests wildly sweep.

And they who perished first, ah, me!
Perforce unburied left, alas!
Are scattered round Kychreia's shore, woe! woe!
Lament, mourn sore, and raise a bitter cry,
Grievous, the sky to pierce, woe! woe!
And let thy mourning voice uplift its strain
Of loud and full lament.

Torn by the whirling flood, ah, me!
Their carcasses are gnawed, alas!
By the dumb brood of the pure sea, woe! woe!
And each house mourneth for its vanished lord;
And childless sires, woe! woe!
Mourning in age o'er griefs the Gods have sent,
Now hear their utter loss.

Although in the above account of the battle of Salamis, I have deemed it proper to confine myself strictly to received authorities, yet I cannot forbear commenting upon the improbability of many of their *facts* nor refrain from giving my own idea of the causes which led to the utter rout of the Persians, in this great engagement, which taking into consideration the magnitude of the interests involved, the number of the combatants, the myriads of the slain, and the results which ensued, is without a parallel in naval history.

It seems difficult to conceive, in the first place, that there could have been so great a disparity in force between the contending fleets as is represented. That of the Greeks, as we have it from themselves, may safely be set down as not below the number estimated, viz., three hundred and eighty triremes; but that the force of the Persians consisted of a thousand of these war-galleys seems altogether improbable; for, after seven years of preparation, during which every "seaport along the whole winding length of coast from Macedonia to Libya was engaged in building ships and impressing seamen," only twelve hundred triremes could be fitted out to accompany the invading army—a mighty work indeed, when we consider the length of time it takes to build and equip a single vessel capable, like the Persian trireme, of carrying two hundred men, but one which sinks into utter insignificance in comparison with the Herculean labor, which the Greek historians would have us believe was afterward imposed upon the Asiatics, of fitting out, during the six months that elapsed between the sailing of the fleet from the Hellespont and its last encounter with the Greeks off Salamis, six hundred triremes, the reinforcement it must have received in order to make its total force in that battle amount to one thousand, for it lost four hundred triremes, in the great north-east gale off Eubœa, and two hundred shortly afterward, according to Herodotus, on the rocks in the dangerous bay of Cœla, "thus," says the historian, "the deity interfered to reduce the Persian force *more nearly to an equality with the Grecian.*" Now supposing one hundred vessels—a very moderate estimate—to have been placed *hors de combat* in the three encounters off Artemisium, and the Egyptian squadron, detached on special service, to have been reduced, by battle and shipwreck, to one hundred triremes, half of its original number, we have remaining of the fleet that sailed from the Hellespont—arguing on the hypothesis of its not having received an accession of force meanwhile—but four hundred triremes; so that to make its effective strength in the battle of Salamis amount to one thousand, a re-inforcement of six hundred, as I have stated above, must have previously reached it. A story that will be discarded at once by every reflecting seaman. If we set down the Persian fleet, then, as consisting, at this crisis, of seven hundred vessels, instead of a thousand, we may feel well assured that we have not under-estimated its number.

Secondly, there seems to be a misapprehension, on the part of Herodotus and those who follow him, of the motives which induced Themistocles to send a message to the Persian King, declaring that "the Greeks were about to fly,"[10] for since, in the last council of war held by Eurybiades, the Grecian commanders had resolved to fight, and not a particle of evidence has been adduced to show that they afterward wavered in their determination, the Athenian leader could have had no fears on this score. On the contrary, it appears more probable that, finding Eurybiades fully prepared to give battle on the morrow, he invented the story which he told Sikinnos to repeat to Xerxes, in order to induce that weak monarch to withdraw a portion of his force from the Grecian front; and we may fancy his exultation, as well as that of all the other Grecian admirals, when Aristides arrived with the news that the squadron sent to Nisæa was none other than the famous Egyptian one, which, shortly before, had distinguished itself, at Artemisium, "by the capture of five Athenian galleys." The artifice of Themistocles produced this additional effect, that it caused the Persian captains, as we have seen, to keep under way all night; so that when day came, their crews—no matter what the number of the "reliefs"—must have been quite worn out with rowing and watching, and in no condition to meet a resolute enemy, fully informed of their plans, and fighting for the liberty they prized more highly than life itself. A due consideration of the above statements, and of the fact mentioned by Herodotus that "the Ionians purposely behaved ill," taken in connection with the disaster which befell the Persians early in the action in the death of Ariabignes, their commander-in-chief, will sufficiently explain to every intelligent mind, I think, the cause of their total overthrow, on this occasion, by the Greeks, *with whom they had previously contended on equal terms at Artemisium.*

That the battle was a terribly severe one there can be no doubt, but that it lasted—fought under oars, as it was—"from daylight to dark" is not probable. As the wind was blowing from the westward, however, it is quite likely that the pursuit of the vanquished was continued *under sail* until darkness concealed them from the victors' view. If we may credit the accounts that have come down to us, the Grecian fleet was admirably handled throughout, while in the Persian, owing doubtless to the causes stated above, disorder reigned almost from the first. Xerxes committed a grave error in fighting at all, and he paid the penalty of his folly in the immediate loss of nearly half his navy, while the indirect consequence of his defeat, as the wise Artemisia had predicted, was the death, by starvation and fatigue, of a quarter of a million of men.

Thus does the Almighty, not unfrequently, visit the sins of nations upon their heads, by appointing a fool or a madman to preside over their councils.

Of the Grecian admirals, Themistocles stands pre-eminent, while Eurybiades seems to have behaved as comported with the dignity of his high position. Sparta acted not unwisely, then, in awarding to the former the prize of wisdom and to the latter that of valor. As nothing is heard of Mnesiphilus after the battle, it is probable he perished in it.

Among those who fought on the Persian side, Artemisia alone is worthy of particular mention. As discreet as Themistocles, and not inferior in courage to the bravest of the Spartans, it is no wonder that the Persian despot, as he beheld her marvellous acts of heroism, leaped from his throne with the exclamation: "The men behave like women and the women like men!" If it be true that she afterward imitated Sappho and took the lover's leap from the Leucadian rock, it only proves that, like the poetess, her head was sounder than her heart. Her wisdom in council and her constancy in battle have, however, rarely been surpassed, and we may therefore rest assured with the enthusiastic Greek that "no braver spirit ever rushed from the embrace of men to that of the immortal gods" than Artemisia, the fair heroine of the battle of Salamis.

The naval victory of the allies, so far from putting a stop to the petty jealousies which had for some time existed among them, gave rise to bitter and endless controversies, each state magnifying the exploits of its own citizens and deprecating those of others. The Athenians, in particular, were very forward in appropriating to themselves the whole credit for defeating the Persians, and, among other falsehoods, did not scruple to affirm that the Corinthians *ran* at the very beginning of the engagement. This the Corinthians indignantly denied, declaring that they had been among the foremost in the action, and "the rest of Greece bore testimony in their favor." The oracle at Delphi, little likely to be at variance with public opinion on this matter, unquestionably gave the palm of valor to the Æginetans; for when the Confederates, after dedicating three Phœnician vessels to "all the gods," sent "a statue twelve cubits in height holding the beak of a ship in its hand to Delphi, they inquired of Apollo whether enough had been given. "All have given enough," was the response, "except the Æginetans, from whom a particular offering is due on account of their superior prowess." The Æginetans accordingly made an offering of three golden stars, on a brazen mast, "which was placed," says Herodotus, "in a corner near the bowl which Crœsus sent to Delphi when he sent there that famous statue of a woman in gold, three cubits high, which the Delphians say is the image of Crœsus's baking woman.

PELOPONNESIAN WAR. EXPLOITS OF PHORMIO AT NAUPAKTUS.

After Salamis, the operations of the Persian fleet were confined entirely to the defensive, while the Greeks, in general, and more especially the Athenians, following the counsel of Themistocles, rapidly added to the number of their fighting ships; yet no sooner did they feel themselves secure against foreign invasion than they turned their arms against each other, and, weakened by continual battles, both by sea and land, became subject in the end, first to Macedon and afterward to Rome. As their sea-fights were, for the most part, however, fought as at Salamis, in line, sometimes with a reserve and sometimes without, I shall limit myself to a description of two of them which took place between the Athenians and the Corinthians, off Naupaktus, in the third year of the Peloponnesian war, and the year before Christ, 429, wherein the tactics of both parties were novel, and where, prior to engaging, strategy was resorted to by the contending commanders-in-chief, each doing his utmost to out-wit and outmanœuvre the other.

From Naupaktus, I shall transport the reader to Sicily, in whose great sea-port, through the defeat of Nikias, Athens lost her supremacy as a naval power over the other Grecian States.

Conformably to the plan of campaign agreed upon by the States of Peloponnesus in league against Athens, a large army was assembled at the city of Ambrakia in readiness to march into the interior of Akarnania, while the combined naval forces of the allies were directed to concentrate at

Leucas in Leucadia, and thence make a descent upon the coast of the invaded province, and get possession of its seaboard towns. The fleet of Corinth therefore proceeded down the Corinthian Gulf until it had rounded Point Drepanum, when it kept to the south-westward and steered for Patræ, intending to cross thence to Etolia, but as it took its departure from Drepanum, Machaon, the Corinthian admiral, was surprised to find that an Athenian fleet of twenty-five triremes was keeping along the opposite shore, on a line parallel to his own, and evidently closely watching his movements; yet as his own force consisted of forty-seven vessels he never for a moment supposed the Athenian commander would have the audacity to attack him; and so when he reached Patræ he bore away north-west for Etolia, expecting to see the enemy stop, as he drew near and suffer him to pass unmolested. But Phormio, the Athenian admiral, who was the foremost sea-captain of his day, had such confidence in the superior seamanship and training of his men that he gladly availed himself of this opportunity of bringing on an engagement; he therefore kept his course with the design, apparently, of breaking through the centre of the Corinthian fleet and doubling upon its rear; seeing which Machaon, in great haste, put about and stood back to Achaia, where he anchored at nightfall at some point between Patræ and Rhium. Toward morning, thinking either that the Athenians had returned to Naupaktus, a garrisoned town not far distant, where they had been for some time stationed, and whence they had got underway the previous day on the report of his coming, or that if they were still near at hand, he might in the darkness elude their vigilance, he got underway and again steered for Etolia; but just as he had arrived in mid-channel day dawned, disclosing the Athenians so close aboard that it was no longer possible to avoid an encounter with them, whereupon he drew up his fleet in the form of a circle, and in this order awaited their onset. The circle was composed of thirty of the largest triremes, placed near enough to each other to prevent the passage of a vessel between them, and yet not so near as to incur the hazard of fouling their oars. An inner circle contained the twelve weakest vessels of the fleet, and between the inner and the outer circle were five very large and fast ships, equi-distant from each other, whose province it was to succor those vessels of the outer circle which should be first assailed by the enemy. The prows of all the vessels faced outward.

Phormio bore down upon the circle in column of vessels, and, keeping it on his port hand, rowed at full speed around and around it, always making a show of attacking it, and yet never coming to actual conflict. In this way it became gradually contracted, for each Corinthian commander, as an Athenian brushed by him backed a little, to avoid collision, until finally the outer vessels impinged upon the inner, and the rowers were compelled to use their oars to fend off with. Then, too, the East wind, as Phormio had foreseen, began to blow strongly from the Gulf of Corinth, and raising quite a sea, huddled the vessels together after such a fashion that all order was lost among them, so that the vessels of the outer line, no longer controlled by either helmsmen or rowers, fell off with their heads towards every point of the compass, and exposed their broadsides to the sharp rams of the Athenian triremes. Then Phormio made the signal to attack in earnest, and the Athenians, putting their helms to starboard, went crashing through the Corinthians in all directions, sinking many of their vessels and driving the others to a shameful flight. The battle, if that may be called a battle where there is no resistance, lasted but a few minutes, and resulted in the complete triumph of the Athenians, who captured twelve of the Corinthian vessels, and, according to the barbarous usage of that day, put their crews to the sword. The conquerors then erected a trophy on the promontory of Antirhium, and dedicated one of their prizes to Poseidon, after which they returned to Naupaktus whence Phormio dispatched a galley to Athens with the news of his signal victory. The galley entered the Piræus decked with flags, her rowers keeping stroke to the sound of martial music, and the officers and seamen standing on the upper deck, with chaplets of flowers upon their heads and chanting a hymn to Apollo,* while all the Athenian people, crowding the docks, filled the air with shouts of welcome and congratulation.

The good judgment and tactical knowledge of Phormio are not more clearly exhibited in the operations off Rhium than is the want of sound sense and nautical ability in the Corinthian Admiral. Machaon, who was a soldier by profession, had no doubt often seen attacks on shore warded off by the circle formation, where each man, kneeling down and resting his shield on the earth, lapped it over that of his comrade on the right, so that the whole formed an almost impenetrable rampart. It was borrowed from the ancient Egyptians, and we shall meet with it again, among the Scandinavians, whose kings and chieftains were surrounded by their "shield-circle men." But nothing could be more faulty than such a defensive order of battle in a fleet, which can never, with impunity, *passively* await an attack. It might seem, from a cursory examination of the subject, that the Corinthian vessels, before their array was broken, had it in their power to sink the Athenian vessels, as they circled round them, by *ramming;* but when we bear in mind that the Corinthians were then lying motionless on the water, we see that such was not the case; for had a Corinthian ship, with this intent, abandoned the line, she must have come in contact with an Athenian before she had well got headway, thus striking her adversary but a feeble blow, while she herself would have been struck full and fair by the Athenian next astern, and almost certainly have been cut down to the water's edge. It has been asserted, however, that a number of broadside artillery ships, ranged in column of vessels and steaming in a circle, would present a very formidable obstacle to a superior force

* On chantait un pœn (hymne) avant le combat, et un autre après ; le premier en l'honneur du dieu Mars, le second en l'honneur d'Apollon.—DuSein.

of *similar* attacking vessels; and much has been said of the "terrible circle of fire," which from such an array, would meet the assailants; but, in reality, the admiral who should thus permit himself to be attacked, would be in the position of a general who has suffered himself to be completely invested in a city or fortress, without hope of succor from without. The fire of the assailants all converging toward a central point, while that of the assailed is divergent and distributed over a wide area, the affair becomes a mere question of time, and victory must ultimately belong to the assailants. Thus, it is evident that, under all circumstances *afloat*, the circle formation, as a *defensive* order, in itself involves defeat.

The discomfiture of the Corinthians caused great indignation among all the Peloponnesian States, and especially at Sparta, where it was attributed, not to the superior tactics and strategy of Phormio, but to the arrant cowardice of his adversaries. Another fleet was therefore at once fitted out, whose commander-in-chief, Knemus, as also its divisional officers, were, by the unanimous voicc of the allies, selected from Lacedæmon; and as each State furnished its quota of vessels or men, it numbered, when ready for sea, seventy-seven triremes, all fully manned and excellently well equipped.

The rendezvous of this imposing force was at Panormus, a small semi-circular harbor of Achaia, just inside of the promontory of Rhium, while Phormio, with his twenty triremes, took station at Molykreium, on the opposite shore.

Thus the two fleets at night were but a mile and a-half apart; and each morning, they got underway—Phormio stretching to the westward, and endeavoring to entice his enemy into the open sea, where he knew that, through the superior seamanship of his men and the greater swiftness of his ships, he would have greatly the advantage of him, while Knemus, conscious of his inferiority in these respects, used every stratagem and art he could devise, to bring on an engagement in the Strait, where there would be no room for manœuvring on either side. Six days were consumed in this manner, but on the seventh, at early dawn, the Peloponnesian fleet left Panormus, right in front, and steered for Naupaktus. Its van, consisting of the twenty fastest vessels, was commanded by Timokrates, its centre by Brasidas, the rear by Lykophron.

As soon as this movement was perceived at Molykreium, the Messinian soldiers, belonging to the garrison of Naupaktus, but now encamped abreast of the Athenian fleet, in readiness to succor it in case of need, became clamorous to return to the city, " within whose undefended walls," they cried, " they had left their wives and children." Phormio too, saw the necessity of repairing thither with the fleet, since he felt that it would be a lasting disgrace to the Athenian navy, to let a city in alliance with Athens, fall into the enemy's hands without striking a blow in its behalf. He therefore got under way as speedily as possible, and taking a course parallel to that of the allies, kept close in shore, hoping to reach Naupaktus ahead of them, although they had at least eight hundred yards the start, and the goal to be reached was not distant more than six English miles.

Along the adjacent heights the Messinian army was marching at the double-quick, and on the walls and towers of Naupaktus were to be seen all the male citizens of the place, fully armed indeed, but few in number, while the roofs of the houses and temples were crowded with women anxiously awaiting the arrival of fathers, brothers, husbands and sons, and as anxiously dreading the coming of the foe.

But soon the general interest centred upon the rival fleets, whose swiftly moving oars made the Corinthian waters white with foam ; for they were now close together, each fleet apparently only intent upon outstripping the other,and Naupaktus, with its trembling watchers, but three miles away. History presents to us few more dramatic spectacles than this.

The excellence of Phormio's training and discipline was

now made manifest, in the steadiness of the Athenian vessels, their uniform speed,and the perfect silence maintained by their crews, while each Peloponnesian trireme, yawing to and fro in unskilful hands, and going first slow then fast, by fits and starts, was a perfect pandemonium of noise and confusion; and as the Athenians had so gained in the race, that the leader of their "columns of vessels" were already lapping the centre file of the van of the Peloponnesian "column of fours," it seemed certain that they must ultimately win. Suddenly, however, at a given signal from Knemus, the allies came by the left flank and headed towards the Athenians, four deep. Phormio, who was leading his column, seeing the danger of being hemmed in between his enemies and the land, shouted at the top of his lungs, and had the word passed from ship to ship, "to pull at full speed and endeavor to pass their right flank." The Athenian vessels now fairly flew through the water, and eleven of them went clear; but Knemus, throwing his whole fleet into line on its leading vessels, by a right oblique, cut off the others and drove them ashore, following them up with his rear and centre divisions, while Timokrates signalled to his division, "by the right flank," and hurried in pursuit of Phormio. Being embarked on board a Leukadian trireme of exceeding swiftness, the Lacedemonian admiral shortly got far ahead of his companions and close upon the rear vessel of the fugitives, which he felt certain of making his prize. But the captain of this vessel was a man of nerve, clear head, and sound judgment, and observing that the course steered by Timokrates would take him close to starboard of a merchantman, anchored at the mouth of the harbor of Naupaktus and heading seaward, he passed himself to port of her, and pulling at full speed, turned short round her stem, just as the Leukadian trireme was coming on a line with it, so that he struck the Leukadian amidships, injuring her so badly that she sunk in less than twenty minutes after the collision. So overwhelmed was Timokrates by this unexpected reverse of fortune, that, lacking the moral courage necessary to enable him to bear it with fortitude, he threw himself upon his sword and instantly expired. The officers and men of the disabled galley, now left without a leader, surrendered without making the slightest resistance, while the captains of the vessels following her, who might easily have snatched victory from the bold Athenian, lost their wits and absolutely backed their oars. For a moment they remained irresolute, but the next a wild shout of triumph, coming from land and sea, decided them, and they turned and fled, hotly pursued by Phormio, while the Messenian *hoplites*, or heavy armed infantry soldiers were seen rushing from the heights to the assistance of their stranded vessels, but one of which had yet fallen into the enemy's hands. Encouraged by their presence, the crews of the others, who, though fearfully outnumbered, were still making a desperate resistance, fought with renewed ardor; and as the *hoplites* wading into the water and climbing on board took their places beside them, Knemus realized that there was still a hard fight before him; yet he never doubted of final success until several of his vessels, hauling out of the action, pulled at full speed for the opposite shore, where a Peloponnesian army was stationed, when, looking toward Naupaktus, he beheld six of his rear division in the hands of Phormio and the rest flying wildly before him. Then a general panic seized his whole command, and victory was justly claimed by the Athenians, who, with the loss of but one of their little fleet, had captured and sunk seven of the Peloponnesian triremes, and put the rest of them—a force still numbering seventy vessels—to a shameful flight.

A few days after this battle, Phormio's force was strengthened by the arrival of twenty vessels from Athens, whereupon, the allies dispersed and returned to their several states leaving Phormio in undisputed possession of the Gulf of Corinth.

The strategical movement of Knemus toward Naupaktus

was well conceived, since it had the effect of forcing Phormio into a disadvantageous position, and his manœuvring to bring on an engagement was admirable and must have secured him an easy victory had his officers and men been worthy of such a commander. The officer to whom the honor of gaining the day properly belongs, is that Athenian Captain whose name has unfortunately not come down to us who sunk the flagship of Timokrates, but this does not detract in the least from the merit of Phormio, who was quick to profit by the enemy's disaster, and who had so completely gained the confidence of all under his command, that they were ready to encounter any odds as we have seen, when he gave the order to advance.

From the fact that, at Salamis, the smaller naval force preferred "narrowness of space," while off Molykreium, it sought "amplitude of sea-room," Mr. Grote concludes "that the improved practice of Athens had introduced *a revolution in Naval warfare.*" The truth is, however, that at Salamis the confederate fleet was not so superior as a *whole* to the Persian fleet, in which it must be remembered, were incorporated the well drilled naval forces of Egypt and Phœnicia, as to enable Eurybiades to calculate with certainty upon out manœuvring it, he, therefore, wisely guarded against being overpowered by numbers by fighting in the strait. At Naupakatus, on the other hand, the Athenian fleet was so far ahead of that of the Peloponnesians in speed and handiness and so much better officered and manned, that Phormio undoubtedly expected to have it in his power, with "amplitude of sea-room," to concentrate his whole force upon one of his adversary's wings or centre and, whipping that, to produce such consternation throughout his whole command as to ensure its utter defeat. That his judgment was correct in this matter after events proved. But this so far from being a revolution in ancient maritime warfare, as regarded the selection of a battle ground, was a confirmation of it. And it may yet be laid down as a naval maxim that, of two fleets equally swift, handy and well manœuvred, the safety of the weaker numerically, lies in seeking such a confined space as shall prevent its being outflanked by the other ; but when the large fleet is composed of slow unwieldy vessels badly handled, while the smaller consists of fast, quick-turning ships in the hands of seamen, the former and not the latter must avoid the sailor's home, the open sea.

At the beginning of the Peloponnesian war, the Athenians were accounted the most expert mariners of Greece, but little by little, under the teaching of such men as Knemus, the allies became accustomed to the deep, until at the siege of Syracuse as we shall see, the palm of superior seamanship was snatched from its former possessors by their ancient and inveterate enemies, the Corinthians.

ATHENIANS AND SICILIANS ; FEARFUL OVERTHROW OF THE FORMER IN THE HARBOR OF SYRACUSE, AND DECLINE OF ATHENS AS A NAVAL POWER.

When the Athenian fleet dispatched to the aid of the little republic of Ægesta, situated near the western end of Sicily first hove in sight of that island, it numbered one hundred and thirty-four triremes, carrying twenty-five thousand seamen and light-armed infantry, and was accompanied by a large number of transports with six thousand pikemen, and a proportionate force of archers and slingers on board, designed to co-operate with it not only in the reduction of Syracuse, the immediate enemy of the Ægestans, but also, according to Thucydides, in the conquest of the whole Island.

As the vessels drew near the land, flags were displayed and trumpets sounded, and the glad shouts of both soldiers and sailors, accustomed by a long succession of victories, to regard defeat as impossible, rent the air, and reaching the shore, smote sadly upon the ears of the Sicilians, who, knowing the defenseless state of their country, watched the approach of this vast armament with the gloomiest apprehensions. Soon however, through the malign influence of those worst of all defects in a commander-in-chief, indecision of character, and a proneness to move slowly where celerity alone could insure success, the aspect of affairs was entirely reversed, the victors became the vanquished, and ancient renown was lost in present humiliation; and the proud fleet which, about a year before the time of which I speak, had entered the port of Syracuse, with great pomp and ostentation, was now actually blockaded in it by the Syracusans, who had moored vessels head and stern, and placed other obstructions across the mouth of the harbor, to prevent its escape.

Such was the condition of affairs, when a retreat by sea having been resolved upon, Nikias intrusted the command of the Athenian fleet to Demosthenes, Menander and Euthydemus, and prepared to fight his last great naval battle ; and, taught by recent reverses, that the beaks of the Syracusan triremes were more powerful than those of his own, he directed his captains to avoid *ramming* as much as possible, and to rely for success entirely upon *boarding*, for which purpose he stationed a large body of soldiers on the forecastle and poop of each vessel, together with a few picked seamen provided with grappling irons, which they were instructed to fasten to such of the enemy's galleys as might collide with them, for the double purpose of preventing them from backing off to ram a second time, and of enabling the Athenian soldiers to gain their decks, and, by the weight of superior numbers beat down all opposition. When everything was ready, the fleet, consisting of one hundred and ten triremes, moved from the dock-yard which the Athenians had constructed, in three grand divisions, with Demosthenes leading, and made directly for the mouth of the harbor, toward which the Syracusans, fewer in number by thirty-four vessels, were shortly afterward observed to be steering. At the first shock, the obstructing vessels were carried by the Athenians, who were proceeding to cut their moorings and clear the passage, when the near approach of their enemies obliged them to desist from their enterprise and form in order of battle. This they did as speedily as possible, and with as much regularity as the narrow limits of the harbor would permit; but they were hardly in line when they were attacked on both wings by the Syracusans under Sicanus and Agatharcus, who, moving down close to the shore — the one on the right, the other on the left side of the harbor, which is semi-circular in form and narrowest at its mouth — were enabled to out-flank them. Their flanks being turned in this manner were necessarily driven in upon their centre; which, at this critical instant, was furiously assailed by the Corinthians, the faithful allies of the Syracusans, who, led by Pythen, one of their own countrymen, had pulled down the middle of the harbor, and inspirited by the remembrance of former successes, rushed with full speed to the attack, with loud shouts of triumph, as if the victory were already theirs. Great confusion now ensued among the Athenians; for many of their triremes had been stove and were foundering, while those that remained were hemmed in by their enemies; so that there was no room for manœuvring, nor did there seem to be any way of extricating them from their perilous situation. To add to their misery, the waters in their midst were filled with their drowning comrades, piteously calling for help, while their countrymen on shore, beholding their sad condition, were beating their breasts and loudly calling out one to another: "They are conquered! they are conquered! Alas! alas! for Athens!" Still they behaved in a manner not unworthy of their former reputation. When the Syracusans, circling round them, bore down upon them for the purpose of ramming, they so plied them with javelins, stones and arrows as often to make them retire. At other times, when they could not effect this, they threw out their grappling irons upon the forecastles of the approaching vessels, and when they found that the irons would not hold (owing to the fact that the Syracusans, in anticipation of this stratagem, had covered their forecastles with bulls' hides), they, nevertheless, did not abandon their design of boarding; but, watching the moment of contact, sprang boldly on the decks of the assailants, and put all who opposed them to the sword. In this manner they got possession of many of the Syracusan triremes; but their own loss, meanwhile, was frightful; and, after the battle had been maintained for many hours, Demosthenes, perceiving that a longer continuance of it would lead to the annihilation of his whole fleet, took advantage of a break in the enemy's line, to make the signal to retreat. This was immediately answered by the other commanders, both of whom saw the necessity for retiring, and the retreat began. At first it was conducted in good order, but the Syracusans pressing upon the Athenian rear, soon converted it into a shameful flight, in which each captain, forgetful of the public safety, thought only of his own. In this disorder the Athenians reached their dock-yard, the entrance to which was securely guarded by merchant ships, having cranes rigged on them, carrying large stones called *dolphins,* which were of sufficient weight to sink any vessel they might be dropped upon. Here the pursuit of the vanquished necessarily ended; and, content with their victory, the Syracusans returned to their city, "with their wrecks and dead," "while the Athenian sea forces," says Thucydides, "as many as were not taken afloat, hastened from their vessels to the camp, where the army, lamenting and groaning, deplored the event, and proceeded, some to succor the ships, others to garrison the dock-yard; while others, and those the greater part, began now to think of themselves, and how they should best provide for their own preservation."

That night, Demosthenes proposed that they should man their remaining triremes, sixty in all, and make another attempt to force their way out of the harbor, alleging, as was true, that they were still stronger than the enemy by ten vessels. Nikias gave his consent to the measure, but when the sailors were ordered to embark, they flatly refused, loudly declaring that their numbers had become so reduced by sickness, battle and scant diet, that there were neither able seamen left to take the helm, nor rowers sufficient for the benches. The last battle, they said, had been a soldiers' rather than a sailors' fight; and such battles were better conducted by land than by sea. They then, with one accord, ran to the dock-yard, carrying torches in their hands, which they applied to it in many places. It was soon in a blaze and the flames rapidly extended to the fleet, the greater part of which became a sheet of fire, while such of its vessels as escaped the conflagration fell into the hands of the Syracusans; who, amid the tumult occasioned by the mutiny, carried them off, if not unobserved, at all events without opposition. Thus the whole of the fleet was lost to the Athenians, and Athens ceased to be a great naval power. Two days after this commenced that melancholy retreat by land, in which love of country was lost in love of life, and which ended in the surrender of the Athenian army, and the stoning to death of Nikias and Demosthenes by the Syracusans. The genius of Socrates was right. Not without cause had the heads fallen from the Hermæ, standing at the doors of the houses in Athens!

A study of all the particulars of the siege of Syracuse, so minutely given by Thucydides, but which it is not our province here to recite; teaches us a useful lesson of what may be gained by determination and promptitude, and what lost by vacillation and delay. Had the Athenians attacked Syracuse on first making Sicily, it must have fallen almost without resistance, while its capture would have been followed by that of the whole island, and have led eventually, it seems highly probable from the political aspect of the times, to the enthrallment of all Greece to Athenian rule. On the other hand, if the Syracusans, justly alarmed by the Athenian armament, had tamely given themselves up as lost, and neglected making those preparations for defence which, with the inventions of Archimedes at a later date for their protection against Marcellus, are still the admiration of mankind, they could not afterward have profited by their enemy's mistakes; in despite of which their city would have fallen, and they themselves have been subjected to the bitter mortification of knowing that it fell, not so much through the valor of the Athenians, as through their own cowardice and inaction. In their last naval combat, following, no doubt, the advice of the Corinthians, who were now accounted the best seamen of Greece, they displayed much tactical skill, while the Athenians fell into a trap from which the merest tyro in his profession should have saved them; for, since their fleet greatly outnumbered that of the Syracusans, their *role* was so to extend their front as to outflank the latter, instead of which they suffered themselves to be drawn into an engagement in the very narrowest part of the harbor, where their numbers were an incumbrance rather than an advantage to them; and where they were outflanked themselves, as we have seen. Had Demosthenes simply dispatched a squadron to remove the obstructions, the Syracusans must either have permitted it to clear them away unmolested (in which case the object of the Athenians, a retreat by sea, would have been attained), or have sallied forth from their city to attack it. In the latter event, Demosthenes could have drawn out the rest of his fleet in line, directly across the harbor, and followed the Syracusans, who must then have faced about to receive his attack in front, while they would have been exposed to that of the detached squadron in their rear. The result may easily be imagined.

Of the military character of Nikias, who lived like a saint, and died like a martyr, it is difficult to make an analysis, but he seems to have been ever of a wavering, irresolute and overcautious temper, and to this, during his Sicilian campaign, was added the timidity natural to an *infirm* old age. He is said to have been the first Commander-in-Chief who made written reports to his government of his military and naval operations; and he was accustomed to indulge in lengthy dispatches, filled with complaints of a want of men and of equipments and munitions of war, and giving an exaggerated picture of the force and resources of the enemy. To this pernicious habit, may doubtless be attributed, in part, his want of success at Syracuse; for it may be laid down as a military and naval maxim that *that Commander-in-Chief will fall short in deeds, who, in the face of the enemy, relinquishes the sword for the pen.* A consideration of what Nikias lost for his country in Sicily, and of the evils which that loss subsequently entailed upon the Athenians, will serve to show *how careful a people should be in the selection of generals to command its armies, and of admirals to conduct its fleets; and especially should the lesson be brought home to us, whose existence as one nation has more than once, within my own recollection, been imperilled by the blind subserviency of the government to "political expediency" or to public clamor.*

The deliberations of the councils of war on both sides, as recorded by history, give us much valuable information with regard to the tactics of the contending parties. The Athenians, it seems, were in the habit of manœuvring to outflank an enemy, and wherever they saw a chance of piercing his line, to seize it and double upon him; or breaking the unity of his fleet, by retreating in feigned disorder, they turned upon its detached parts, when they had become so widely separated as not to be within supporting distance of each other, and crushed them, one after the other, by superior forces. To accomplish these objects great speed was necessary, and they therefore lengthened the prows of their vessels to such a degree as seriously to impair their strength, so that they never ventured to run straight at an enemy, but endeavored by an *oblique* blow to carry away his oars or steering gear, and thus put him at their mercy. The Corinthians, on the other hand, and the Syracusans, copying after them, struck full and fair with their massive beaks, sometimes cutting a vessel down to the water's edge, sometimes so careening her as to cause her to founder from the quantity of water taken on board, at first through the row-ports and finally over the rail, on the side opposite to that struck. The excellence of their *method* became apparent, so soon as the Athenians from a want of sea-room were unable to avoid their attacks; and it would be well for us to adopt it, since in our "long ships" propelled by steam, we can have strength and speed combined, or, in other words, a *steam ram*, the shock of which is much more to be dreaded than that of the heaviest projectiles thrown by cannon or the explosion of the "horrid torpedo," about which all the world is just now exercised. The great importance attached to *ramming* by the ancients, generally, is shown in the fact that of "forty-two undoubted specimens of ancient marine architecture, taken indiscriminately as they could be collected," by John Charnock, more than three fourths are representations simply of the prows or beaks of ships.

Of the many marvellous stories about the disaster to the Athenians in Sicily, not the least singular is that told by Plutarch of the manner in which the news of it was carried to Athens. "It seems," says he, "that a stranger who landed in the Piræus, as he sat to be shaved in a barber shop, spoke of it as an event already known to the Athenians. The barber no sooner heard it, than he ran into the city and communicated the intelligence to the authorities in open court. The magistrates, in alarm, immediately summoned an assembly and introduced the informant, who not being able to produce the stranger was considered as a forger of false news, and fastened to the wheel, where he suffered torture for some time, till at length some credible persons arrived from Sicily, who gave a distinct account both of the march and the defeat. With so much difficulty was it that the misfortunes of Nikias found credit among his countrymen, though he had often forewarned them that they would certainly happen."

ROMANS AND CARTHAGINIANS. FIRST NAVAL VICTORY OF THE ROMANS, OFF MYLÆ. A ROSTRATED COLUMN OF MARBLE ERECTED TO DUILIUS AT ROME. GREAT ENGAGEMENT OFF HERACLÆA OF MINOS AND TOTAL DEFEAT OF THE CARTHAGINIANS. POOR SEAMANSHIP OF THE ROMANS.

While the Phœnicians were serving as mercenaries in the Persian fleet, a colony, planted by them in Africa, was rapidly rising in the scale of nations, raising vast armies and equipping mighty fleets; and everywhere adding to that petty territory which according to a most agreeable fiction was originally confined within the narrow limits of an ox's hide.

To this aggressive power, which seemed to be aiming at the sovereignty of the world, was opposed a city in mid Italy, founded by illiterate warriors and herdsmen, weak in comparison with its rival, as regarded its military and naval resources, but all-powerful in that which constitutes the real strength of a State, its exalted national character. This enabled it to grasp victory without elation, and with fortitude to bear defeat, and was the direct offspring of that public virtue for which the Romans, under the republic, were conspicuous, above all other people of their time.

Pyrrhus, during his invasion of Italy, is said to have remarked to his officers, "that the boundless ambition and clashing interests of Rome and Carthage must soon involve them in war, and to have designated Sicily as their first battle-ground." The prediction was verified, fifteen years afterward, in this manner: A body of Campanian mercenaries, who had been serving against Carthage, in the army of Agathocles, tyrant of Syracuse, found means on their return from Africa, of introducing themselves, as friends, into Messina. They had not been there many days, however, before they treacherously took possession of the place, and, putting the men to the sword and seizing upon their wives, children and effects as their own, commenced leading a life of lasciviousness and debauchery. For a while, supported by a Roman legion, which, in imitation of their villanous example, had with like perfidy, seized upon Rhegium, a free city, opposite Messina, on the Italian side of the Strait, they not only retained possession of what they had stolen, but made frequent raids upon the neighboring towns, from which they exacted large contributions both of money and provisions. But when Rome had revenged its outraged faith by taking Rhegium by storm, and putting to an ignominious death all that remained of its infamous garrison, the Campanians or Mamertines, as they now arrogantly styled themselves, began to tremble for their own safety, and, being hard pressed by Hiero, King of Syracuse, applied to both Rome and Carthage for assistance. While the Roman Senate, reflecting not only upon the baseness, but upon the inconsistency of affording aid to an army of robbers and assassins, whose crimes were precisely similar to those which they had but just punished so rigidly in the persons of their own citizens, refused to listen to their appeal, the Carthaginians, deterred by no such scruples, and obeying only the voice of ambition, promptly dispatched a force to the scene of action, which was placed by the Mamertines in charge of their citadel; hearing which the Roman people, in whom the sovereignty of the republic was vested, and who exercised, in their assemblies, the powers of legislation, passed a law directing Appius Claudius, one of the consuls, "to pass over to Messina and expel the Carthaginians."

Such was the beginning of the first Punic War, during the first year of which the Romans, although almost always successful on land, found themselves exposed to continual insults from the Carthaginian fleet, which not only overawed all the seaports of Sicily, but made frequent descents upon the Italian shores. This induced that truly great people, who, at this time, to use the strong language of the Greek historian, "were not in possession of a single shallop they could call their own," [12] to undertake the building and equipping of a fleet which should be able to cope with that of Carthage, then the undisputed mistress of the seas. Fortunately for their design, a Carthaginian quinquereme, in attempting to prevent Appius Claudius, with his legion from crossing the straits, in *borrowed* boats, had grounded upon a shoal near Rhegium, and fallen into the Consul's hands. This served as a model to the Romans, who, in an almost incredibly short space of time, put afloat one hundred quinqueremes, and twenty triremes. As these war-vessels, however, were exactly like those of the Greeks and Persians already described, which were modelled, as we have said, after the galleys of the Phœnicians, the remote ancestors of the Carthaginians, no further description of them is necessary. While they were building, a large force of landsmen was assembled at the dock-yard, and put under the care of such able seamen as could be persuaded to enter the Roman Navy from the neighboring maritime States. These instructed the landsmen in the exercise of the oar, by placing benches in the water along the shore, arranged as in a galley, to the extremities of which were secured upright pieces of timber, with *thole pins* attached, to which the oars were fastened with *grummets* or *beckets*, as in our large cutters and launches. Then the rowers, seated in pairs upon the benches, "accustomed themselves to perform all the necessary motions of the body; to fall back together and again to bend forwards; to contract and extend their arms; to begin or leave off according to the signals."

When all things were in readiness, the Romans put to sea, and steered to the southward and eastward, along the Italian shore, exercising diligently in fleet tactics, as they went, and finding their vessels sluggish in their movements, they foresaw that they would easily be out-manœuvred by the Carthaginians, and therefore determined, when in action, to close with them at once, and place their whole dependence in boarding. To this end, they erected on the prow of each vessel a machine, called afterward *corvus*, most probably from some real or fancied resemblance of its grappling iron to the claws of a crow or raven. This was invented by a mechanic of the fleet, and is described by Polybius as a round pillar of wood, of about twelve feet in height, and of three palms breadth in diameter, with a pulley at the top. To this pillar was fitted a kind of stage, eighteen feet in length and four feet broad, which was made ladder-wise, of strong timbers laid across, and cramped together with iron, the pillar being received into an oblong square, which was opened for that purpose, at the distance of six feet within the end of the stage. On either side of the stage lengthways was a parapet, which reached just above the knee. At the farthest end of this stage, or ladder, was a bar of iron, whose shape was somewhat like a pestle; but it was sharpened at the bottom, or lower point; and on the top of it was a ring. The whole appearance of this machine very much resembled those that are used in grinding corn. To the ring just mentioned was fixed a rope; by which, with the help of the pulley that was at the top of the pillar, they hoisted up the ladders, and as the vessels of the enemy came near, let them fall upon them, sometimes on their prow, and sometimes on their sides as occasion best served. As the ladder fell, it struck into the decks of the enemy, and held them fast. In this situation, if the two vessels happened to lay side by side, the Romans leaped on board from all parts of their ships at once. But in case that they were joined only by the prow, they then entered two and two along the ladder; the two foremost extending their bucklers right before them, to ward off the strokes that were aimed against them in front; while those that followed rested the boss of their bucklers upon the top of the parapet on either side, and thus covered both their flanks."

I have been particular in giving Polybius' description of the *corvus*, in full, because to this is mainly to be ascribed, as we shall see, the naval victories obtained by the Romans over a people much more at home upon the water than themselves.[13]

During the time thus occupied in making preparation for battle, the consul, Cn. Cornelius, who had gone, with seventeen ships, to Messina, to provide stores and provisions for the fleet, was seduced, by false reports, into making an attempt upon Lipara, where he and all of his vessels fell into the enemy's hands. This disaster to their arms, however, was more than counterbalanced to the Romans, not long afterwards, by the capture of the greater part of a squadron of fifty ships, with which Hannibal, the Carthaginian commander-in-chief, had presumed to attempt a close reconnaissance of the strength and disposition of their armament.

When Duilius heard of the misfortune that had befallen his colleague, he left the army in Sicily to the care of the Tribunes, and hastened to assume command of the fleet; and as he was anxious to signalize his consulship, then drawing to a close, by some important service to the State, which should entitle him to the honors of a triumph, he had scarcely displayed his flag afloat when he got under way, and shaped his course for Mylæ, where the hostile fleet, under the command of Hannibal, was then lying at anchor.

When the Carthaginians beheld the Romans approaching, they congratulated themselves upon having secured, as they supposed, so easy a prey, and pulling out of the harbor in a straggling manner, made no effort whatever to secure unity of action among their vessels. "What need have we, the favored sons of Neptune," they cried contemptuously, "to form in order of battle, for the purpose of engaging with these landsmen. Let us close with them at once, before their courage evaporates, and they turn their prows towards Italy!" Encouraging each other in this manner, they steered directly for the enemy, their fleet of one hundred and thirty quinqueremes being soon broken into detachments of various strength, according to the speed of the vessels. Thus, the van, composed of thirty of their fastest quinqueremes, and led by Hannibal, in an immense ship of "seven banks of oars," which is said to have originally belonged to Pyrrhus, came in collision with the Romans, drawn up in line to receive it, while the rest of the fleet was still at too great a distance to render it the least assistance. Then the Carthaginians, engaged in this unequal contest, seeing themselves attacked on all sides by the Romans, began to repent of their rashness, and turned to fly; but flight was no longer possible; for the *corvi*, descending upon their decks, held them fast in their iron grasp, while the Roman soldiers advancing along the ladders or gangways, two and two, in the manner described by Polybius, put all who opposed them to the sword. Thus, the whole van-division fell into the hands of the Romans, without the slightest loss on their part. Hannibal, however, who had made his escape, with great difficulty, in a small boat rowed by four seamen, now hastened to repair his error by forming the remaining vessels of his fleet into line, in which order it awaited the shock of the victorious Romans who were rapidly approaching. During the interval that elapsed between this time and the moment of actual combat, the Carthaginian commander passed from vessel to vessel, exhorting each man to stand firm and to fight as if the event of the battle depended upon himself alone. But nothing could restore the drooping courage of those who had just witnessed the destruction of their comrades by so novel a mode of warfare, and they were scarcely attacked before they broke and fled, leaving fifty more of their vessels in the enemy's hands.

So ended the first great naval engagement between the Romans and the Carthaginians, the news of which filled Rome with joy and hope, and Carthage with grief and despondency. Duilius obtained the honors he coveted, at the hands of his countrymen; for in commemoration of his glorious achievements, a marble column, "adorned with the beaks of ships, and having his statue on top," was erected in the Roman Forum, while Hannibal, who suffered himself to be surprised, not long afterward, by the enemy, in one of the harbors of Sardinia, was seized by his own seamen and crucified.

In the course of the ensuing year, there were several slight engagements between the hostile fleets, in which victory inclined first to one side and then to the other; but no decisive battle was fought. At length, however, the Roman, as well as the Carthaginian government, became convinced that ultimate success could only be achieved by that nation which should obtain the mastery of the Mediterranean, and each resolved to put forth its utmost strength, to effect this object. Thenceforth, in pursuance of this resolution, the dock-yards and work-shops of both countries resounded, for many months, from daylight to dusk and from dusk to daylight, with the sound of the hammer and saw, and the hum of a busy multitude, of which some were engaged in building ships and in making masts and oars, some in cutting out sails and awnings, and in fitting and overhauling rigging; and others in providing water and provisions, and in collecting together, and storing away under sheds provided for this purpose, an immense quantity of naval stores of every description.

Their united efforts gave to the Romans three hundred and thirty, and to the Carthaginians three hundred and fifty quinqueremes, with which these bitter rivals took the sea early in the summer of the year 260 B.C.; the former sailing to join their army at Ecnormus, with a view of embarking it and shifting the scene of action from Sicily to Africa; the latter, in order to thwart this design, which their able leader Hamilcar had readily divined, making all haste to form a connection with their own soldiers at Heraclæa of Minos, and keeping a sharp lookout for the Roman fleet, from the high lands of Caena, with the fixed determination of forcing it to an engagement should it endeavor to pass their place of anchorage. They were not kept long in suspense; for, on the second day after their arrival, its coming was announced by their sentinels; whereupon Hamilcar ordering his officers and men to hold themselves in readiness to weigh anchor at a moment's notice, himself repaired to a neighboring eminence, whence he beheld, with the delight of a soldier, but the anxiety of a general, that magnificent military array of the Roman vessels, which has never been surpassed, if indeed equalled, by any combination of modern times. For two ships of six banks of oars, with the standards of the Consuls Manlius and Regulus flying from their flag-staffs, and placed abreast of each other, at such a distance from each other as should afford room simply for the free use of their oars, acted as leaders of the starboard and port columns of the fleet, which composed, respectively, of the van and centre divisions, with the first and second legions on board, and formed into echelon of vessels, constituted what in military parlance, was termed a *wedge*, and rested upon the rear division, carrying the third legion, as a base, so that the whole made an isosceles triangle, "strong and proper for action and not easily to be broken." Following the rear division and towed by it, were the transports, and last of all came the reserve, with the colors of the *Triarii*[14] displayed, which, divided into two equal squadrons, served as a guard for the right and left rear flanks of this imposing military and naval armament.

As Hamilcar scanned the disposition of the enemy, with an experienced eye, he perceived that the movements of their third and fourth divisions were fettered by the transports, and resolved to try by stratagem to separate the first and second from them, believing it would then be an easy matter to fall upon and capture, in succession, the disjoined parts, and thus whip the whole fleet in detail. With this intent, he drew out his force in four divisions, of which he disposed three in line, at right angles to the course the Romans were steering, and heading south-east, and the fourth, in the order which was called the *forceps;* posting this last a little in the rear, and well on the left of the main body. Thus prepared, he passed through the fleet in his barge, reminding his countrymen of their descent from a long succession of illustrious seamen, and assuring them that victory was easy over their inexperienced foe, if they would but do their whole duty to themselves, their country and their general. "Your former defeat," said he, "was owing not to the nautical skill of the Romans, but to your own rash valor, which prompted you to rush headlong into action with a warlike people never to be despised. Let us now profit by our past misfortune, and, avoiding the prows of the Roman galleys, strike them amidships or on the quarter; thus shall we either sink them or disable their oars, besides rendering the machines, on which they principally rely for safety, wholly inoperative." This speech was received with loud acclamations by the Carthaginians, who, with the fullest confidence in their general, demanded to be led at once against the enemy; whereupon, Hamilcar, taking his station in their midst, ordered the advance to be sounded, at the same time signalling to all the vessels of the centre division, which he observed would be the first to engage, to retreat in apparent disorder, when they came within fifty yards of the enemy. In obedience to this command, the Carthaginian centre no sooner came near the Romans, than, as if terrified by their appearance, it turned, in well-simulated flight, and steered for Heraclæa, hotly pursued by the enemy's starboard and port columns, which, as Hamilcar had foreseen, rapidly drew away from the rest of the fleet. When they were so far separated from it as to preclude the possibility of its coming to their support, the Carthaginians, upon a signal from their flag-ship, put about and attacked them with great ardor and resolution, making a desperate effort, from their exterior lines, to force the two sides of the wedge together; but these, facing outward, and always presenting their prows to the assailants, remained unbroken and immovable; and if, by chance, a Carthaginian vessel succeeded in ramming one of their number abeam or on the quarter, as directed, instantly her next on the right or the left, as the case might be, came to her relief, so that the Carthaginians, turn which way they would, found the dread *corvi* always suspended above them. Thus furiously did the battle rage in the centre, when Hanno, who commanded the right wing, instead of falling upon the enemy's port column in flank, and thus making victory sure in that quarter, stretched far out to sea, and bore down upon and engaged the *Triarii.* The Carthaginian reserve, too, making a similar mistake with regard to the Roman right, now changed from its first order into line and advanced with loud shouts upon the third division, incumbered, as we have said, with the transports. Thus there were three naval combats going on at the same time, and all maintained with equal valor and constancy; but at length the *Triarii*, overcome by the double duty of having to protect the transports, as well as themselves, from the attacks of the enemy, were about to yield, when they observed that the Carthaginian centre was in full retreat, chased by their van division, while their second division was hastening to their own assistance. This inspired them with new courage, and, although many of their quinqueremes had been sunk and not a few taken, they continued to fight with great gallantry until the arrival of their friends compelled Hanno to make the signal for flight. In the meantime, the Roman third division, embarrassed by its convoy, had been gradually forced to give sea, until it found itself close to land; in which situation it resembled a beleaguered fortress; for, while attacked in front and on both flanks by the Carthaginians, a more terrible enemy, in the shape of sharp-pointed, surf-beaten rocks appeared in its rear; and it was falling, vessel by vessel, into the Carthaginians' hands, when Manlius, perceiving its critical condition, gave up his pursuit of the fugitives, and went to its support. His presence converted defeat into victory, and thus insured the complete triumph of the Roman arms.

Then the whole sea was covered with the Carthaginians scattered in flight, while the Romans, towing their prizes stern foremost, as was their custom after a successful action, entered and took possession of the harbor of Heraclæa.

Such was the termination of this sanguinary engagement, in which thirty of the Carthaginian, and twenty-four of the Roman quinqueremes were sent to the bottom with all on board. Not a single Roman vessel was carried off by the enemy, while the Carthaginians, who, by all the rules of war, should have come off victorious, had sixty-four vessels taken with their crews. *The lesson it teaches us is, that the ablest strategist can effect nothing, if the officers next to him in rank, upon whom he has to rely for the execution of his orders, fail either through ignorance or arrogance, or a spirit of insubordination, to carry out his plans.* Had Hanno and the commander of the Carthaginian reserve done their duty faithfully and intelligently, on this occasion, the Roman van and centre must have been doubled up and defeated, almost instantly; after which it would have been an easy matter to get possession of the third and fourth divisions with the transports. Thus the Carthaginians would have gained a decisive victory, the effect of which would have been perhaps, to deter the Romans from again making their appearance in force upon the sea; and then, with such leaders as Hamilcar, Hasdrubal and Hannibal to shape her policy and conduct her armaments, Carthage, instead of Rome, might have been the mistress of the world. Such are the great issues sometimes impending over contending armies and fleets!

It seems singular that the consuls who had the foresight and ability to adopt an order of battle, so admirably suited to ward off the attacks of the Carthaginians, obliged from the force of circumstances to assume the offensive, should have been betrayed into the grave error of breaking that order, in the ardor of pursuit, before the battle had really begun. This, however, is doubtless to be attributed to the impatience of their subordinates, whose impetuosity, in all probability, could not be restrained. On the other hand it would be difficult to explain, on any plausible supposition, why the Carthaginians, who, in former encounters, had seen the bad effect produced upon their men by the *corvi*, had neglected in fitting out this new armament, to guard against these formidable instruments of war, which, while they entirely neutralized their own superior nautical skill, enabled the Roman soldier to fight on the decks of the enemy, with as much confidence as on the land. These, and these alone, prevented the two columns of the wedge from being forced together, and saved the Roman van and centre.

A careful study of this great sea-fight, in all its details, cannot fail to prove instructive to the naval officers of the present day, *when steamers have taken the place of the ancient war galleys, and, with proper turning-power, without which a man-of-war, whatever her speed, armament, or armor, is unworthy of a place in the line of battle, may and should be manœuvred on precisely similar principles.*

As soon as the consuls had repaired damages, they set sail for Africa, where they arrived in safety, and disembarked the army, which was then put in charge of Regulus, while Manlius, after selecting forty of the best ships to remain behind, as auxiliaries to the legions, returned with the rest of the naval force, having all the prisoners on board, to Rome.

After the defeat of Regulus, the Roman fleet, being again dispatched to Africa, to take off some two thousand of his soldiers, who, escaping from the field of battle, had fortified themselves in Aspis, a small town on the sea-coast, fell in with the Carthaginian armament, inferior to it in strength, off the promontory of Hermæa, and, after a trifling engagement, captured one hundred and fourteen of its vessels. Then taking on board the troops at Aspis, its leaders, the consuls, M. Emilius and Servius Fulvius, determined to return to Italy along the Southern shore of Sicily, against the urgent remonstrance of their pilots, who wisely argued "that, at this dangerous season, when the constellation of Orion being not quite passed, the Dog Star was just ready to appear, it were far safer to go North about." The consuls, unfortunately were not to be shaken in their determination, and, Sicily reached, a course was shaped from Lylybeum to the promontony of Pachymus. The fleet had accomplished about two thirds of this distance, and was just opposite the Camarinian coast, where there are no ports and the land is high and rocky, when, with the going down of the sun, the North wind, which had been blowing steadily for several days, suddenly died away; and, as the Romans were engaged in furling their flapping sails, they observed that they were wet and heavy with the falling dew, the sure precursor of the terrible *sirocco.* Then the pilots urged them to pull directly to the Southward, that they might have sea-room sufficient to prevent their drifting ashore, when the storm should burst upon them; but this, with the dread of the sea natural to men unaccustomed to contend with it, they refused to do, not comprehending that although their quinqueremes were illy adapted to buffet the waves, anything was better than a lee shore, with no harbor of refuge. The North wind sprang up again, after a little, *cheering the hearts of the inexperienced*, blew in fitful gusts for an hour or more, then faded nearly away, again sprang up, and finally, died out as before. Next a flash of lightning in the Southern sky; then a line of foam upon the Southern Sea—the roaring of Heaven's artillery in the air above and of the breakers on the beach below—and the tempest was upon them! From this time, all order lost, and the admonitions of the pilots unheeded; the Roman fleet was completely at the mercy of the hurricane, and the veterans who had borne themselves bravely in many a hard fought battle with their fellow-men, now, completely demoralized in the presence of this new danger, behaved more like maniacs than reasoning beings. Some advised one thing, some another; but nothing sensible was done; and, when the gale broke, out of four hundred and sixty-four quinqueremes, three hundred and eighty had been dashed upon the rocks and lost. The whole shore was covered with dead bodies, and the fragments of vessels; and that which Rome had been years in acquiring, at the cost of so much blood, labor and treasure she lost in a few hours, through the want of experienced seamen.

During the remainder of this and the succeeding Punic wars, the Romans and the Carthaginians met in several well contested naval engagements, in which the former were usually successful, although Adherbal gained a glorious victory for his country off Drepanum, on the North-west coast of Sicily, where he captured ninety-four of the Roman vessels; but the details of these actions are too meagre, to allow us to form a just estimate of the tactical ability displayed in them by either party. What the Romans gained in battle, however, was soon snatched from them, through their ignorance of seamanship, by repeated shipwrecks on the coasts of Sicily and Italy; so that at the end of the first Punic war, which lasted twenty-four years, they had lost seven hundred quinqueremes, the vanquished Carthaginians but five hundred.

CIRCUMNAVIGATION OF AFRICA BY HANNO THE CARTHAGINIAN.

We shall now give an account of the cruise of the latter, under Hanno, on the West coast of Africa, after which, bidding them adieu, it is our intention to return to the Romans under the empire.

Of the precise time, when Hanno set out on his famous voyage, history fails to make mention, and this circumstance, taken conjointly with the fabulous accounts contained in the *periplus*, a Greek translation of the story of the cruise, said to have been written by Hanno in the Punic language, has caused a few authors, to attempt to throw discredit upon the whole matter, but the weight of both evidence and opinion is overwhelmingly against their hasty conclusions; and nothing, certainly, would seem to be more probable than that an enterprising maritime people, like the Carthaginians, should make some effort to become acquainted with the form, extent, resources, and character of the country which they inhabited. As to the discrepancy between the number and capacity of Hanno's vessels and of the people said to have been carried by them to colonize certain parts of Africa, this may very well be an error of the translator, or the sixty *penteconters* mentioned may have simply accompanied the grand fleet "capable of accommodating thirty thousand persons, with their arms, provisions and effects," for the purpose of facilitating as Ramusio suggests, the landing of its crews and colonists, on such parts of the coast as might not be safely approached by the larger vessels.

According to Hanno's narrative, he got underway from Cadiz, and having passed the pillars of Hercules, steered to the southward and westward, two days, when he anchored opposite to a wide spreading, well watered plain, bounded on three sides by high hills, where he built a city called Thymatheerion. Resuming his voyage, he planted four other colonies, at such points on the coast as he deemed favorable for commercial purposes, and hove to, and sent for water off the river Lixio, where Hercules, lifting the giant Antæus from his mother earth, crushed him to death in his arms, and near which he found the golden apples of Hera, in the garden of the Hesperides. *Filling away* again, Hanno kept to the southward, and after many long months had elapsed, reached the native settlement of Salen, where, although the land was fertile and the climate fine, owing to the prevalence of fresh sea-breezes, he was deterred from landing, because of the wild beasts which coming thither from the Libyan deserts terrified the inhabitants "with their frightful howling."

From here the Carthaginians continued onward by that dreadful Cape, which the sailors for many ages regarded with superstitious awe, saying that he who with mad daring should pass its southern limit, might never more hope to put his foot on land, and that many a phantom ship of the old Phœnicians, manned by a phantom crew, was there condemned to cruise till the end of time, ever engaged in the weary, hopeless task of endeavoring to get to the Northward, and ever looking upon the land beyond the Cape with wistful eyes. Sometimes these ghostly mariners, with sails close furled, passed days and weeks, laboriously tugging at their oars, at others, under sails and oars combined, they endeavored to make their toilsome way; but oftenest, according to the legend, they were descried when skies were dark and the ocean lashed into fury by Southern gales, running madly before the blast with all their canvas spread, as if the breeze were light and the waves at rest. Yet ever, as they neared the Cape, an invisible hand bore them backward towards the South.

Arrived at the high lands of Blanco, Hanno founded there the town of Cerne, now called Arguin, whence he proceeded across the gulf of this name to the River Niger, where, "in the midst of crocodiles and sea horses, were seen mermen and mermaids playing in the limpid waters." Next came the islands of the Gorgons, "serpent tressed and hating men, whom mortal wight might not behold and live." And this danger left behind, there burst upon the view of the admiring Carthaginians, a high mountain, which with one voice they pronounced "The chariot of the Gods," for it was all alight with flame and resounded with never dying thunder. "The top of this mountain," says Mariana, "from its great height is ordinarily resplendent with lightning, and the inhabitants on its slopes, who, owing to the excessive heat, keep close within their subterranean dwellings by day, when twilight appears, sally forth with burning torches, to seek their food; thus at night the whole mountain side seems wrapped in a garment of fire. This gave rise to the marvellous story told by Hanno and his companions, on their return to Carthage (*after the manner of most travellers, who speak of that which they alone have seen*) of their having beheld, in this place, rivers of fire running down the mountain side, and making the country sterile for miles around. With all deference, however, to the precise old friar, it seems highly probable that this was some volcano, in full eruption as the Carthaginians hurried by. The next discovery was the Island of Gorillas, now called St. Thomas, situated on the equator, where the mariners landed and gave chase to a number of "naked men and women covered with hair," capturing three of the latter after a long run, but none of the former, who proved to be too vigorous and swift-footed to be overtaken, and finding their captives "sullen, silent and intractable," they cut their throats on the spot. Then filling their carcases with straw, they stowed them securely away in the holds of their vessels, until their arrival at Carthage, when they were carried ashore with great pomp and ceremony, and hung up in the temple of either Juno or Venus, it is impossible to say which, as on this important point authorities differ. They also differ in relation to the terminus of Hanno's cruise; some asserting that he turned back, through a scarcity of provisions, from Gorilla Island. others, that he kept on to the Arabian Gulf, whence he sent messengers home by land. From these conflicting statements, many of the learned are of the opinion that he made two voyages, in the second of which he completed his circumnavigation of Africa. They also gravely give it as their opinion, that the females captured were not women, but monkeys of large size, of which they say there are various races and "all alike distinguished for sagacity and cunning." On one point all are agreed, namely, that Hanno was absent from Carthage five years, and that, when he returned to it, in addition to what is given above, he delighted the people of that city with wondrous accounts of the dangers he had experienced by land and sea, and of the curious birds, beasts and fishes he had seen, during his wanderings. His *log-book* was deposited in the temple of Saturn. It was entitled "An account of the voyage of Hanno, Commander of the Carthaginians, around the coasts of Libya, beyond the Pillars of Hercules.

ANTONY AND OCTAVIUS. BATTLE OF ACTIUM.

We left the Romans a free people, virtuous and patriotic. We come back to them, after the lapse of two centuries, when Marcus Brutus and Caius Cassius being dead, and public virtue fast expiring, an arbitrary government was in process of erection upon the ruins of the republic, and an image of Liberty, usurping the place formerly occupied by that deity herself, mocked the betrayed citizens from the centre of the Roman forum.

The triumvirate had been dissolved; and Octavius and Antony, at the head of vast armies and fleets, were preparing on opposite sides of the Gulf of Ambracia, to submit the quarrel in which they had long been engaged, to the arbitrament of the sword. In this emergency, Antony's old officers and soldiers, who had often been led to victory by their general, naturally indulged the hope that, drawing out his legions, he would assume the offensive, and, by his superior strategy, force his adversary from the field; but in this they were destined to be disappointed: for, giving up his judgment to that of the "Strange Woman" who had bewitched him, and disregarding the advice of his tried counsellors and friends, *the greatest captain of the age—now that Cæsar and Pompey were no more*—had consented to abandon his faithful army and place his whole reliance upon his fleet, which, although equal to that of Octavius in numbers, was much inferior to it in discipline and drill, and in that experience of actual combat—the most valuable of all—which the latter had acquired in the naval war just concluded between the *Imperator* and Sextus Pompeius.

It is asserted, indeed, by many historians that Antony only contemplated fighting, in case his retreat by sea should be intercepted by Octavius, and that, following Cleopatra's advice altogether, he intended to fall back into Egypt, with both his sea and land forces, and there, re-enforced by all the power of Asia, make his final stand against his formidable rival; and, in support of this assertion, they adduce the fact that he directed his vessels to be supplied with masts and sails, which could be only an incumbrance to them in action. On the other hand we may quote Antony's own words: *they will be useful to me in pursuit;* and, as a proof that his soldiers believed a battle was decided upon, the remark of one of his centurions, who, as he marched by him, at the head of his company, on the way to the place of embarkation, exclaimed, pointing with his sword toward the fleet: "*Why will you, general, rest your hopes on those villanous wooden bottoms. Let the Egyptians and Phœnicians skirmish at sea; but give us the land, where we have learned to conquer or to die.*"

After all his preparations were made, Antony was detained in port four days by a violent storm; but, on the morning of the fifth day, the weather being fair, he got under way and proceeded to the Straits of Actium, where he deployed his whole force in line, with the Egyptians in reserve. On the right was Poplicola; on the left Cælius; in the centre Marcus Octavius and Marcus Justeius. In his front, at the distance of a mile, the fleet of the enemy could be plainly seen, drawn up in parallel order, with Larius opposed to Cælius, Agrippa to Poplicola, Aruntius to Octavius.

Then Antony calling his officers together addressed them, at some length, upon the magnitude of the interests depending upon the battle in which they were about to engage. "If we win," said he, "you will find that your leader well understands how to reward those who have assisted him to rise to power; if we lose, you know what to expect from the man who has never yet pardoned friend or foe who has presumed to thwart his inclinations. This is certainly one of the cases where death is preferable to defeat. The incapacity and cowardice of Octavius you have all had the opportunity of testing, and since his armament is not superior to ours, surely you have every reason to expect to wrest victory from his grasp, when led by him to whose care Julius Cæsar intrusted the left wing of his army at the great battle of Pharsalia. Be assured, then, that the gods will be propitious to us this day, and that your general will share with you its fatigues and dangers."

While Antony was haranguing his officers in this manner, Octavius passing through his fleet, reminded his veterans that they were not fighting against his colleague, but *against the Egyptian sorceress, her eunuchs and waiting women*, who having submitted that once famous warrior to their will, now aspired to the control of the Roman government. *As to Antony, he had lost his wits, as they would see in the engagement, and was no longer responsible for his actions. War, therefore, had been declared not against him, but against his mistress Cleopatra, whose he was, body and soul:* and it remained for them to decide whether they too would be her subjects, or whether they would bring her to justice in the name of the Roman people, whose majesty she had dared to trifle with, in the person of one of their chief magistrates."

At the conclusion of his address, Octavius took his place in the rear of Larius; Antony was already in position alongside of Poplicola. About noon the sea-breeze sprang up, and Antony's men becoming impatient, the left wing was set in motion, whereupon Octavius finding himself embarrassed through a want of room, retired seaward, until he was distant about three miles from the mouth of the Gulf of Ambracia, when he turned and again confronted his adversary.

Then Antony's whole line moved forward, while Agrippa made a flank movement with the design of doubling upon the enemy's right, but, being foiled in this, by a similar manœuvre on the part of Poplicola, the action may be said to have been begun by the two fleets, on equal terms; for although Antony's vessels were larger and stronger than those of Octavius, these advantages were counter-balanced by the superior swiftness and lightness of the latter, which, manœuvring in pairs about the former, assailed the defenders of their towers with javelins and other missile weapons, and the towers themselves with fire, while, from the turrets, in return, darts and javelins were hurled upon the assailants, and huge stones rolled down upon the decks of the light galleys that bore them to the assault. On the one side was a chain of forts, on the other an army of soldiers, organized into companies as on shore, gallantly endeavoring to carry the forts by storm. *Roman against Roman, victory inclined to neither side.* Suddenly, however, a fire-brand thrown by a veteran who had served with Cæsar in Gaul, set fire to one of the towers, and in an instant it was all ablaze. Aruntius, too, observing an opening in the centre of Antony's line, dashed through it with his *liburnians* and attacked the enemy in rear. Then Cleopatra, who, at a little distance behind her friends, was gazing with throbbing heart upon the sanguinary strife from the gilded poop of her luxurious galley, became seized with an irresistible terror, and hoisting her purple sails to the breeze, which shortly before had veered to the north, she steered directly through the contending fleets towards Alexandria, followed by all the Egyptian vessels, and—alas that a great soldier should have sunk so low!—by Antony himself.

Thus Octavius with his "cool head and unfeeling heart," was left in the undisputed possession of the Roman empire. The "*good fortune*"[15] *which had greeted him in the morning continued with him throughout the day; and not the least of the favors of the conservatrix was the giving him Agrippa—a much abler commander than himself—to manœuvre his fleet and lead it to that victory which had been presaged.*

Of Antony, it is enough to say that with all his great qualities, *his baser part so predominated at the last, that he deserted his companions in arms in the heat of battle, and resigned the dominion of the world for the embraces of a woman.* While, therefore, we cannot withhold our admiration for the military genius of one who, in the field, was "inferior only to Cæsar," *we look with contempt, after the battle of Actium, both upon the general and the man.* The character of Cleopatra is not so despicable as his, "As a woman," says Merivale, "she deserves neither love nor admiration; but as a queen, her ambition was bold, and her bearing magnanimous. She contended gallantly for the throne of her ancestors with the weapons which nature had given her." To this we may add that she died royally, according to the public sentiment of her day, lying in state upon her golden bed, and attired as became a queen, with her dainty fingers covered with jewels of priceless value, and on her head the proud diadem of the Pharaohs of Egypt.

What would have been the result of the battle of Actium had Antony but remained true to his former renown, is a question more easily asked than answered, but from the obstinacy with which his faithful soldiers and sailors maintained the combat after his base desertion of them, it seems highly probable that, had he remained, victory would have been his. He undoubtedly committed a great error, however, at the outset, in suffering himself to be decoyed, with his unwieldy vessels, into the open sea;[16] and Agrippa fairly earned the rostral crown that was adjudged to him. The disposition which Anthony made of his forces, prior to engaging, furnishes an additional argument against those who say his flight was premeditated; for had this been so, nothing would have been easier for him than to have adopted, in imitation of Manlius, a wedge-like formation for his fleet, and then putting Cleopatra in the centre, he could readily have beaten off his assailants, and retired whithersoever he pleased.

After Actium, Egypt being reduced to a province of the empire, the Romans had no enemy to contend with upon the sea; yet the transportation of armies, and the protection of commerce from the depredations of pirates, still made it necessary for them to maintain three fleets, one of which was stationed at Ravenna, one at Forum Julii, and the third at Misenum. From this period, however, fortunately for themselves, their naval annals offer nothing worthy of notice.

ARMS AND ENGINES OF WAR OF THE ANCIENTS, AND THEIR MANNER OF USING THEM.

Of the weapons, offensive and defensive, used by the combatants in the myriad sea-fights from Salamis to Actium, it may be briefly remarked, that with some unimportant modifications, they were such as had been in use ages before in the Egyptian navy. Their grappling-irons were shaped much like the modern kedge, and not unfrequently had a *gangway-attachment* to them for the purpose of boarding, like the *corvus* described by Polybius. The name αρπαγγ or *corvus*, seems, indeed, to have been applied indiscriminately to a variety of machines, some of which were used simply for holding on to a vessel while throwing troops on board, others for dropping heavy weights upon her deck, like the *crane* or *dolphin*, and others again for raising vessels up to a considerable height, and then dashing them to pieces against the walls or towers of a beleaguered city, or by suddenly letting them fall stern foremost into the water below, ensure their sinking with all on board. The first *corvus* mentioned in history was invented by a Rhodian architect named Diognetus. Their catapults and balistœ—the former throwing javelins and darts, the latter immense stones —supplied the place of our modern artillery, while their archers and slingers may be said to have represented our small-arm men. "Rigged out on the ends of poles fixed obliquely to the prows of their galleys, and forereaching their beaks," the Rhodians carried large kettles filled with live coals and various combustibles, which, by means of a chain fastened to the bottom of each kettle, they capsized upon the decks of their enemies; and, by not a few writers, it has been confidently asserted that they possessed a knowledge of certain chemicals, which, thrown together, produced a flame, resembling the Greek fire invented by Callinicus, the Syrian, in the 7th century, and, like it, inextinguishable by water.

Fire ships were often used successfully in attacking fleets at anchor, and the Tyrians delayed for some months the fall of their city by destroying with one of these vessels, an immense mole that Alexander had constructed in their harbor. The use, by Hannibal in his war against Pontus, of "earthen pots filled with snakes," seems to have been a solitary instance of this kind, and was, undoubtedly, a mere stratagem of his to gain victory through the power of the imagination, (a very serviceable ally to a commander who knows how to make the best use of it in battle), while the "pipes of metal emitting noise and inflamed smoke," said to have been used in the "early ages of naval warfare," were very probably *the inventions of the writers by whom they have been reported to us.*

In the course of a few centuries after the Christian era, the corvus, the catapult, and the balista were seen no more afloat, and the archers and slingers had given way to cross-bow-men, while the Greek fire "came flying through the air like a long-tailed dragon, with the report of thunder and the velocity of lightning." Some centuries more and the invention of gunpowder revolutionized everything. With a veneration for antiquity, however, which would excite the contempt of a Japanese, Europe and America still continue to "serve out" to their seamen an inferior kind of Egyptian lance called a "boarding-pike."

A ROMAN TRIUMPH.

Of the mixed military and naval triumphs celebrated at *old* Rome, the greatest by far was that of Pompey the Great, after his successful termination of the war against the pirates and the Mithridatic war, wherein several hundred wagons—some loaded with the beaks of ships, and others carrying paintings and sketches of naval battles—were dragged through the *Forum* attended by thousands of the captives, dressed in their national costumes, and followed by many legions of Roman soldiers, and all the seamen that could be collected from the fleet. A placard borne along with the procession, according to custom, informed the lookers-on that this triumph was celebrated "because the maritime coasts had been cleared of pirates; *the dominion of the sea restored to the Roman people,* and the kings of Asia and Pontus subdued.

Out of the spoils obtained in these wars Pompey erected a temple to Minerva, with this dedication, "Cneius Pompey, Captain General and Admiral—the thirty years' war being ended, two millions one hundred and eighty-three thousand men vanquished, put to flight, killed or taken prisoners, eight hundred and sixty-six ships sunk or taken, fifteen hundred and thirty-eight fortified towns and fortresses forced to capitulate, and all the countries between the lake Mæotis and the Red Sea subdued—in gratitude dedicates this temple to Minerva."

VENICE.

The question as to which of the European nations is entitled to the honor of having revived commerce and navigation after the fall of Rome will never perhaps be satisfactorily settled; but the Italians seem to have the fairest title to this distinction. It is to them, then, and especially to Venice the Beautiful, whose palaces anchored in the sea, with St. Mark in the centre for their flagship, may not inaptly be compared to a fleet of galleys fettered together and moored head and stern, that the attention of the naval chronicler must now be directed.

At the head of the Adriatic are a large number of marshy islands, separated by narrow channels or lagoons, which were originally the abode of none but rude fishermen, who gained a scanty subsistence by the sale of fish and salt to their neighbors of Venetia, a province on the mainland of Italy, rich and fertile, and numbering within its limits fifty cities, of which Aquileia and Padua were the most conspicuous. Upon the invasion of Venetia by Attila, in the middle of the fifth century, many of its principal families took refuge among the fishermen of the Adriatic. The Paduans settled in Malamocco and Rialto; the Aquileians in Grado, and dispersed throughout the other islets, were to be found refugees from every city and town of Venetia. These *water-fowls*, as Cassiodorus fancifully styles them, soon became united under a Republican form of government, and, in imitation of ancient Rome, gave the name of consuls to their chief magistrates; Alberigo Faliero, Zeno Dandolo and Tomasso Candiano, formerly of Padua and now residing in the Island of Rialto, being the first to fill this high office. Thus the seat of government was established at Rialto. In a few years the consuls gave way to tribunes elected annually, and these in 697 were supplanted by a Doge, whose office was to be for life. From this period Venice rose rapidly in power and wealth, until in the early part of the ninth century, it had become so strong as to set at defiance the son of the Emperor Charlemagne, whom it utterly defeated at the Canaglia d' Orfano, in the fierce battle which was called in after times the battle of Albiola.

The army of Venice was composed almost entirely of foreign mercenaries, the command of which was entrusted, not to one of her own citizens, lest he should acquire such influence over it as might enable him to subvert the government should he be so inclined, but to some soldier of fortune, who made a trade of war, and whose lust was not for empire, but for fame and gold. The Venetians therefore like the Carthaginians, although they engaged in many wars by land, never became a military people, and the importance of the Venetian commonwealth must be estimated, not by the number of armies it could put into the field, but *by its naval and commercial resources.* "*Nothing was apprehended from the navy*," says Robertson, "*that could prove formidable to liberty.* The Senate encouraged the nobles to trade, and to serve on board the fleet. They became merchants and admirals. They increased the wealth of their country by their industry. They added to its dominions by the valor with which they conducted its naval armaments."

In the year 829 the body of St. Mark, *carefully and tenderly covered with herbs and pork*, was conveyed in a basket at the masthead of a Venetian galley from Alexandria to Rialto, where, being visited by pilgrims from every quarter of the Christian World, it contributed greatly to the national prosperity, in gratitude for which the Venetians transferred the guardianship of the Republic from St. Theodore to the Evangelist, whose name and image were thenceforth stamped upon her coins and her colors; and the battle cry of *Viva San Marco!* was thenceforth as formidable throughout the Mediterranean and Euxine Seas, as became some centuries later the war-whoop of the Spaniards *Santiago y cierra Espana! on the battle fields of two continents.*

VENETIANS AND SARACENS. SEA-FIGHTS OFF CROTONA, IN THE GULF OF TARANTO.

Thirteen years after the translation of St. Mark to their city, the Venetians, at the solicitation of the Emperor Theodosius, co-operated with the Greeks in a naval expedition against the Saracens, whose name was then a terror to every Christian merchant who had a venture upon the sea. The hostile fleets met at Crotona, on the Gulf of Taranto, and although the Greeks fled at the first onset of the *unbelievers*, leaving their ally to contend against vastly superior numbers, the battle seems to have been maintained by the latter, with great courage and constancy, for many hours, and until indeed their loss both of ships and men was so heavy as to make further resistance impossible. But few of the sixty galleys that had left Venice only a few days before in triumph, returned to tell the tale—alike piteous for the vanquished to narrate and for Christian ears to hear—that forced to fly, yet looking back, they had beheld the flag of the Prophet waving above the Lion of St. Mark.

This is the first sea-fight of the republic, and although but few details of it are given they suffice to show us that the vessels of the three powers engaged in it closely resembled each other both in design and construction, and, in fact, differed but little from the galleys that had been in use for war purposes, on the Mediterranean for *two thousand years.* After they began to carry cannon, their sides were raised and made to " tumble home," so that their upper decks were much narrower than they had been previously. Jal (Archéologie navale, mémoire No. 5.) gives a very particular description of the manner of building a galley in the 14th century, taken from a Venetian manuscript, which the reader who desires minute information on this subject will find well worthy of his perusal.

The remembrance of their humiliation in the Gulf of Taranto, rankled in the breasts of the Venetians for a quarter of a century, when a signal victory obtained over the enemy in the very spot that had been the scene of their former discomfiture, enabled the sturdy republicans once more to hold up their heads in the presence of the hated Saracen. In this, as in the previous engagement, if the Venetian historians are to be believed, the Greeks behaved in a perfidious and cowardly manner.

VENETIANS AND GENOESE.

The fights at Crotona were but the first of countless battles which the republic found it necessary, for the protection of her commerce, to maintain against the followers of the Prophet, and to these she undoubtedly owed her development, as a vast naval power, but, as the accounts of them, by contemporary chroniclers, are vague, contradictory and confused, and as we shall have ample opportunity of making ourselves familiar with the tactics of the *infidel* when we come to the great battle of Lepanto, I prefer to pass them over in silence, as well as other conflicts in which Venice was engaged with opposing *Christian* States, and shall therefore commence my story from the period when the long-existing, ill-disguised hatred between her and her commercial rival, Genoa the Proud, had broken out for the third time into open war, and at the very moment—two hours before sunset, on the thirteenth of February, thirteen hundred and fifty-three—when the allied forces of Venice, Arragon and Constantinople, numbering seventy-five galleys and commanded in chief by Nicolo Pisani, were preparing to attack, in the vicinity of Constantinople, the Genoese fleet of sixty-four galleys, led by the redoubtable Paganino Doria.

VICTORY OF THE GENOESE LED BY PAGANINO DORIA, OVER THE VENETIANS, SPANIARDS AND GREEKS, NEAR CONSTANTINOPLE.

The line of battle of the allies was formed about two in the afternoon, with the Catalans on the right, the Greeks on the left, the haughty Republicans in the centre; but the wind was so high, and the sea so rough and irregular, that no line could long be preserved, and when the battle was actually joined, there was but little more order in the allied fleet than in that of Doria, who, taken completely by surprise, scarcely had time to signal to two of his squadrons, cruising at some distance from him, on his flanks, *close with all speed*, before the enemy was reported to be bearing down upon him. But the Genoese was a thorough master of his art, and, observing that Pisani, in his eagerness to intercept one of the detached squadrons, had extended his centre and right wing so far to the right, as to isolate the Grecian vessels, eight in number, on the left, he determined to concentrate on these his whole disposable force, which, with this object in view, he now formed into a wedge, the port column of which was instructed to keep its course, right through the gap between the objective aimed at and the Venetian left, and assail the Greeks in rear, while the starboard column was to be thrown, at the instant the head of the wedge should be seen passing the Grecian right, quickly into line in its front. This disposition being made, he signalled to oblique, at full speed, four points to the right. The Greeks, however, did not await his coming; but, adopting the mode of warfare for which, under the empire, they had become notorious, they *reversed their order, by an exceedingly rapid evolution*, and, spreading their canvas to a fair southerly gale, were soon snugly anchored under the fortifications of the Golden Horn, whence the imperial admiral, Constantine Tarchoniota, enjoyed an undisturbed view, while daylight lasted, of the prowess of those whom he had so *prudently* deserted. Beholding the bad conduct of the Greeks, Pisani made no effort to recall them; but moving first by the right flank, and then deploying, on the centre of his column, into line, he entirely encompassed the squadron he was pursuing, whose captains, seeing no chance of escape, made for the Asiatic shore, where they set fire to their vessels with their own hands. The destruction of ten Genoese galleys being thus effected, Pisani faced about to receive Doria, who, having collected all his remaining strength, was now coming up in his rear, in three divisions, each in double echelon, with the design of piercing his van, centre and rear, failing in which, because of the close array of the Venetians and Arragonese, he deployed into line, on his leading vessels, just as the last glimmer of light had faded from the western sky; after which there was no attempt at manœuvring, on either side, and the battle degenerated into a melée. The Genoese now attempted to carry the Arragonese and Venetian vessels by boarding, and the officers and crews of these, in their turn, often gained the decks of the Genoese. In one quarter were heard appeals to the saints for strength to strike, in another prayers to the Virgin for protection. Here, by the light of their own burning vessel, might be seen a few wretched mariners, surrounded by the blood-stained corpses of their comrades, vainly endeavoring to escape death by leaping into the sea—there a disabled galley, drifting into the breakers under her lee, which lashed into fury by the prevailing storm, threatened with annihilation both the bark and her crew. Thus fearfully did the battle continue, at intervals, throughout the night, and, when day dawned, Pisani, who was slightly wounded, discovering that twenty-six of his galleys had either been captured or sunk, gave the order to retreat; and Doria could justly boast that he had gained a glorious victory; since, with his inferior force, he had beaten off his assailant, with a loss to himself of but thirteen vessels. The number of killed, wounded and drowned on both sides was fearful, and both Venice and Genoa had to lament the death of many of their most eminent citizens. Arragon, too, suffered greatly in this respect; and the brave Marquis of La Paz, who had led her fleet, died shortly afterwards in Constantinople, of a broken heart, it was said, at the evil event of the battle, and the rejection, by Pisani, of his own strategical plans.

When the news of their defeat in the East reached the Venetians, an inquiry into its causes was instituted, which led to the exoneration of Pisani, whom they were at first inclined to censure, from all blame. He was accordingly continued in command of the Venetian fleet.

UNGRATEFUL TREATMENT OF PAGANINO DORIA BY THE GENOESE—HE IS DEPRIVED OF HIS COMMAND, WHICH IS GIVEN TO HIS BITTER ENEMY, ANTONIO GRIMALDI.

Far different was the treatment experienced by Doria, at the hands of his ungrateful countrymen; for, returning to

Genoa, where he had every right to expect an ovation, he met with the coldest reception. The Grimaldi faction, the bitter foes of himself and his house, had been actively at work during his absence, and the silence that reigned in the streets through which he passed, on his way from the quay where he landed to the stately mansion which still bears his family name, told of grief for the dead, while there was not one word of greeting for the living, *no one to doff his cap or extend his hand to the gallant old admiral who had so nobly sustained his country's honor on a distant sea.* So far, indeed, had the malice of his enemies prevailed over justice and honor that he was actually removed from the command of the fleet, to make room for the most unscrupulous of his slanderers, Antonio Grimaldi.

UTTER DEFEAT OF GRIMALDI OFF THE ISLAND OF SARDINIA BY THE VENETIANS AND SPANIARDS.

Shortly afterward, Grimaldi was dispatched by his government, with fifty-nine sails, to the relief of Alguiero, a seaport of Sardinia, belonging to Genoa, which was then closely blockaded by the Arragonese admiral, Bernardo de Cabrera, with twenty-two galleys.

Upon the approach of the Genoese, in such overwhelming numbers, Cabrera raised the blockade, and endeavored to make off under all sail, but, finding the enemy gaining on him, he took in his canvas, between Lojera and Cape Cagliari, and forming in line, in close order, with (it may be presumed) a reserve to resist any attempt to turn either of his flanks, he resolutely awaited their attack. The onset of the Genoese was fierce in the extreme, but fortunately for the assailed, the assailants seem to have regarded victory as certain, and to have been *careless of their array;* Grimaldi's signal being *engage as fast as you come up with the enemy;* thus their van was in action some time before their centre, their centre some time before their rear; and, for perhaps an hour, the battle was rather in favor of than against the Arragonese. At length, however, numbers began to prevail, and Cabrera saw nothing but defeat before him; for the decks of his vessels were covered with the dead and the dying; five had been forced to strike and as many more sent to the bottom, while all were more or less disabled in oars or hull. Yet he bore himself bravely, as became one of his rank and race, and encouraged all about him, both by speech and action. *If we cannot win*, said he, as he bore down upon Grimaldi, *we can die with honor!* Scarcely were the words spoken when a seaman near him called out: *Thanks to Saint Barbara, here come the Venetians!* and at the same instant his signal officer, respectfully removing his cap, and pointing with it toward Cape Cagliari, reported: "The Venetian fleet is in sight, sir! Yonder comes the admiral's vessel round the point!" Cabrera looked in the direction indicated, and beheld—*a glorious sight for a sailor's eyes at all times to rest upon, and especially at a time like this*—rounding the Cape, not two miles away, and sailing in column of divisions, a magnificent fleet of more than fifty ships, all coming to his relief, and all displaying from their tall mast-heads, the *grim old Lion of St. Mark.* Even while he looked a signal went up from the flag-ship, in obedience to which sails were taken in, and in another instant, their van swept through the Genoese fleet, and turning short round took position by his side, while their rear and centre obliquing to the right and left, assailed the enemy in flank. The Venetians and Catalans now vied with each other in deeds of daring and valor, and the air resounded with the cries of *Down with the Genoese! Pisani to the rescue!**

The resistance of the Genoese was sharp but could not long be maintained, and but little time had elapsed, from the coming of the Venetians, ere their vessels were to be seen, on all sides, hauling down their colors, or, where these were

* Charnock says Rufino commanded the Venetian fleet; but in this he errs. Rufino was appointed *proveditore* of the fleet, but Pisani remained in command.

gone, *trailing their oars in token of submission.* The victory of the allies was so complete that but eight of Grimaldi's galleys escaped, among which was the one bearing his flag. His loss in killed, wounded and drowned was reported to be five thousand.

"It would not have fared with us thus," said a weather-beaten tar, who having survived the action, was relating the particulars of it, on one of the quays of Genoa to his distressed and now repentant countrymen. *It would not have fared with us thus, had we been led by our brave old Doria.*

Such was the consternation of the Genoese at the result of the battle of Lojera, such their terror of the Venetians, for whom they cherished the most deadly hatred, that, false to five centuries of independent government, they threw themselves into the arms of Giovanni Visconti, Lord of Milan, who was accounted the most powerful Italian prince of his time.

ABJECT TERROR OF THE GENOESE UPON THE NEWS OF GRIMALDI'S DEFEAT.

"The surrender of Genoa, subject to the enjoyment of her civil rights in their full integrity and the provision by Milan of the means for prosecuting the war against the Signory with unrelaxed vigor, was accepted without delay (October 1353). Count Palavicini was sent by Visconti with a garrison of seven hundred cavalry and fifteen hundred infantry as governor of the city, and the requisite sums were simultaneously drawn from the Milanese treasury to defray the cost of a new campaign." But another fleet was to be fitted out and an army raised, and so the wily Lord of Milan felt it necessary to amuse the Signory with overtures of peace, until he should be ready to assume the offensive; for which purpose he selected, as his embassador to the Venetian Government, the illustrious Petrarch, who undertook the mission most willingly, since he honestly believed himself the first diplomatist of his day. He reached Venice, at the beginning of the year thirteen hundred and fifty-four, "buoyant in spirits and sanguine of success." But the lover of Laura was not so well versed in State-craft as in the composition of love sonnets. He had several long interviews with the Doge Andrea Dandolo—himself a man of letters and personally much attached to Petrarch in which he discoursed most fervently on the blessings of peace and the horrors of war; but he had no rational plan to submit for securing the one or avoiding the other; and Dandolo, who perfectly understood his *weak side*, treated him with the utmost courtesy and paid him many compliments on his learning and eloquence; yet, when pressed for a direct answer to the proposals of Visconti, he firmly replied:

"The Genoese, in their attempt to deprive us of our rights upon the sea, have driven us to arms. To them belongs the responsibility of this war; and if the Milanese choose to espouse their cause, the republic has no choice but to enrol them also among the number of its foes.

"*Arma tenenti omnia dat qui justa negat.*"

So the friend of Boccacio left the Rialto somewhat crestfallen, and in July thirteen hundred and fifty-four, war was formally declared against Milan.

GENOA INTRUSTS THE COMMAND OF HER FLEET AGAIN TO DORIA, WHO GAINS A GREAT VICTORY OVER NICOLO PISANI, IN THE HARBOR OF PORTOLONGO.

While this fruitless negotiation had been pending, Doria, who was again in command of the Genoese fleet, had not been idle. Early in May he ascended the Adriatic and ravaged the districts of Lesina and Curzola, and before Pisani, who had put to sea from Venice with forty-one galleys, could intercept him, he had left the gulf and was seen steering to the Westward. Pisani followed him (as he supposed) as far as Sardinia; but the great strategist was lying all the while among the Ionian islands, and no sooner had his enemy passed him than he returned to the gulf and took Parengo, which he burned to the ground. This so alarmed the Venetians that they called out the whole force of the state, appointed Paolo Loredano captain general of the city, and sent a peremptory order to Pisani to return without delay to its defense. To attack it, however, formed no part of Doria's plan; and before Pisani had commenced his return from Sardinia, he was already on his way to the shores of Asia, where he made sad havoc with Venetian commerce. Searching for him here, Pisani fell in with him off Scio, and endeavored to bring him to action; but the Genoese was much inferior in strength to his adversary; and although he may have felt fully confident of his ability, if attacked, to ward off his blows as in the Bosphorus, yet he regarded with the abhorrence natural to a great commander a battle from which no decisive results could be expected, and studiously avoided a collision. Thus the summer and fall passed away; and, toward the end of November, Pisani went into winter quarters at Portolongo, opposite the island of Sapienza. Doria was about to follow his example, when he learned that Pisani, trusting for defense to the narrowness of the port, at the mouth of which were anchored twenty galleys under Nicolo Quirini, had had the imprudence to dismantle the rest of his vessels, some of which were actually in dock. "Now I have him," he remarked quietly; and steering for Portolongo with all dispatch, he arrived off the place before any one there had the slightest intimation of his coming.

A hasty reconnoisance convinced him that there was room for a galley to pass between the Venetian guard-vessels and the land on the right side of the harbor, and he directed his nephew, Giovanni Doria, to take advantage of it to get in the enemy's rear. Giovanni carried out his orders with gallantry and zeal; and the Venetians found themselves attacked on all sides, while they were yet in the act of getting under way. Resistance, under these circumstances, would have been madness; and the officer temporarily in charge of the division—for Quirini seems to have been on shore at the time, so unforeseen was the attack—reluctantly gave the order to strike; not, however, before four hundred and fifty of his officers and men were either wounded or slain.

The whole of the Venetian fleet was captured, with an immense quantity of naval stores of every description. The number of the prisoners was six thousand. Pisani and Quirini made their escape to Venice, where they were brought to trial, and convicted of the grossest neglect of duty. The former was disqualified forever from holding the supreme command of the Venetian forces by land or sea; the latter suspended from duty for six years, and each compelled to pay a fine of one thousand *lires.*

This was the last exploit of the great Doria,—*an admiral to whom battle and victory were synonymous terms.* He died not long afterward, and was soon forgotten by the people he had served so faithfully and well; but he will live in the hearts of seamen of all nations and of every clime, while the earth and the sea exist.

The disaster at Portolongo was a fearful one for Venice; yet there was no cry of abject fear throughout her streets, such as had disgraced Genoa after the battle of Lojera. On the contrary, she at once began to levy fresh forces, and to equip for sea the new galleys in her dockyard, as well as all the merchant ships belonging to her which happened to be lying in her harbor. So firm, indeed, was her attitude that, on the 8th of January, Milan and Genoa entered into an armistice with her for four months, preparatory, it was hoped, to a lasting peace.

A VENETIAN TRAGEDY.

While negotiations were going on for this purpose, an event happened in Venice which startled the civilized world, and which, as it had its origin in the person of a Venetian admiral and at the naval dockyard, must be regarded as in some degree belonging to her naval annals.

On the morning of April 3rd, Marco Barbaro, a wealthy nobleman, called on the Commandant of the dockyard, Admiral Stefano Chiazza, with the view of getting employment for a favorite of his in one of its workshops; and being told by the admiral that there was no place for his *protegé*, he became greatly enraged, and, after using much abusive language, so far forgot himself as to strike the old officer in the face with his clenched fist. So violent was the blow, that Chiazza fell fainting to the floor; and, when he recovered his senses, Barbaro had disappeared. Wild with rage at the indignity put upon him, he rose to his feet and paced slowly back and forth in his office, wrapped in thought. What course to pursue to obtain satisfaction he knew not. The *duello* was not then in vogue in Venice; and even if it had been he—a *commoner*—could not hope to measure swords with a *patrician*, notwithstanding his high official position. At length his face lightened. A bright thought seemed to have struck him. "These men have tried our patience too long," he muttered. "Faliero cannot like them any better than I. Jealousy is an all-absorbing passion—especially in an old man, who has a young and beautiful wife." So saying, he left his office, and took his way to the Ducal palace, where he narrated to the Doge what had occurred.

"Admiral," said the Doge, as Stefano ceased speaking, "I assure you, you have my fullest sympathy."

"I came not for sympathy, your Serenity," was the reply; "I demand redress!"

"Redress!" exclaimed the Doge, rising hurriedly from his seat. "How can I obtain redress for another, who cannot obtain it for myself?"

"Do you refer to the case of Michele Steno, your Serenity?"

"To whom else could I refer, Admiral, than to the ribald knave, who had the assurance to place on the outside wall of my house, in letters so large that all passers-by might read it, this choice inscription?—

"*Marino Faliero della bella moglie; lui la mantiene, ed altri la godono.*"

And as the old man recited these galling words his eyes flashed, and his face became livid with passion.

Stefano looked at him steadfastly, and without speaking for some minutes. Then he said, almost in a whisper—

"If my neighbor has a biting dog, and will not chain him, why—then—" and here he hesitated.

"Then what?" asked Faliero, stamping his foot impatiently on the floor.

"Why, then," continued Chiazza coolly, "I kill him."

"How might such a thing be done?" asked the Doge, in a low tone, as if communing with himself.

"Readily enough," replied Chiazza quickly. "The commoners of the better class, whose wives and daughters are insulted daily by the profligate young nobles, hate them with a bitter hatred; and the *rabble* here, as elsewhere, can be *bought with gold!*"

Up to this time, Faliero may have contemplated the killing of Steno only; and, indeed, it seems hardly credible that he could have desired the extirpation of that whole order, of which his own family formed so conspicuous a part; but he had gone too far to recede.

That night he entered into a conspiracy with Chiazza and others, for the complete overthrow of the government. On the fifteenth of the month the nobles were to be murdered to a man, and Marino Faliero declared the *Head of the State, with absolute power.*

It happened, however, that one of the conspirators, Beltramo de Bergamo, had a noble patron, Nicolo Lioni, whom, from motives of gratitude, he was most unwilling to see among the proscribed; and it being arranged that the massacre should take place in the streets, as the nobles were on their way to the Square of St. Marks, whither they were to be summoned upon the pretence that a Genoese fleet was approaching the city, Beltramo went to Lioni's palace on the evening of the fourteenth, and darkly insinuated *that it would be well for the Signor not to stir out of his house on the morrow.*

Words so pregnant with meaning were not lost upon Nicolo, a man of sound judgment, and, as the event proved, of prompt action, who, giving orders to his servants to detain Beltramo a close prisoner until his return, repaired with all speed to the Doge, by whom, to his utter amazement, his story was characterized as utterly absurd. But while Faliero spoke thus, his confused manner and faltering voice betrayed him, and Liōni left him with the firm conviction that some tragedy was about to be enacted, in which his Serenity was to play a principal part. He, therefore, called upon two of his most intimate friends, Giovanni Gradenigo and Marco Cornaro, and persuaded them to go to his house with him, where the three nobles subjected Beltramo to such a searching cross-examination as compelled him to expose the whole conspiracy.

The six Privy Councillors and the Council of Ten were at once assembled, and Marino Faliero was cited to appear before them; and, having confessed his guilt, he was sentenced to be beheaded, at the head of the great Staircase of St. Marks.

Accordingly, on the morning of the seventeenth of April, he was conducted under guard from his apartment to the place of execution, where he begged pardon of the people for his grievous offense, and denounced himself as the worst of criminals. His scarlet cloak was now taken off, and replaced with a black one, and a black cap substituted for the ducal bonnet or *beretta.* Then the unhappy old man laid his head upon the block, and, with a single stroke, the executioner severed it from his body. At the same time the infamous Chiazza and some ten others were beheaded between the *red columns,*—the usual place of execution,—where, to the horror of the people, who looked upon the act as ominous of evil, Faliero upon being first invested with the *beretta* had landed by mistake, instead of at the Doge's landing-place, the *Riva della Paglia.*

The remains of the Doge were interred at San Giovanni e Paolo, behind the monastery; and the words, *Let it not be written!* at the head of a blank leaf in one of the books containing the "Transactions of the Ten," afford the sole clue to a great crime and its appropriate punishment.

The portrait of Faliero was at first hung up in the Senate Chamber, beside the portraits of his predecessors in office; but, twelve years after his execution, by a decree of the Ten, it was removed, and a black crape curtain drawn over the place which it had occupied; above which was inscribed, in letters still to be discerned, *Hic est locus Marini Faliero decapitati pro criminibus.*

Three centuries later, some workmen at San Giovanni, engaged in preparing a foundation for a building about to be erected, accidentally excavated a marble sarcophagus. One of their number, more curious than the rest, raised the lid, and, peeping in, started back aghast.—*A skeleton with the skull between the knees, was all that was left of the man who, through marrying a young woman in his old age, had been led into crime, and brought shame upon that great house which had given three Doges to Venice.*

WAR AGAIN DECLARED BY VENICE AGAINST GENOA. SHE PLACES HER GREAT ADMIRAL, VETTORE PISANI, IN COMMAND OF HER NAVAL FORCES.

In June, a treaty of peace was concluded between Genoa and Venice, by which the ships of the latter were excluded for three years from every port in the Black Sea, except Cafta. This serious blow to her commerce in that quarter, the republic endeavored to counterbalance by the improvement of her trade with Flanders, Egypt and Barbary. This peace lasted until April, 1378; when a dispute having arisen between the rival States in relation to the island of Tenedos, which the Venetians had taken possession of, the Signory formally declared war against Genoa, which it denounced as false to all its oaths and obligations.

On the twenty-sixth of this month Vettore Pisani was invested with the supreme command of the naval forces of the republic by the Doge in person, who, delivering to him the great banner of Venice, in the Square of St. Mark, thronged with spectators, thus addressed him: "Admiral, in the name of all the people, I intrust to your care this glorious standard, which, for more than seven centuries, has waved in triumph over the Adriatic. Look to it that it receive no stain in your hands!"

Then the Admiral, kneeling down and reverently uncovering his head, swore to defend it and the republic with his life. After which the banner was carried in procession to his flag-ship, where it was unfurled with great pomp and ceremony, amid the cheers of the whole fleet. The new commander-in-chief was the son of Nicolo Pisani, and had held a commission in the Navy for twenty-five years. He had been in many actions, both afloat and ashore, in all of which he had distinguished himself for coolness, courage and sound judgment. Although of a somewhat passionate nature, he was a man of warm heart and of great amiability of character; and his courteous manners and chivalric bearing had gained him the respect and affection of all who had had the good fortune to serve under him. He was greatly beloved by the people, and consequently not looked upon with favor by his own class, the patricians, who regarded him certainly with jealousy,—perhaps even with fear. Of the seamen he was the idol; and it was a common saying of theirs that victory followed where Vettore Pisani led. Such was the man to whom Venice now intrusted her destinies, and to whom, as we shall shortly see, she afterwards owed her safety, when the enemy was even *within her lagoons*, threatening to hoist the Genoese flag over the *Campanile of St. Mark*.

PISANI DEFEATS THE GENOESE ADMIRAL, FIESCHI, OFF ANTIUM.

Pisani sailed from Venice early in May, with fourteen galleys; and, on the thirtieth of the month, while cruising off Antium came across a Genoese squadron of ten galleys, commanded by Admiral Fieschi. It was blowing a gale at the time, and five of Pisani's vessels, which had parted company with him, and fallen to leeward, were unable to rejoin him, while one of Fieschi's drifted ashore, and was wrecked. Thus, the battle which immediately ensued, was between equal forces; but the Genoese admiral was no match for Vettore Pisani, who, having the weather-gage of his opponent, ranged in line under oars, bore down upon him under all sail, as if intending to engage him squarely in front.

Just before he reached him, however, and while moving with great speed, he obliqued to the right, and concentrated upon his centre and left wing, which were doubled up and beaten almost as soon as assailed,—Fieschi himself being taken prisoner. Four of the Genoese vessels were taken possession of by the Venetians, together with their officers and men, amounting in all to eight hundred souls.

During the summer, Pisani captured great numbers of the enemy's merchantmen; but was unable to find their fleet, which, under Luciano Doria, was actively engaged in cutting up Venetian commerce in the East.

In November, he asked permission to return to Venice to refit his vessels, which were in a very bad condition, but this was denied him; and, being kept constantly cruising through the winter, at its expiration only six of his vessels were found to be seaworthy. Twelve others, however, were fitted out at their own expense, and sent to him by his friends, who perceived that his political enemies were making an effort to ruin him.

At the end of February, thirteen hundred and seventy nine, Michele Steno and Donato Zeno were appointed by the Government *proveditori* of the fleet. These officers, like the field deputies of the Dutch republic in later times, were set as spies over the commander-in-chief, whose operations they entirely controlled.

PISANI BEING FORCED, BY THE *PROVEDITORI*, TO FIGHT A BATTLE AGAINST SUPERIOR FORCES, OFF POLA, IS ALMOST ANNIHILATED BY HIS ADVERSARY, LUCIANO DORIA, AND ON HIS REUURN TO VENICE, IS LOADED WITH CHAINS, AND CONFINED IN A DUNGEON.

On the first of May, Pisani left Brindisi, bound to Venice, having a large number of merchantmen in charge, laden with wheat; and, on the sixth instant, as the weather looked squally, put into Pola, with his convoy for the night.

On the following morning, at day-break, it was reported to him that Doria was off the port with twenty-five vessels; whereupon he determined not to leave his anchorage until Carlo Zeno, whom he was expecting with a re-enforcement of ten galleys, should be seen approaching. But the *Proveditori*, loudly denouncing such a determination as a reflection upon the valor of his officers and men, ordered him, peremptorily, in the name of the Senate, to engage the enemy without delay. Pisani, therefore, got underway; and as he knew the dread that the name of Doria inspired in Venetian breasts, he passed in his flag-ship within hail of every vessel of his fleet, exhorting their crews to bear themselves bravely in the coming fight; and *to remember that the stripling Luciano was a very different person from his father, Paganino.* "Were it not so," said he (wisely and patriotically concealing from them the difference of opinion between himself and the Proveditori), "your admiral would not be so ready to lead you against his superior force. Strike, then, this day for Venice and St. Mark! and with one blow we will end the war."

He now sailed down the harbor with a fair wind; and at its mouth observing Doria's vessels to leeward, drawn up in line with a strong reserve in rear, he formed his own fleet also into line, and bore down upon the enemy as fast as oars and sails could carry him, obliquing to the right when near, and concentrating upon their centre and left wing, as at Antium. Luciano Doria, however, had anticipated this movement, and hurried up his reserve to the support of his menaced flank; while his right wing, swinging to port, threatened with annihilation Pisani's left. But the Venetians, thus beset, fought with more than their usual gallantry; and wherever their spirits flagged there was heard the cheering voice of their admiral, calling upon them *to remember Venice, and fight courageously.* Thus the battle raged for three hours, and several Genoese vessels had been forced to surrender; when Doria, trained in his father's school, resolved to resort to stratagem. Signalling to have everything ready for making sail, he seized a favorable moment to bear up, and spreading all his canvas, was a mile away before the surprised Venetians were prepared to follow him. They then made sail one after the other, in pursuit; and Pisani, who saw, from the good order prevailing in Doria's fleet, that this retreat was but a ruse, vainly endeavored to stop them. Signal after signal was made and disregarded; and Michele Steno encouraged the general disobedience by his own bad example; seeing which, Pisani made all sail himself, trusting by his presence, perhaps, to avert the impending disaster. But this was now impossible; for Doria no sooner perceived his enemy extended in a long irregular column, than he put about, and commencing his attack at the head of the column carried everything before him, virtually ending the fight just as Pisani ran along side of him with the intention of boarding; when, raising his visor, he shouted at the top of his voice: *Victory, victory!—the battle is ours!* These were his last words. Donato Zeno, seizing the favorable moment, buried the point of his lance in his throat, and the brave Doria fell to the deck a corpse. Pisani now called out: *Courage, comrades—Doria is dead!* But, looking up, he observed the Genoese colors flying above the banner of St. Mark throughout almost his entire fleet, whereupon he made the best of his way to Parenzo, followed by five of his galleys, which were all that were saved from this most terrible engagement, wherein eight hundred Venetians, perished and two thousand were taken prisoners. All of the grain vessels, too, fell into the enemy's hands.

This signal triumph was dearly purchased, however, by the Genoese, who had reason to lament for many long years the death of Luciano Doria. A thousand masses were offered up, in the cathedral at Genoa, for the repose of the deceased hero's soul; while his body was placed tenderly to rest, by his mourning comrades at his father's right hand, in the family vault, *where the old and the young warrior are still lying side by side.*

The defeat at Pola filled Venice with amazement and consternation; for Carlo Zeno, it seems, instead of being sent to join Pisani, had been dispatched on a cruise to the Black Sea; so that the six galleys at Parenzo were all that were at the immediate disposal of the republic in this fearful crisis, when the enemy was within a day's sail of the lagoons.

Pisani was now violently assailed by his enemies; although they well knew that he had fought the battle of Polo against his own judgment, and agreeably to the wishes of the government, as made known to him by its accredited agents, Michele Steno and Donato Zeno. The Great Council decreed his immediate removal from the supreme command, and he was brought to Venice *loaded with chains.* Dragged before the Senate for trial, one of its members had the infamy to move *that Vettore Pisani be beheaded between the Red Columns;* and this motion being negatived, he was finally sentenced to six months' imprisonment in that fearful dungeon, over the door of which, as over Dante's entrance to hell, might well have been inscribed: *Leave here all hope, O ye who enter in!*

THE GENOESE, AFTER TAKING AND BURNING SEVERAL VENETIAN TOWNS, APPEAR OFF VENICE.

While this mockery of justice was being enacted in Venice, the Genoese had burned Grado, Omago, Rovigno and Coorlo; and on the sixth of August their fleet of forty-seven galleys, commanded by Pietro Doria, a cousin of the late admiral, appeared off the "City of the Sea," whose relative situation, with regard to its immediate dependencies, must now be given, in order that what follows may be clearly understood.

Of the natural channels which existed in the fringe of land surrounding Venice," says Hazlitt, "the northernmost was that of Treporti. It separated the islets of San Erasmo and San Nicolo; and it was adapted only for craft of the smallest description. The next aperture was that which lay to the south of San Nicolo, and which disjoined the latter from Malamocco; it was known as the port of Lido. To the south of Malamocco, in a nearly straight line of five miles, lay Pelestrina; and the space between the two islands formed the port of Malamocco, or the principal harbor of Venice. It was here that the deepest soundings were taken, and that vessels of the largest draught were able to ride. Below Pelestrina was Brondolo, behind which stood Chioggia. The southern point of Brondolo all but touched the Terra Firma.

"Chioggia, more anciently known as Sotta Marina, was thus placed at the southern extremity of the Dogado. It was bisected by the Canal of Santa Caterina into Chioggia, Piccola, and Chioggio Grande, which communicated by a draw-bridge of a quarter of a mile in length. Great Chioggia was nearly two hundred and fifty yards square, with a circumference of two miles. A canal, running the whole length of the lagoons, connected it with the capital, from which it was distant five and twenty miles. The configuration of Venice, and the narrowness of its superficial area, make it easy to imagine the anguish with which the intrusion of a foreign invader on Venetian ground inspired the Senate and the people."

Upon the approach of the Genoese all the above mentioned channels had been obstructed with sunken vessels, booms and chains, except the very narrow one between Brondolo and the mainland, through which, to the surprise and consternation of the Signory, the enemy now penetrated, landing an army and taking possession of Little Chioggia without resistance, and preparing to continue their march to Great Chioggia, the fall of which they confidently expected would lead to that of the coveted capital. But upon reaching the long narrow street leading to the bridge over which it is necessary to pass to come at Great Chioggia, they found it commanded by a small fort, bristling with cannon which were now coming into general use all over Europe, and having made a reconnoisance of the work, they wisely determined to await the arrival of the troops of Carrara, their ally, already near at hand, before attempting further operations. On the tenth the expected re-enforcement arrived; and on the eleventh the army of the allies, twenty-four thousand strong, commenced its assault upon the fort, which continued without intermission for five days; and the assailants, who had suffered fearfully, were beginning to relinquish all hope of carrying it; when a fire broke out on board a vessel in the canal of Santa Caterina, which gave rise to a rumor among the defenders of the fort that the bridge was in flames in their rear; whereupon they deserted their guns, and fled over it in a panic, thinking that there were but a few minutes left to them to secure their safe retreat. So great was their disorder that they neglected to raise the draw after they had passed it; and a free passage was thus given to the enemy, who were not slow in taking advantage of it; so that Venetians, Genoese and Carrarese entered the gates of Great Chioggia almost side by side. Of the garrison in the town, eight hundred were put to the sword, and four thousand taken prisoners.

GREAT CHIOGGIA BEING TAKEN BY THE ENEMY, THE VENETIAN PEOPLE INSIST UPON PISANI'S BEING INVESTED WITH THE CHIEF COMMAND. HE SAVES VENICE. HIS ADMIRABLE CONDUCT AND CHARACTER.

The terror which now reigned in Venice no language can describe. The bell of the *Campanile* was tolled,—a signal that danger pressed, and the foe drew near,—and the great Square of St. Mark was soon filled with armed men. The Doge, Andrea Coutarini, who was then in his seventy-third year, made his appearance on the balcony of the palace. "My children," said he, "this is sad news that we hear; but the new Captain-General does not despair; and for myself I can say that, so long as there are men enough left to garrison a fort or man a galley, so long will I continue to defend the city."

But a veteran, who had served under Pisani from youth to old age, now came forth from the crowd, and replied respectfully but resolutely: "Giustianni, we all know, your Serenity, comes of a good race, and has often approved himself a gallant officer; but God has not gifted him with great ability. There is but one man in Venice who can save her in this her hour of peril; and that man is Vettore Pisani!"

These were brave words, and bravely were they spoken; for Giustianni was one of the most powerful of the nobles, and his followers and dependents frowned darkly upon the speaker. But his speech had found a responsive echo in the breasts of the populace; and a cry arose that went from mouth to mouth, through every street and every canal of the city,—penetrating at last even through the walls of the loathsome dungeon, where the admiral lay upon his bed of straw,—of *Pisani to the front. Giustianni to the rear! Long live Vettore Pisani!* The members of the Council of Ten next appeared on the balcony, and, taking their places on either side of the Doge endeavored to address the multitude; but their voices were unheeded, and, finding that the people would not be denied, they reluctantly promised that Pisani should be released. It was growing late, and the citizens retired to their homes. At day-break, on the following morning, a Committee of the Senate repaired to the dungeon, and, bringing Pisani forth, escorted him to the palace, where the Doge received him most affectionately. He accompanied Contarini to the Chapel of St. Nicholas, and, after hearing mass, betook himself to his house at San Fantino. On his way thither he was met by an immense concourse of his fellow-citizens, headed by a certain Marino Corbaro, a great grumbler, but a good seaman, who had served under Pisani in the capacity of pilot, and was greatly attached to him. This man ran up to the admiral, waving his hat in the air, and shouting at the top of his lungs: "Seize the opportunity, Pisani, to make yourself the Head of the State! We are heartily tired of our incompetent rulers!" But the loyal admiral, reddening with anger and mortification, and giving way to the impulse of the moment, dealt Corbaro a heavy blow with his fist, indignantly exclaiming: "*How dare you thus insult me! Who told you your old commander was ready to turn traitor?*" Then facing the crowd, which had now become so dense that, "from St. Marks to San Fantino, there was not an unoccupied spot of ground large enough to hold a grain of millet," and, raising his voice to its highest pitch, he called out: "Let him who loves *Pisani cry: Long live St. Mark and the Signory!*" The people obeyed; and Venice was spared the horrors of an intestine strife, which must inevitably have led to its capture by the enemy, to whom we will now return.

Had the advice of the Carrarese general been followed, who, after the taking of Chioggia, desired to move at once upon Venice, it seems highly probable that the fall of the former would have preceded that of the capital by only a few hours; but, fortunately for the republic, Pietro Doria, who was in supreme command, was not possessed of talent either as an admiral or a general; and he wasted two whole days in useless preparation for an advance upon Malamocco, between which place and Chioggia there was not a gun nor a man to oppose him. Arrived at last at Malamocco, he found the Venetians drawn up in readiness to dispute his further progress; when, giving up all idea of attempting to carry Venice by storm, he pitched his camp where he stood, and erected a battery within four miles of the Ducal palace. This was as near as he ever got to it; Pisani and St. Mark proved abler tacticians than Doria and St. George.

Aroused to action by their country's peril, the artist left his studio, the student his closet; the courts were closed, and judges and lawyers were seen organizing companies of brawny mechanics and laborers to go to the front, where Pisani was overseeing everything with untiring energy. Two wooden towers raised by Giustianni, on either side of the port of Lido, were demolished as worse than useless, and two stone ones were directed to be built in their stead; but the masons had been tampered with, and no one stepped forward to obey the order; so Pisani seized a trowel himself, and crying out: "Let him who loves St. Mark follow my example!" he laid the foundation stones with his own hands. A murmur of approbation went up from the by-standers; and in another instant a thousand strong arms were at work upon the towers, which were actually completed in four days. They were mounted with cannon, and known as the Castles of St. Andrew and St. Nicholas. Pisani's next work was to surround the city with a double wall; and when this was done, he felt secure against every enemy but famine, whose insidious attacks now began to be felt by all classes.

The allies seem not to have comprehended Pisani's plans until it was too late to thwart them, when, after an unsuccessful assault upon the castles, the Carrarese general retired in disgust, and marched his men home, leaving Doria, who had boasted that he would "put a bit in the mouths of the horses of St. Mark," to continue the siege after his own fashion. Six weeks later, the Genoese withdrew to Chioggia; where, with thirty thousand men, forty galleys and some eight hundred boats, he concluded to await the fall of Venice by starvation, which seemed to be near at hand. Pisani, however, now formed the bold design of besieging the besiegers. With this intent, he procured a number of old hulks; which, on the night of October twenty-first, he put in charge of a brave and enterprising officer, named Giovanni Barberigo, giving him directions to tow them to the mouths of the various channels and canals, leading from Chioggia, and there sink them, while he created a diversion in his favor by landing with an army at Brondolo, and moving upon the enemy's works. The whole operation was completely successful, and when day dawned, on the twenty-second, Doria, who had been congratulating himself, upon having gained a great victory, because he had repelled the attack of Pisani, discovered, to his alarm and chagrin, that he had been completely out-witted, and was in fact a prisoner within his own fortifications, having been caught "like a rat in a trap;" for the hulks being sunk as directed, served as foundations for the great stones with which the boats used in towing them into position had been freighted, and these being piled upon them, layer after layer, and firmly cemented with mortar, made a solid barrier across all the outlets to the Adriatic. The Venetian engineers now erected a fort at Fossone, which they called the Lova. It was directly opposite to the Convent of Brondolo, which Doria had converted into a fortress, and mounted guns of the heaviest calibre known at that day. One of these, the "Trevisan," threw a stone ball weighing 195 lbs., and a second called "Victory" one of 190 lbs., but *neither could be discharged oftener than once in twenty-four hours.*

Such, however, was the exposure of the Venetians during these fatiguing operations, obliged, as they often were, to work knee-deep in water, with the pitiless winter rains beating upon their heads, such their suffering from the pangs of hunger, that a fearful malady broke out in their camp, and, weak and dispirited, they demanded to be led back to Venice.

Pisani, who now realized the fact that the courage and endurance of his men had been taxed too far, sent the most urgent messages to Zeno, who was reported to be not far distant, to hurry to his relief; at the same time solemnly assuring his command that, if the Venetian fleet did not make its appearance by the 1st of January, he would on that day raise the siege of Chioggia.

The evening of December 31st arrived, and "in twenty four hours it was to be decided whether a state, which, through a perspective of eleven centuries, could look back upon the rise and decay of so many empires, should retain or should renounce its independence."

So great was the anxiety of Pisani, that he passed the whole night upon the battlements of Fort Lova eagerly looking towards the sea.

Daylight came: the sky was unclouded and the weather clear, and yet nothing was to be seen; and despair had almost taken possession of the brave admiral's soul, when an officer directed his attention to something that appeared like a fleecy cloud, on the distant horizon. Soon another, and another cloud came into view; and as the sun rose and threw his gilded rays upon the scene, it became evident that the clouds were sails—sails rising grandly over stately galleys, manned by stout hearts, and guided by experienced hands, whose Venetian nationality was proclaimed by the proud old banner of St. Mark. The "sea-gulls" had flown back to their nest: Carlo Zeno was at hand; and "Venice the Beautiful" was saved!

Six months after this, the enemy, reduced by famine, made an unconditional surrender of his fleet and army, with all his munitions of war—a blow from which Genoa never recovered.

PISANI MAKES A CRUISE TO THE COAST OF ASIA, AND ON HIS RETURN VOYAGE FALLS SICK, AND DIES AT MANFREDONIA. GREAT MOURNING AT VENICE.

Pisani next devoted himself to fitting out the Venetian fleet; and on the 3d of July, left Venice with forty-seven vessels in search of the Genoese admiral, Gaspar Spinola, who was cruising in the East. After looking for him in vain on the coast of Asia, he concluded that Spinola was retracing his steps to Genoa; and thinking it more than probable that on his way thither he would look into the Adriatic, he determined to shape a course for Manfredonia, that he might be near at hand should danger threaten the capital. As he approached Manfredonia he became seriously ill, and although he made light of his illness, declaring "it was only a bad cold," his officers became alarmed at his extreme debility, and the flag-ship's anchor was no sooner down on the morning of August 3d, than they insisted upon carrying him to the house of Guido da Fojan, commandant of Manfredonia, where he was a tonce put to bed, and attended by the most eminent physicians of the place. His constitution, however, had been greatly impaired by overwork in the service of his country, even before the battle of Pola, and his three months' imprisonment, with the subsequent ten months' labor at Malamocco, and in the trenches before Chioggia, had completely destroyed it. His medical advisers counselled perfect repose of mind and body, but his restless spirit could not be controlled; and he had not been an hour on shore ere he dictated a letter to the Signory, detailing his operations since his departure from Venice, and concluding with a promise "to make Genoa rue the day when she entered upon the war of Chioggia." After his secretary had sealed this dispatch, he called for water, which he drank with feverish eagerness. He then took a morsel of bread, but as he was in the act of swallowing it, he became deathly pale, gasped convulsively for breath, with a violent effort threw himself from the bed and stood erect, and the next instant fell in a swoon to the floor. His attendants hurried to his assistance, but their efforts to revive him were of no avail. The great admiral was dead. His remains, after embalmment, were conveyed to Venice, where they lay in state for many days, during which time the Senate was convoked and passed a decree "that a public funeral be given to the Great Citizen." On the day of his burial, the city was draped in mourning, and no man within its precincts covered his head while the old bell of St. Mark's announced, in muffled tones, that the body of Vettore Pisani was being conveyed from San Fantino to the church of Saint Anthony, where his father's ashes already reposed. As the funeral *cortege* was leaving San Fantino, several persons called out that the remains of the Saviour of Venice should rest nowhere but in the Ducal Chapel. The procession stopped: the crowd took up the cry, and a tumult seemed inevitable, when a gray-haired seaman, one of twelve who were carrying the bier, said sadly, while the tears trickled down his weather-beaten cheeks: "Our good admiral is far above all earthly honors now. We, who have been faithful to him even unto death, are carrying him to his father Saint Anthony: in his arms let him rest." The people acquiesced, and the funeral moved on. After the burial service was over, the citizens gathered in knots about the streets, bewailing the loss they had sustained; and Venice, on that day, might have been likened to Jerusalem after the death of Maccabeus, when all the people wept and said: "Why is that great man dead, who saved the people of Israel?" A magnificent mausoleum was erected over the ancestral vault at San Antonio; upon which was placed a statue of Pisani, habited in the uniform of a captain-general, and grasping in his right hand an ensign surmounted by a cross.

Such were the death and burial, such the honors paid to the memory of Vettore Pisani, than whom, it may be justly said, Venice, throughout an independent existence of over a thousand years, produced *no greater admiral, no better man.* What nobler epitaph could a sailor desire?

As I shall have no more sea-fights between the Venetian and the Genoese to chronicle, I desire briefly to call the reader's attention here to the masterly manœuvres of their great admirals, in some of those which I have attempted to describe. At the battle of Constantinople, for instance, what could have been more brilliant than Paganino Doria's movement to cut off the Grecian vessels, or his double-echelon formation, in his effort to pierce the Venetian line. See him again, at Portolongo! where, with unerring judgment, he decides at a glance that there is room enough for a galley to pass between the Venetians and the land, taking advantage of which he gains a great victory, thereby setting an example to future admirals, which possibly the inimitable Nelson profited by at Aboukir.

What a magnificient spectacle of good order and discipline the Venetian fleet presents to us at Cagliari, going into action in column of divisions and obliquing to the right and left, with the precision of soldiers on parade!—and what could be finer than the "doubling up" of Fieschi by Vettore Pisani at Antium, or the *feint* of Luciano Doria, and the tactical ability displayed by both Pisani and himself in the stubborn fight off Pola?

Let every naval student, then, study carefully the contest between the rival republics, well assured that there have been no abler strategists and tacticians than the old Venetian and Genoese admirals, and perhaps no better regulated and organized navy than that of the "City by the Sea."*

* See article on the Venetian Navy, from the able pen of John Knox Laughton, M.A., Naval Instructor, R.N., in Fraser's Magazine, October, 1875.

FORCED INTO A WAR AGAINST FRANCE, SPAIN, GERMANY AND THE PETTY ITALIAN STATES, BY THE LEAGUE OF CAMBRAY, VENICE DEFENDS HERSELF WITH GREAT SPIRIT, BUT IS FINALLY OBLIGED TO CEDE ROMAGNA TO THE POPE.

After the successful termination of the war of Chioggia, Venice increased rapidly in wealth and influence, until, at the close of the fifteenth century, she had acquired so great an extent of territory as to excite the envy and apprehension of all the other European powers; which, instigated by Pope Julian the Second, notwithstanding that His Holiness owed his elevation mainly to the Venetians, united in that formidable League to crush "*the great republic*," which was signed at Cambray on the 10th day of December, 1508. The civilized world now beheld with astonishment, not unmingled with awe, Venice contending single-handed, yet undismayed, against the combined forces of France, Germany, Spain and the petty Italian States; and at the same time replying with spirit and dignity to the bitter fulminations of the Vatican. The Emperor Maximillian, at the head of a hundred thousand men, besieged Padua; the King of the French with his army descended like a mountain torrent upon Lombardy; and dispersed throughout the rest of her territory, at various strategical points, Venice had to confront the soldiers of Spain and of misguided Italy, which, hearkening to the voice of the tempter, had invited the representatives of tyranny to invade the soil that, for so many centuries, had been sacred to freedom.

The Venetian army, beaten on the Adda, yet still facing the enemy like a lion at bay, retreated slowly and sullenly upon the capital.

The main-land was lost, but not the love of its inhabitants for Venice; and so, little by little, after the first shock of war had passed, the republic recovered its former possessions, with the exception of Romagna, which, upon the termination of hostilities, it was obliged to cede to the Pope forever, in order to obtain the revocation of his infamous sentence of excommunication against her citizens, which had produced so terrible an effect upon the minds of the vulgar in Venice, as to cause the Signory to apprehend an outbreak on their part against the authorized government in favor of the priesthood.

The republic now enjoyed some years of repose, which were devoted to the embellishment of the capital; and the magnificent private dwellings erected there about this period, are looked upon with admiration by the traveller of the present day, rich as they are in marbles, painting and sculpture, in curiously carved furniture, walls clothed with tapestry, and ceilings adorned with frescoes of priceless value.

WAR WITH THE TURKS. FEARFUL ATROCITIES COMMITTED BY THEM IN CYPRUS.

But a more terrible enemy than any with which Venice had yet contended appeared on the political horizon in 1566, in the person of Selim II., the youthful Emperor of the Turks — that barbarous nation which, in 1453, had taken Constantinople by storm, and learning there the sad truth that "the rapine of an hour is more productive than the industry of years," had assumed the aggressive ever since, wresting from the republic by degrees the whole of the Morea, and now demanding from her the cession of the Island of Cyprus (which Selim greatly coveted) as the price of peace.

The Signory, which had for some time been pursuing a temporizing policy towards the Turks, of which this demand was the legitimate fruit, now resolutely prepared for war, and despatched embassies to all quarters in quest of aid.

The Christian princes of Europe, however, lent a deaf ear to the story of a danger menacing them from the distant Bosphorus, and coldly turned their backs upon the embassadors of a power which they had always hated and often feared.

But, fortunately for Christianity, there was one great man among them, who fully sympathized with the republic in this her hour of need, and comprehended clearly that as Sicily, in ages gone by, had served as a breastwork for Italy against the advances of Carthage from the west, so Venice now rose from the sea as its bulwark against the barbarians approaching it from the east.

This great man was Pius the Fifth, one of the best and ablest pontiffs that ever filled the apostle's seat.

Gifted with eloquence and discernment, and possessed of an enthusiastic temperament and a religious fervor, which gave to all he uttered the force of inspiration, his opinions had great weight with Philip the Second of Spain, whom he now earnestly besought, in the name of the Holy Catholic Church, of which His Majesty was so distinguished and devout a member, not to be a passive spectator of a strife that, unless he took part in it, must inevitably result—to the shame of Christendom — in the triumph of the Moslem over a neighboring Christian State.

Thus urged, Philip, who, it is probable, foresaw on his part that the establishment of the naval supremacy of the Turks on Mediterranean, would endanger the safety of every Spanish colony inside the Pillars of Hercules, and even of the maritime districts of Spain itself, filled as they then were, with disaffected Moriscoes, readily consented to unite with Venice and His Holiness in an effort to check their further encroachments; provided the League was considered as binding against the Moors also, the inveterate enemies of Spain. This coalition was formally announced from the chair of St. Peter in 1570,* and resulted, during the following year, in the great battle of Lepanto, where the Christian called out

* Prescott says: "Although a draft of the treaty had been prepared in the latter part of the preceding year, it was not ratified until 1571; but La Fuente (vol. 7, p. 265) mentions two distinct treaties, one made in 1570, and the other in 1571."

to the Moslem from the midst of the sea, as he had declared to him eight centuries earlier from the centre of France: *Hither shalt thou come, but no farther; and here shall thy proud course be stayed!*

But, in order that the characters in this great naval drama may be properly brought upon the scene of action, it is necessary that a *résumé* of the events immediately preceding it should be first presented to the reader.

The conquest of Cyprus was resolved upon by Selim, according to La Fuente, from the moment he succeeded to the throne of his father, as an enterprise worthy of the son of the Great Solyman; and this, no doubt, was the ground upon which this conquest was urged upon him by the commander-in-chief of his army, the infamous Mustafa; for it is the very language flattery would use in addressing a youthful sovereign; but as Selim, brought up in the seraglio, although fully imbued with the thirst of military glory, was not possessed of the warlike spirit which had prompted his ancestors to *lead* their armies to battle, and was so addicted to the wine-cup withal, notwithstanding its prohibition by the law of Mohammed, as to have been nick-named by his subjects the "wine-bibber" and "the inebriate,"—we cannot but think with Hammer, that the wines of Cyprus acted as a powerful stimulant to the ambition of the young Sultan; and we are not, therefore, disposed to pass over in silence the remarkable tale told by him, in his history of the Ottoman Empire, of the influence exercised by a certain Joseph Nassy in bringing about the war of Cyprus and the events consequent thereon, which is, in substance, as follows:—

During the lifetime of his father, Selim conceived a great friendship for a Jew named Joseph Nassy, a pretended convert to Mohammedanism, who was in the habit of making him rich presents of wine and money, "thus giving the young Prince a taste for the ducats of Venice and the wines of Cyprus;" and one day, when the two boon companions had indulged for many hours in the pleasures of the table,

Selim rose, staggering to his feet, and holding up his glass to the light, exclaimed: "By the great Prophet! when I come to the kingdom, I will take possession of the island which produces this rare nectar; and you, Nassy, shall be the governor of the island, and have charge of its vineyards."

The acquisition of Cyprus, then—from whatever cause—being now resolved upon, it was not difficult for a government which maintained that, wherever a mosque had once been erected, there the standard of Mohammed should fly forever, to trump up a claim to that island which had been formerly in the hands of the Saracens. Besides, although the Ottoman Empire was at peace with the republic, it had long been held as a maxim with the former that no treaty of peace should be considered as binding upon it whose rupture would enlarge the bounds of Islamism, and redound to the glory of the Sultan.

In honor of the Prophet, too, a magnificent temple was in process of erection at Adrianopolis, to which the revenues of Cyprus were to be appropriated. So the demand for the cession of the island to Turkey was made, as we have seen, and great was the rejoicing at Constantinople at its indignant rejection by the Venetians; for the Turks, at that period, were a nation of military fanatics, delighting in nothing but war, and especially in war with those, of whatever nation they might be, who inscribed on their banners the sacred emblem of the Crucifixion.

A force of fifty thousand infantry and artillery, under the command of Mustafa, was soon landed in Cyprus, and laid siege to Nicosia, its capital, striking terror within its walls; a squadron of Turkish infantry, scouring the roads in all directions, spread havoc and desolation through the country far and wide; while a fleet of one hundred and eighty galleys, whose admiral was the Bashaw Piali, one of the instigators of this war, entirely encircled the island, cutting off all hope of succor from without.

Nicosia fell, after an obstinate resistance, on the 13th of September, 1570; and in August of the following year, Famagusta capitulated, after a protracted siege, during which the most heroic valor was displayed on both sides; for it had withstood six general assaults, and buried fifty thousand Turks beneath the ruins of its levelled walls: while, of the Christian garrison within it, one-half had perished, either by famine or the sword.

The accounts given us of the cruelty of Mustafa, after the reduction of Famagusta, towards those officers who had stood foremost in its defense, would be deemed incredible, were they not attested by numberless authorities, whose evidence is indisputable.

The *Seraskier*, it seems, had expressed a wish to become personally acquainted with these gallant men, and sent them a message to this effect, adding that he should feel complimented if they would make him *a call of friendship*.

To this kindly summons Marco Antonio Bragadino, the former military governor of the city, General Baglioni, Colonel Martinego, and a young artillery officer, named Quirini, at once responded, by making their appearance at the Turkish head-quarters, dressed in full uniform, and wearing their swords, which they had been permitted as a special mark of honor to retain.

Mustafa received his visitors graciously, and courteously asked them to be seated by his side.

Soon, however, a dispute arose between him and Bragadino, in relation to one of the articles of Capitulation, which Bragadino accused him of being about to break. "Wretch!" cried the enraged Turk, springing hastily to his feet, "have you forgotten that I am the conqueror, and you the conquered? A slave must learn to be respectful to his master!" As he spoke, he made a sign to his guards, and, almost simultaneously, three naked scimetars flashed before the eyes of the astonished governor, and three Christian heads rolled upon the rich carpet at his feet.

9

Then, with a cynical smile upon his sallow face, Mustafa bade him look upon the quivering trunks of his comrades, and rest assured that theirs was a happy fate in comparison with that which awaited him.

Accordingly, Bragadino's nose and ears were cut off; and in this pitiable condition he was obliged, for ten days, to labor like a beast of burden, in carrying earth to one of the bastions of the surrendered city, which the Turks were already engaged in repairing. While thus employed, each time that he passed Mustafa, who took pains to put himself in his way, he was forced to bow his head, until his lips touched the ground. Finally, after being tortured in various other ways, he was lashed to the slave's whipping-post, and flayed alive.

His skin was then stuffed with straw * and carried in derision through the streets of Famagusta and the camp under a red umbrella, which, among the Turks, is the symbol of power and dignity, while his head, severed from his body, and placed in a box with the heads of Baglioni, Mastinego and Quirini, was sent as a present to the Sultan. A tablet in the Church of St. John and St. Paul,† at Venice, commemorates the virtues, the heoric bravery, and the sad fate of the Christian warriors, over which many a tear has been shed by their tender-hearted countrymen. But the "deep damnation of their taking off" will cling to the memory of Mustafa, and awaken a feeling of detestation for his character in every generous breast,—whether of Christian or of Moslem,—until time shall be nó more; for even the false law which taught him to make war against all those

* Que su piel, relleno del heno, fuera passeada por el campo y la ciudad bajo el mismo quitasol encarnado que habia llevado la tarde que se presento a Mustafa etc., etc. Le Fuente, p. 273. Pellem que carnifices misero detraxissent, eampaleis stramineque repletam, etc., etc.—Stufano.

† San Giovani e Pablo. Here also is the urn of the heroic Marc Antonio Bragadino, the champion and martyr of Cyprus ; containing his skin ransomed by his family at enormous cost from the Moslem.

Flagg vol. 1st, page 140, La Fuente, vol. 7, page 237.

who were accounted enemies of the Prophet, yet bade him "be merciful to the suppliant and the vanquished."

With the taking of Famagusta, the Turks remained masters of Cyprus.

This enabled the Porte to give its undivided attention to the fitting out of a great fleet, which, as soon as it was fully equipped in every particular, sailed from the Golden Horn in quest of that of the Holy League, now gathering reinforcements from all directions, and preparing, under the invincible Don Juan of Austria, to bring the infidel to a decisive action.

BATTLE OF LEPANTO*.

Don Juan left Barcelona for Messina, which had been assigned as the rendezvous of the Christian forces, on the 20th of July, 1571, and, on the 9th of August, put into Naples, where Cardinal Granvelle presented to him the great banner blessed by the Pope, which as Generalissimo of the League, he was to hoist at the masthead of his royal galley.

The presentation took place in the chapel of the Franciscan convent of Santa Chiara, amid as brilliant a concourse of knights and nobles as had ever been gathered together.

"It was a striking scene," says Prescott, "pregnant with matter for meditation to those who gazed on it.

"For what could be more striking than the contrast afforded by these two individuals; the one in the morning of life, his eye kindling with hope and generous ambition as he looked into the future, and prepared to tread the path of glory under auspices as bright as ever attended any mortal; the other drawing near to the evening of his day, looking to the past rather than the future, with pale and thoughtful brow, as of one who, after many a toilsome day and sleepless

* Although this battle is known in history as the battle of Lepanto, it was really fought at the mouth of the Gulf of Patras, on the northern shore of which, about eight miles from port Petala, the Christian left rested.

night, had achieved the proud eminence for which his companion was panting and had found it barren."

Sailing from Naples on the 21st of August, Don Juan reached Messina on the 25th, where he found the Papal and Venetian fleets anxiously awaiting him.

The former, although it consisted of but eighteen vessels, was in admirable order, and gave promise of good service on the day of battle, but the latter presented a slovenly appearance, indicative of a want of discipline, and greatly disappointed the expectations Don Juan had formed of the armaments of the ancient Queen of the Adriatic.

His disgust may be gathered from a letter written by him on the 30th of August to Don Garcia de Toledo, former Viceroy of Sicily, in which, after speaking of various matters and asking Don Garcia's advice in relation to some of them, he says: "I must add that the Venetians are badly fitted and equipped, and, worse than all, there is no order or discipline among them, every captain of a galley doing just what pleases him best; a nice condition of things, truly, when one reflects that it is in their cause we are about to do battle." Finding, in addition to their other defects, that the Venetian vessels were poorly manned, Don Juan incorporated with their crews several battalions of Spanish infantry, a measure which gave great offence to Veniero, the Venetian admiral, and laid the foundation for a serious difficulty that afterwards occurred between him and Don Juan, which, but for the intercession of Colonna, the Pope's admiral, might have been productive of evil consequences to the Venetians.

By the fifth of September, the various contingents of the powers engaged in this new crusade against the Mussulmans had arrived and taken their places in the divisions to which they were assigned, and Odescalco, the Pope's legate, in the name of His Holiness, conferred upon all the Christian warriors special blessings and dispensations, conceding to them the same favors and indulgences as had been conceded in former times to the defenders of the Holy Sepulchre.

Officers, soldiers and sailors now confessed, and received absolution, and the great fleet, lightened of its sins, prepared to take its leave; but owing to bad weather, it did not get away from Messina until the sixteenth of the month.

Odescalco watched it from one of the balconies of the convent where he was lodging, till the last sail disappeared below the eastern horizon, when he hastened to Rome to give information of its departure to his master, who was anxiously and impatiently awaiting the tidings.

Reaching Corfu on the twenty-sixth of September, the confederates remained there two days, and on the twenty-eighth again put to sea, bound to Cephalonia, where they anchored on the first of October.

Here news reached them of the fall of Famagusta, and of the horrible atrocities committed by Mustafa; and bitter were the imprecations heaped upon the Seraskier's head by the whole Christian host, but most especially by the Venetians, who made many a solemn vow to avenge their slaughtered countrymen.

Before daybreak on the morning of the seventh, Don Juan got under way, and about sunrise, as the van of the allied forces, led by the Genoese admiral, Andrea Doria,* was rounding the island of Oxia, at the mouth of the Gulf of Patras, it suddenly came in sight of the Turkish fleet standing toward it, and signalled its approach to Don Juan, who at once ordered a gun to be fired from his flag-ship—an announcement to the Christians of the proximity of the foe, and of the determination of their youthful admiral to bring him to action.

The sacred banner of the League was now given to the breeze and forthwith confronted by that of the Prophet, waving above the flag-ship of the Bashaw Ali, the Turkish Grand-Admiral, and both commanders-in-chief began actively to marshal their forces for the coming engagement.

* This was Gran-Andrea Doria, a nephew and namesake of the celebrated admiral whom Barbarossa had defeated in the Gulf of Ambracio, about thirty years before.

While this was going on, some of the division commanders, on both sides, endeavored to dissuade their leaders from giving battle.

On the part of the Turks it was urged, not unwisely, that the conquest of Cyprus, just completed, should not now be left to the hazard of an hour. "The allies," they argued, "have here assembled the most powerful Christian fleet that has ever been seen in the Mediterranean. "If left to themselves they will quarrel and separate, as on former occasions, and may then safely be attacked in detail."

But Ali was young and ambitious of fame; and although, it is said, his countenance fell when he beheld the whole extent of the Christian fleet, which he had been led to believe much inferior to his own, yet he masked his fears—if, indeed, he had any—under a forced smile, and cried, with real or affected cheerfulness: "O commanders of the Faithful, this night we shall either have conquered the unbelievers, or be supping with the houris in Paradise! 'To God we belong, to God we must return'—what matters it?"

On the other hand, Don Juan, who had the good sense to see that it was no longer possible for either party to avoid an engagement, addressed his would-be advisers in a few pithy sentences: "Repair to your vessels, gentlemen," said he, "and encourage all under you to fight courageously. The enemy is in our front and a narrow sea behind. We have, therefore, neither the time nor the place, now, for further deliberation."[1] Then, observing that the upper parts of the beaks of his galleys, which projected far above and beyond their prows and served for ornament rather than for use, interfered with the full sweep of his artillery, he directed that they should be sawed off, and at the same time, ordered the trumpets of the whole fleet to sound the call to quarters.

In truth, God willed that this fearful battle should be fought; and each chief was impelled to it not less mysteriously, it would appear,—for each was led to seek for the other by false reports of his adversary's strength and condition

PLATE II.

ALBERT ROSS. LIEUT. U.S.N.

—than was Alaric to the capture of Rome by that weird voice which, he averred, ever whispered in his ear: "Go and destroy the capital of the Cæsars!"

The forces of the combatants are so variously given that it is difficult to form a correct estimate of them. The Turks seem to have had about two hundred and seventy vessels, the Christians some thirty less; but this disparity of numbers, the latter more than made up by the greater size of six of their ships, called galleasses, which not only carried guns on their poops and forecastles, as did the galleys, but also in *broadside.*

This rendered them extremely formidable, and they no doubt contributed mainly to the defeat of the Turks, a fact which the majority of Spanish historians, in their too evident desire to exalt national and individual prowess, have studiously ignored.

In *personnel*, the Turks were numerically the superiors, their force being nowhere stated at less than one hundred thousand men, while that of the Christians was but little over eighty thousand.

But it was a great element of weakness with the former that their vessels were impelled by Christian captives chained to the oar, enfeebled by scant diet, and not only dispirited, but doubtless made sullen and refractory by blows and other abuse; and although Ali, with the generosity natural to him,, for even his enemies speak of him as a man of humane disposition and of true greatness of soul—promised them their liberty if he should prove to be the victor in the fight, thus "inspiring them with a momentary enthusiasm for his cause;" yet it would have been strange if sundry misgivings had not possessed him as his eye glanced upon the opposing galleys, rowed chiefly, as he well knew, by men in the vigor of health and manhood,* who had been taught from their infancy to

* On this occasion a large number of the oarsmen in the Christian fleet were volunteers, and not the ordinary galley slaves, while *all*, it must be remembered, were *Christians.*

abhor all the various followers of the Prophet who were here gathered together under the bloodstained flag of Stamboul.

And to some ill-defined foreboding of evil, may surely be ascribed the shade of sadness which is said to have rested on his face during the whole time he was resolutely preparing for action, *even while he smiled.*

And now each fleet was in order of battle, in the form of a half moon with its horns in advance.

On the right of the Christians was the famous Doria, with some sixty Sicilian, Genoese and Maltese galleys ; on the left the *proveditore* Barbarigo, with a like number of Venetians, while the centre, or *battle*, as it was then called, composed of eighty of "the best vessels that had ever been built," was led by Don Juan himself, with the great Colonna on his right hand and the veteran Veniero on his left, who, notwithstanding his disagreement with his commander-in-chief, seconded him on this occasion, loyally and well, thus setting the seal of honor upon a long life devoted to the service of his country.

The reserve of thirty-six vessels was conducted by the chivalric Don Alvaro de Bazan, marquis of Santa Cruz ; and just astern of the *Real*—the designation then given to the ship of a Spanish admiral-in-chief—was Don Juan's old preceptor in the art of war, Don Luis de Requesens, commander of Castile.

The battle of the Turkish fleet consisted of ninety-six vessels, of which the right centre was led by Ali, the left centre by the Bashaw PERTEW.

The right wing was intrusted to Mehemet Sirocco, Viceroy of Alexandria ; the left to the Calabrian renegade, Uluch Ali, Dey of Algiers.

In rear of the battle was a strong reserve [2] commanded by Amurath Dragut, an officer of approved capacity, experience and valor.

When the two fleets had approached within a mile of each other they ceased rowing in mutual admiration. [3]

For the day was bright and beautiful. Not a cloud disturbed the repose of the blue sky above, nor a solitary ripple that of the placid waters below, and the mid-day sun shone with resplendent lustre upon lance, and shield, and scimetar —upon glittering breast-plates and helmets of burnished steel.

The great banner of the League with its piteous crucifix, at the foot of which were to be seen the arms of Venice, Spain and the Pope, bound together by an endless chain, was not more conspicuous than the green standard of the Prophet, all covered with verses from the Koran, in letters of silver and gold.

The red flag of the corsairs of Algiers, with its hateful device, the head of the fierce Hali,[4] son-in-law of Mohammed and the dreaded enemy of all the Christians of his day, was well met by that of the knights of Saint John, whose presence on the battlefield was ever a terror to their foes.

And along the whole infidel line the ancient Byzantine crescent, now appropriated by the Turk, and suggestive of devastation and death, was nobly opposed by the pure, white cross, inscribed on every banner in its front, teaching the story of the life to come.

A gun was fired by Ali and, as if aroused from slumber by its report, the Christian fleet began to move, and opening from the wings and centre, unmasked its six leviathans—for such the Venetian galleasses must have appeared to the eyes of the astounded moslimim—which, passing through the gaps left for them, now rowed slowly and majestically forward until they had got a half mile in advance, when they lay on their oars, while the vessels that had made way for them resumed their stations, and the line was closed as before.

Then a deafening cheer arose from the whole Christian front, followed by cries of bitter reproach and insult to the Moslem; yet, not for this did the Turks, who were already in motion, cease for a moment in their career.

On the contrary, brandishing their weapons, and striking their shields together, after the manner of their remote ancestors when engaged in battle, they replied to the taunts of their enemies with loud shouts of, *God is great! Mohammed is his Prophet!* and, urging their galleys to their utmost speed, advanced steadily and in splendid order to the encounter.

Their extreme right, piloted by a Genoese renegade, who knew the soundings of every foot of the Gulfs of Patras and Lepanto as an astronomer knows the stars, boldly dashed through a narrow and intricate passage [5] between two coral reefs, over which the sea was even then breaking, and assailed the Venetians in flank, while Uluch Ali, rapidly extending toward the left, endeavored to turn the Christian right.

Foiled in this by his adversary, the descendant of a long line of distinguished admirals, and himself the most experienced of the Christian commanders, the redoubtable corsair, who well deserved the name afterward bestowed upon him by the Sultan, of Al Kilich, or the Scimetar, made directly for the Maltese galleys, which during the manœuvring necessary to prevent the flank being turned, had become widely separated from their consorts, and sinking some of them and disabling others, carried off their largest vessel in triumph.

Then, passing through the line and attacking it in rear, he forced Don Alvaro de Bazan with all his strength, to hasten to the relief of the out-numbered and overpowered Genoese, whose vessels, sorely beset on all sides by the Algerines, were fast falling into infidel hands.

While such was the success of the Turks on the left, on the right, where they had commenced the fight under such favorable auspices, fortune was preparing to set her face against them; for the *proveditore*, far from being dismayed by the approach of his enemies through a channel which his own pilots had told him was impracticable, ordered his flanking squadron to make a half-wheel to the left, in readiness to receive them; while he himself, with his remaining squadrons, advanced, in unbroken line, to attack Mehemet Sirocco, who had opened a tremendous fire on his front.

For three long hours the battle was carried on, in this

quarter, in the most vindictive spirit by both parties, while the old lion of St. Mark, restlessly impelled by the breeze to and fro, above Barbarigo's head, glared fiercely down upon the crocodile, whose distended jaws served as a beak for the Egyptian Viceroy's galley. The fight between the flag-ships was sustained with equal valor on both sides, and each Admiral was gallantly supported by all the vessels of his command; but, Barbarigo falling to the deck, pierced through the eye by an arrow, the crews of his vessels become disheartened, and, disregarding the remonstrances and threats of their officers, prepare to strike their flags to the Egyptians.

The cry for a surrender has passed from ship to ship, and, in a few moments, on the left as on the extreme right, the cross will cease to fly in presence of the crescent. What hope then of saving the Christian centre?

"Christ will descend to save his people"! [6] cries an Italian friar, who, holding aloft the crucifix, opposes his single person to the hosts of Egyptians now pouring aboard of their fancied prize—the Venetian flag-ship.

A hundred arquebusses are levelled at his breast—a hundred scimetars flash above his head; but lo! unscathed, he still remains, erect, waving the holy symbol high in air. Encouraged by the *miracle*, the Christians now furiously turn upon their assailants, while the Turks, seized with mortal terror, first waver, then fly? Sirocco and his chief captains nobly endeavoring to rally them, are either slain or desperately wounded, and victory at last declares in favor of the Venetians [7].

The centre vessels of the Turks, opening to the right and left [8] and pulling at full speed by the galleasses [9], whose broadside batteries made sad havoc among them as they passed, now formed in close order, and steered for the Christian centre, from which, when the infidel drew near, a single galley, having carved upon its bow the armorial bearings of the House of Austria, rowed forth, and, in token of defiance, fired a blank cartridge in the air, as in the late rebellion of the Moors of Granada, which Don Juan had brought to a termination so glorious for himself and his country, when hostile forces met, a solitary Spanish cavalier was wont to ride to the front of his command to dare to single combat the Moorish knight who appeared as the leader of the opposite party.

Stung to the quick by the *bravado*, the impetuous Ali bore up at once for Don Juan, and, as his vessel was under full headway when she struck the *real*, the bow of the latter was severely injured by the collision, and Don Juan, who was standing on the forecastle at the time, must have been crushed thereby, had not an old seaman picked him up and carried him in his arms as far aft as the fifth bench of rowers.

Ali's galley felt the shock from stem to stern, and his officers and men suffered fearfully from the fire of the *real*, whose defenders were also fast falling under the deadly aim of the Turks.

To right and left now, along the whole line the battle raged with terrific fury.

The roar of the artillery was incessant, and heard for many miles, and volley after volley of small arms sounded the death-knell of hundreds of gallant soldiers and seamen both of the Turks and of the Christians. The Marquis of Santa Cruz, occupied, as we have seen, with Uluch Ali, could render no assistance to Don Juan ; while the Turkish reserve was fully engaged, it appears probable, in preventing the galleasses from falling upon Ali's rear ; for upon no other hypothesis can we account for our not hearing any thing of it at this most important juncture when the addition of a few fine ships to the Turkish centre must inevitably have turned the scale against the Christians, and caused the defeat of that portion of their fleet upon which the safety of the whole depended ; for the battle had now become a *melée* wherein everything hung upon the numbers and strength of the contending vessels, and the courage, endurance and discipline of their crews.

In such a conflict the great point was to keep the head of one's galley ever pointed toward the foe, and the crew well in hand, in readiness to board or to repel boarders, as opportunity might offer or occasion require. If a vessel became disabled in her motive or steering power, straightway she was *rammed* by several enemies at once, and went to the bottom with all on board; or fire brands and burning darts were thrown at her from every direction, and in an instant she was all ablaze, her men either perishing miserably in the flames or jumping overboard to be despatched by the sweeps of some hostile galley. Here was seen a Christian vessel—her decks covered with the dead and the dying—whose flag was being lowered by unchristian hands; there, a Turkish galleon, with battered sides and scuppers running blood, borne off in triumph under the banner of Venice or Castile. Ere long, however, the fleets were so enveloped in smoke that these piteous spectacles were no longer visible; yet the noise of the cannonade continued, intermingled with that of falling masts and spars, the crash of colliding vessels, and the fierce cries of the combatants of "Down with the unbelievers!" "Strike for Christ and the Virgin!" and ever and anon was borne upon the breeze the triumphal shout of the vengeful Venetian.—"No quarter to the flying Turk! Remember Famagusta!"

The fight had lasted many hours, and the sun was fast declining, when the rival chieftains, the beaks of whose galleys had long been interlocked, like the antlers of two stags in mortal combat, mustered their forces on the upper deck, each with the intention of carrying the other's vessel by boarding.

On the one side were the Janissaries—those renowned warriors whose proud boast it was that they had never turned their backs to the foe; on the other that invincible Spanish infantry, trained and disciplined by the great Duke of Alva.

Many times did the intrepid Ali spring on board the *real* at the head of his men, only to be driven back by the withering fire of the arquebusiers; Don Juan as often gained and lost the deck of the Bashaw's galley. Foot to foot and hand to hand the bravest soldiers of the East and West contended for the mastery.

The Spaniard fought for glory in this world and endless bliss in the world to come; while, beyond the serried ranks of the Christians, the Moslem beheld the dark-eyed houris of Paradise waiting to welcome the warrior who should lose his life in the service of Mohammed and the Sultan. At length Uluch Ali, regarding Doria as whipped, and recognizing the fact that the final issue of the battle depended upon the struggle then so fiercely pending between Ali and Don Juan, steered for the Christian centre, followed by all his Algerines, and, although stoutly opposed by Don Juan's supporters, was fast nearing their admiral's galley.

Inspirited by the sight, Ali put himself at the head of his Janissaries, and, crying out, "O Yengicheri, this day God has delivered the unbelievers into your hands!" he prepared to board the *real* at the moment when Ulich Ali's vessel should collide with her.

Victory seemed indeed within his grasp, and all was dark with the Christians!

At this critical instant, so pregnant with the opposite emotions of fear and hope, the smoke cleared away, as if by enchantment, and Don Alvaro de Bazan, with the reserve, was descried coming at full speed to the relief of his chief, while Doria, supported by a few of his best and fastest galleys, was making an effort to get in Uluch Ali's rear.
[10] Seeing this, the wily Algerine gave up all as lost, and, signalling to his squadron to withdraw from action, retired in the direction of Zante. "Curses on him, for a coward!" cried the indignant Ali. "Soldiers, we must conquer without him!"

As he ceased speaking, a bullet fired by an unknown

hand, went crashing through his skull, and the gallant Turk, more fortunate than his comrades who survived this disastrous day, fell back, senseless, but with honor, in the arms of his nearest follower. Profiting by the confusion incident to his fall, Don Juan boarded his magnificent galley from the bow simultaneously with Veniero and Colonna, who threw their crews on board on either side.

Thus over-powered, the Janissaries, true to the principle which had been instilled into them from their earliest childhood, resolved to die under their colors.

Not one of them threw down his arms or asked for quarter ; on the contrary, each man, fighting to the last, fell in the ranks, covering with his body when dead that portion of the deck which he had occupied while living. As the last man fell, a Spanish volunteer, cutting off Ali's head, carried it with him to the poop of the *real*, whither Don Juan had betaken himself, and, placing it on the point of his lance, held it far above his head that all the Turks might see it, and from the helmet with which it was covered, bearing the insignia of his rank, become cognizant of the fact that their grand admiral was slain.[11]

At this dismal sight, however, a cry of horror went up from friend and foe alike, and Don Juan sternly rebuked the barbarian who had perpetrated the outrage ; then, turning to Requesens, who stood near him, the youthful victor directed him to have the colors of the Bashaw's galley hauled down—an order that was joyfully complied with.

As the great standard of the Prophet was lowered to the deck, fear and dismay seized the whole Turkish host. God had given a great victory to the Christians.

One hundred and thirty of the enemy's vessels, with their crews, fell into the hands of the allies, and twelve thousand Christian captives were rescued from bondage.

The rest of the vast Turkish armament, with its myriads of brave men, was consumed by fire or swallowed up by the waves.

The Christian loss was fifteen vessels sunk and eight thousand officers, seamen and soldiers killed, of whom the most noted were the *proveditore*, Augustine Barbarigo, who died a few days after the battle, universally regretted, and Don Juan, Ponce de Leon, a scion of that illustrious race whose blood has ever been poured out like water in the service of Spain.

Among the Turks who, next to the lamented Ali, most distinguished themselves in the action, the Bashaw Pertew, who for three hours sustained, unaided, the attacks of four Christian galleys, stands pre-eminent.

Finding himself at last without oars or rudder, this indomitable officer leapt overboard and swam to a small fishing craft, where he was overtaken by the Venetians and barbarously murdered.[12]

Of the Christians, three names come down to us invested with especial interest: those of Don Juan of Austria, whose whole life was a feverish dream of ambition, to end in a melancholy death; of Alexander Farnese, prince of Parma, destined to be the first general of his age; and of Miguel de Cervantes Saavedra, then but a common soldier in the field of Mars, but shortly to become a leader and a guiding star in that wider and nobler field where the sword yields precedence to the pen.

Such was the ever-memorable battle of Lepanto, which gave the *coup de grâce* to the naval supremacy of the Turks on the Mediterranean, and filled their capital with mourning.

That the allies did not gain from it all the advantages they should have gained, history makes apparent.

The fact is undeniable, and is to be attributed partly to a want of harmony among the commanders of the allied fleets, and, in part, to Philip's jealousy of his half brother, which thenceforth began to manifest itself in all his conduct toward him; but the assertion of many chroniclers that Don Juan might have taken possession of the splendidly fortified and strongly garrisoned city of Constantinople, had he made sail for it immediately after the action, is best answered by the Turkish Vizïer Sokolli himself: "Your Excellency wishes to know," said he to the ambassador of Venice, "what our temper is since our defeat.

"Let me tell you then, that you, in losing Cyprus, have lost an arm, while the destruction of our fleet is to us as the cutting off of our beard.

"A limb cannot be replaced, but the beard, you may assure the Signory, will grow thicker with each clipping."

And this was not a vain boast; for early in the following summer more than two hundred admirably built and well equipped vessels were put afloat by the Turkish government; and when Uluch Ali, who had been appointed to the command of the fleet, expressed his astonishment at its "marvellous fittings" Sokolli assured him that the resources of the Sublime Porte were such that they could have been furnished if necessary, "with silken cordage, velvet sails and spars of silver."[18] The disaster, then, that befel the Turks at Lepanto, consisted, not in the vast numbers of men and galleys lost, for these, as we have seen, were easily replaced, but in the loss of prestige, *that breath of life to a nation, without which it may be likened to an unburied corpse.*

From that moment the Mohammedans were placed on the defensive; and the historian of the Ottoman Empire, in recognition of this fact, does well to head the chapter following that which gives an account of their defeat, *Epoch of the decadence of the Turks.* Slowly but steadily has their light been declining ever since, and but a short time can now elapse ere it will be extinguished forever; for no nation whose religion is purely material may hope long to survive the enlightenment of the nineteenth century.

No wonder, therefore, that the Pope, shedding tears of joy when he heard of Don Juan's victory, should have exclaimed in the language of the gospel: *There was a man sent from God whose name was John!* or that a statue should have been erected at Rome to Colonna.

No wonder that the pencil of Tintoretto and the chisel of Vittoria were employed by the Venetians to illustrate that great action which seemed to revive the ancient glory of the republic.

The victory of Lepanto was the final and permanent triumph of the Cross over the Crescent.

Philip received the tidings on All Saints' Day, in the chapel of the Escurial, just as vespers were commencing, and, with his usual impassibility remained on his knees, during the whole service, engaged in prayer, without vouchsafing a word of reply to his chamberlain, Don Pedro Manuel, who was the bearer of them.[14]

At the conclusion of the service he ordered the officiating priest to have the *Te Deum* chanted—the first intimation received by his courtiers of the triumph of one whom they all loved, and whose chivalric deeds Spanish historians and poets have ever since vied with one another in celebrating.

The helmet of Ali and the armor of Don Juan were hung up side by side, in the Royal Armory at Madrid, where they are still exhibited; and, as the death of the former was lamanted not only by the Turks, but by the Christians, on account of the kindness he had shown to many of their faith while in captivity, so was that of the latter which occurred but eight years afterward, greatly regretted, both by the Christians and the Turks; for the Mohammedans long remembered Don Juan's courteous treatment of the son of Ali, and his generosity in restoring him without ransom to his sister Fatima.[15]

The hero of Lepanto was in fact no ordinary mortal and well deserved the affection and respect which were accorded to him by all classes while he lived, and the deep lamentation which accompanied his remains to the grave.

"He conquered the Moors," says Bentigvolio, "while but little more than a child, humbled the Turks in the flower of his youth, and, at the early age of thirty-three departed this life with a reputation second to that of no other captain of his day." [16]

After his death he was compared by many of his countrymen to Germanicus, by others to the conqueror of Jerusalem; but the rude soldiery, knowing nothing of the past, declared that there was but one warrior whose image was worthy of a place beside that of their deceased general, and that warrior his own father, the renowned Emperor, Charles the Fifth.

In praise of the *marshalling* of the two great fleets at Lepanto, preparatory to engaging, too much cannot be said; but Don Juan committed a tactical error in not imitating Julius Cæsar (to whom he was extravagantly compared by Alva) at Pharsalia, by placing his reserve in rear of his right-flank, since as he considered his left secured by the shoals of coral and sand off point Scropha he might reasonably have anticipated an attempt to turn his right. His disposition of the Galeasses was admirable, and to the moral effect of these great ships and their destructive fire, which sunk two Turkish vessels at the very commencement of the action, the victory of the Christians, as we have said before, was mainly due. In small-arms, too, the Christians had greatly the advantage, since of the Turkish soldiers not more than one third carried arquebuses, the rest being armed with the arbalest and bow.

As Ali knew, it is to be presumed, of the channel between the reefs on which the Christian left was resting which in military parlance might be called the key of the position, his great effort should have been directed towards getting by means of it, in rear of the confederates, concentrating, with this design, such a force on their left as would have enabled him to annihilate Barbarigo, and making a bold *feint* at the same time toward their centre and right.

Motley is mistaken in supposing that "the Turks committed the fatal error of fighting on a lee shore." They came out of Lepanto, in fact, under sail and running large, and although the wind hauled ahead, as they were forming line of battle, it was very light while the swell raised by an easterly gale which had prevailed the preceding day had so entirely subsided as "to leave the waves," according to Rosell, "in complete quietude" (*quedando las olas en completa calma.*) There was then no lee shore, properly speaking for either party; but the night after the engagement, a violent tornado swept over the Grecian seas, during which a few disabled and deserted Turkish galleys, which had not been taken possession of by the Christians, and some of those that were making the best of their way toward Constantinople, with Uluch Ali, were blown ashore and destroyed. Several Turkish vessels, which had grounded on the Scropha shoals after they turned to flee, were also broken up by this storm.

The bravery displayed by the combatants on both sides in this world-renowned fight has rarely been equalled and *never* excelled. But though fortune declared against them, the meed of heroic valor must be awarded to the Turks, who fought from their open decks, while a vast number of the Christians were under cover, in "towers," "turrets," and "castles," and behind improvised mantalets.

THROUGH THE DISCOVERY OF THE CAPE OF GOOD HOPE, VENICE CEASES TO BE THE GREAT MARITIME POWER OF THE WORLD.

With Lepanto properly ends the Naval history of Venice and the other Italian states. The discovery of the Cape of Good Hope, in 1497, had opened a new road to India, and thenceforth Italy was no longer the commercial centre of the world. From this period, Venice gradually declined, until, on the 12th of May 1797, through the abdication of the Grand Council of the Republic, she ceased to exist as an independent power. With regard to her form of government, much has been written by her enemies, little by her friends; but if we may judge of its character by the works it achieved, we shall conclude that it could not have been without great merits, whatever its defects. And who is there on this continent who does not rejoice that the bride of the Adriatic has returned to the home of her fathers—the land of Columbus and Galileo, of Galvani and Volta, of Michael Angelo and Leonardo da Vinci! that wonderful land which has "extracted glory from every department of human knowledge, and adorned every art"?

What man is there among us whose heart does not throb with emotion, as, looking toward the East, he observes "the dark cloud, fringed with irradiations, which for a thousand years has hung over that beautiful peninsula," slowly but surely rising at last, and revealing in letters of light, on the distant horizon, these words of brighest promise to mankind; *United Italy is again resuming her place among the great nations of the earth.*

OF THE PEOPLE WHO DWELT ALONG THE SOUTHERN SHORE OF THE BALTIC AND ON THE SEABOARD OF GERMANY.

Before proceeding to treat of the maritime affairs of those States which succeeded Venice as rulers of the waves, it will be well to turn our attention for a brief period to the nations dwelling along the shores of those inland waters, which, situated in the frigid regions of the North, and wrapped in Cimmerian darkness during many months of the year, were objects of superstitious awe to the Greeks and Latins, who reveling in the light of their own sunny skies, shuddered with horror at the bare mention of a frozen sea, and a people dwelling in the "gloomy caverns of the North Wind."

That their descendants in the Middle Ages inherited their antipathy to cold, is shown by Dante, who at the very bottom of the *inferno, as his hell of hells*, places an *icy lake.* Perhaps, however, much of the dread of the North among the Latins arose from a vague fore-shadowing of the future. Leaving the banks of the Araxes some centuries before the birth of Christ, the Scythians had gradually made themselves masters of northern Europe, from the Arctic to the river

Rhine, and from the Ural Mountains to the German Ocean. Like the Romans, "where they conquered they inhabited," and thus the Scandinavians, Jutlanders and Germans became eventually a kindred race. "The Germans," says Tacitus, "can recount their triumphs over Carbo, Cassius, Scaurus Aurelius, Servilius Cæpio and Cneius Manlius, all defeated or taken prisoners. With them the Republic lost five consular armies; and since that time, in the reign of Augustus, Varus perished with his three legions.

"Many of our generals, it is true, have beaten the Germans in great battles; but how much blood have their victories cost us? The mighty projects of Caligula ended in a farce. From that period an interval of peace succeeded, until roused at length by our internal dissensions, they stormed our legions in their winter quarters, and even planned the conquest of Gaul. We forced them indeed to repass the Rhine; but from that time what has been our advantage? We have triumphed and Germany is still unconquered." In another place the great historian, as if beholding in prophetic vision, the triumphal march of "Northern barbarians" through the streets ot Rome, offers up a prayer that the arms of the Germans may be turned against each other.

Some centuries had passed, however, from the death of Tacitus before the western empire was finally overthrown, and its last emperor—a pensioner upon the bounty of his lord—banished to the Castle of Lucullus, which had originally served as the Villa of Caius Marius! A Roman cherishing the traditions of the Republic and standing on the Capitoline Hill amid the monuments of its greatness, might well have expected in this sorrowful hour to see the walls of the Eternal City crumble, and the graves open and send forth the old soldiers of the "army of Numidia," to forbid the approach of him who was contemptuously styled *Augustulus* by his countrymen, to the home of the conqueror of Jugurtha, the Teutones and the Cimbri!

About a quarter of a century before the taking of Rome

by Odoacer, the East Germans or Saxons who dwelt along the seaboard of Germany, from the Rhine to the Skager Rack, gained a foothold in Britain, and after a bloody strife of one hundred and fifty years, the events of which every child knows, succeeded in subduing the whole island. Their rule lasted about four centuries, during which time their kinsmen in Germany, under the various names of Ostrogoths, Visigoths, Franks and Vandals, had obtained possession of almost every foot of Europe south of the Baltic, which sea we shall now cross in search of that northern branch of the Scythian family, whose fame as a maritime people was soon to be heralded throughout the world.

SCANDINAVIA.

The earliest reliable accounts that we have of the Norse men come from Snorro Sturleson's *sagas* or old stories, "written down as they were told to him by intelligent persons, concerning chiefs who had held dominion in the Northern countries, the truth of which is not doubted by wise men." Snorro prefaces what may be considered his historic record, however, by a rapid sketch of the Yngling dynasty, which, beginning in fable, ends with the death of Olaf, King of Westfold, about the middle of the 9th century, from which date authentic narrative takes the place of fiction, in the unwritten annals of the North. A *resumé* of this portion of Snorro's work will serve to give us some idea both of the romantic character and the superstitions of the people inhabiting that weird land, supposed by the ancients to be encircled by a *stagnant* sea," whence the sun rose with a sound that was "distinctly audible," exhibiting to view the gorgeous palace of Apollo, and the god issuing forth for his western drive, standing erect in his chariot, surrounded by the nymphs, and with a blaze of fire about his head.

"It is said," remarks Sturleson, "that the earth's circle which the human race inhabits is torn across into many bights, so that great seas run into the land from the out-ocean. Thus it is known that a great sea goes in at Niorva-sund and up to the land of Jerusalem. From the same sea a long sea-bight stretches towards the North-east, called the Black Sea, which divided the three parts of the earth; of which the eastern part is called Asia, the western Europa or Enea. Northward of the Black Sea lies Swithiod the Great or the Cold.

In Swithiod are many wonderful races of men and many kinds of languages. There are giants and there are dwarfs, and there are also blue men.

There are wild beasts and dreadfully large dragons. The country east of the Tanaquisi in Asia was called Asasland, and its chief city Asgaard. In that city was a chief named Odin—a great and very far travelled warrior—who conquered many kingdoms; for victory was with him in every battle. It was his custom before fighting to call down a blessing on his men, laying his hand upon their heads, and whenever they felt themselves in danger, whether by land or by sea, they called upon his name, knowing that where he was aid was near. Having subdued an extensive kingdom in Saxland, Odin left his sons to defend it, while he himself crossed the sea and took up his abode on the Mælare Lake, where he erected a large temple and began to teach the people magic arts. He conversed so cleverly that all who listened to him were charmed with him; and being enabled to change his form and color at will, he appeared beautiful to his friends and fierce and dreadful to his enemies, whom he sometimes made blind, sometimes deaf. At other times he struck them with a panic terror, or dulled the edge of their weapons at the very moment when his own men were rushing upon them like wolves or mad dogs. With words alone he could quench a fire, still the ocean in a tempest, and turn the wind to any quarter he pleased. He died in Sweden and the Swedes said he was gone to the ancient Asgaard. Then they began to call upon his name and it was believed that he often showed himself to them before any great battle, promising victory to some and inviting others to himself."

From Odin to Halfdan, who, on account of the blackness of his hair, was called Halfdan the black, we have an account of more than thirty kings who ruled over the Norse land, and, doubtless many reigned whose memory has not been handed down to us in song or story. The government of Norway, after its various districts were united under one head, consisted of a king and an open-air parliament, or assembly of the people called a Thing. The Great Thing which met at Drontheim was the Congress of the Nation, while the district Things, of which there were four, may be likened to State legislatures. In addressing a Thing, the speaker rose, if he were a king, and its members were in the habit of showing their respect for such of their orators as were agreeable to them by crowding around them, and listening attentively to every word that fell from their lips, while the voices of others were drowned by their rude clamor.

The bonders (land-owners) alone had a seat in these Things, and so influential was this class in Norway that it was not considered a misalliance for the sister or daughter of a king to marry a powerful bonder. Beside the Great and District Things, there were Petty Things, established in all the many sub-divisions of the kingdom, which were presided over by men venerable from age and experience, and had cognizance of such cases as are with us carried before magistrates. For all offenses, from the murder of the king down to the maiming of a thrall, fines were fixed by law, but it was optional with the aggrieved party, or, in case of his death, his next of kin to accept compensation or take vengeance for injuries received.

Next to the land-owners came the freedmen or manumitted slaves, who enjoyed the full protection of the laws, but had no *say* in their enactment, and lastly, the *thralls* or captives in war, over whom their masters exercised the authority of life and death.

The summons to a General or District Thing was by a piece of wood, with a spike in the upper end of it, called a bod or a bodstickke, which was passed from neighbor to neighbor according to established rules. When the bearer of it arrived at a house where the people were from home, he laid it " on the house father's great chair at the fireside," if he could gain entrance to the dwelling, but, if not, he fastened it by the spike to the front door; and either of these modes of delivery was held to be legal. When the lower end of the bod was fashioned like an axe it denoted that the king would be present at the council, and an arrow, split into four parts and sent forth North, South, East and West, summoned the bonders in all haste to the place of rendez-vous, armed to the teeth.

The dwellings of the Northmen were of wood and of one story, with a sleeping loft above constructed like the garrets of our ordinary farm houses. The most important room was the dining-hall, which, with the wealthy land-owners, must have been very large indeed, as in it they entertained, not unfrequently, fifty guests. Their hospitable boards groaned with the weight of boar's flesh and every variety of game, and the mead went round, during the long winter nights, without stint or cessation. That drunkenness and gluttony were their vices is shown by the number of queer stories, found in the sagas, of witches, warlocks, dwarfs and dragons seen by the revellers, on various occasions, upon rising from table, and of the visits paid to them by *Mara* (the northern night mare) after they had retired to their lofts. In the lower rooms of some of the houses great casks were placed reaching to the flooring above, which was cut away to accommodate them; and it is narrated that a certain king named Fiolner, who had been so well entertained by his friend Frode that he became " very sleepy and exceedingly drunk," fell into one of these hogsheads, as he was groping his way to his bedchamber, and was drowned. Thiodolf of Huine thus rhymes of it :

" The cry of fey denouncing doom,
Was heard at night in Frode's home :
And when brave Frode came, he found
Swithiod's dark chief, Fiolner drowned.
In Frode's mansion drowned was he
Drowned in a waveless, windless sea."

The house-frue or house-wife, an important personage in Norway, was noted for her industry and thriftiness. " You have been taught little good," cried one of them angrily, as she hastily pulled away a towel from a man calling himself Vandraade (luckless mortal.) " You have been taught little good, you wasteful fellow you, to wipe your face in the middle of a cloth when the ends of it are still unspotted!"

Among a people ignorant of the art of writing, and yet, like the Norwegian bonders, *udal-born*, that is, having certain inherited rights to property, a class of persons would naturally arise whose sole occupation should consist in committing to memory accounts of the pedigrees, births, deaths, and intermarriages of all the land-owners of the kingdom. These oral-recorders—" the living books to be referred to in every case of disputed ownership to land or cattle "—were of two kinds, the prose-relators or saga-men and the rhymers or *scalds*, who being from Iceland and without hereditary feuds, and the educated men of the day withal, when experience of men and manners and not books formed the mind, were employed by kings as their envoys, counsellors and historiographers. Thus their traditions, which have come down to us, through Snorro Sturleson, in written form, are of great value to us in forming a judgment of the people to whom they relate; and as we realise that their songs and stories are but the reflex of the popular mind, it is interesting to observe, pervading the whole of them, a bold spirit of freedom such as was natural to men having a voice in the national councils, and which carried with them into England, " formed the foundation stone," as Laing well says, " of the British constitution, representative legislation, trial by jury, freedom of mind and person, and freedom of the press." As a proof of the boldness of their satire, nothing could be stronger than the following lines composed in the tenth century and aimed at king Harold Gormson of Denmark and his bailiff Birgir, for seizing upon a wrecked Icelandic vessel as *treasure-trove.* So keenly did the king feel the force of public opinion in the matter that, after the first explosion of his wrath was over, he endeavored to throw the whole odium of it on his unfortunate bailiff:

The gallant Harald, in the field,
Between his legs, let's drop his shield;
Into a pony he was changed,
And kicked his heels and safely ranged:
And Birgir, he who dwells in halls,
For safety built with four stone walls,
That these might be a worthy pair,
Was changed into a pony mare.

This biting lampoon was got by heart by half the children in Scandinavia, and even repeated under the king's very roof with a courage truly republican. To this brave spirit, bequeathed to us through our English ancestry, the United States is largely indebted for all that she at this day possesses of religious and civil liberty; and, in view of this fact, the early history of Scandinavia cannot but be of great interest to every citizen of the republic. It is, however, with the Norsemen as a naval people solely that this volume has to deal, and as the great battle fought off the isle of Rugen, in the year one thousand, between Olaf Tryggvesson king of Norway and the kings of Denmark and Sweden, is narrated by Snorro with so much minuteness of detail as to have served the purposes of learned antiquaries in their investigations into the ships, weapons, &c., &c., of that day, I propose to give a full description of it here, prefacing it with such an account of marine matters and of the life of Olaf Tryggvesson, the hero of the fight, as may seem necessary to explain and illustrate it, and supplementing it with a brief sketch of the deeds of two other famous sea-kings, Olaf the Saint and Harald Hardrada.

THE NAVAL POWER OF THE NORSEMEN. THEIR FONDNESS FOR THE SEA. THE VIKINGS.

In a country like Norway, where in some places the ocean runs up hundred of miles into the land, forming those beautiful fiords, whose crystalline waters abound in fish, it was naturally to be expected that the inhabitants would take to the sea; and we are, therefore, not surprised when Tacitus informs us that in his day they had a powerful naval force.

The whole land, in fact, was divided into ship districts, each of which upon a summons from the king, was to furnish its quota of vessels manned, armed and equipped according to law; while the province of Viken, where the hard round stones used in battle abounded, gave name to that fearless race of mariners known as *Vikings* who had their first harborage there.

With the vikings it was a maxim that "a man should attack a single enemy, fight two, and not yield to three, but that he might, without disgrace, fly from four;" and as, by degrees, they spread themselves over the Baltic, taking possession of many of its largest islands, they became so powerful as to set all law at defiance, and no vessel or coast was safe from their depredations.

Viking and sea-king, it must be remembered, are by no means synonymous titles, though the majority of writers use them as such.

All the *Great* kings of Norway were sea-kings, but many of them were far from being vikings, who, stripped of the romance with which for ages they have been invested, and viewed in the light of historic truth, must be characterized as most atrocious pirates.

It may justly be urged in their behalf, however, that the law of *meum* and *tuum* was but little heeded in the "good old times" by the Norwegians generally, with whom it was as much the fashion to go to the sea-side, during the summer months, "to gather property," as it is with us to go there to lose it.

It seems indeed to have been their chief solace in affliction; for we read of a mighty chieftain who was so inconsolable for the loss of his wife that he could neither eat nor sleep, and so "he assembled his war-ships," says the Saga, "and went a plundering."

So truly Nautical were the norsemen in their ideas that they spoke of the dividing-ridge or water-shed of a country, as its *keel*, since, with its sloping sides, it appeared to them like a huge boat turned bottom upward.

In times of trouble, their chieftains took to their ships, as the old German barons took to their castles; and, indeed, in a country where all the habitations were of wood and consequently could be assailed with fire, an intervening sea-fosse was a man's only protection against surprise from his enemies.

Their war-vessels which were sharp at both ends, were of two classes, the *drakar* or dragon, so moulded as to represent the ideal form of a dragon or winged serpent, and the *snekar* or snake, which, with hissing tongue protruding from its long, narrow prow, glided stealthily through the waves, as its prototype on land glides through the grass.

The largest of these vessels of which we have any account pulled one hundred and twenty, the smallest sixteen oars, (all in one tier) and the rowers sat two abreast as with us.

Beneath their fleet was a shifting deck, along which large chests were placed fore and aft, some of which were filled with stones and others with arms of various kinds whose uses are made known to us in Olaf's battle.

It seems to have been their custom to make a harbor every night and sleep ashore under *tilts* or ships-tents, but when necessity obliged them to remain afloat, the rowers found a safe shelter amidships under "tented" awnings,

PLATE III.

ALBERT ROSS. LIEUT. U.S.N.

while the officers and petty officers took refuge under the poop and forecastle decks.

In some of the finest of their vessels, however, there was a poop-cabin occupied exclusively by the captain or commander-in-chief.

Such were the marine dwellings of these famous seamen during their lives, and such the sepulchres of some of them when dead.

In commemoration of his victories at Fradarberg for instance, King Hakon the Good put the corpses of his slain in the ships captured from the enemy which were then drawn up on shore and covered with earth and stones.

"These tumuli," says Snorro, "are to be seen at the present day."

DESCRIPTION OF THE HULL OF A NORSE VESSEL, EXCAVATED, A FEW YEARS SINCE, FROM A MOUND NEAR FREDRIKSTADT, NORWAY, AND NOW IN THE UNIVERSITY OF CHRISTIANIA.

The best account I have seen of the construction of the boats or galleys of the Norsemen is to be found in a tract published by the society for the preservation of Norwegian antiquities, and translated into English by Mr. Gades, our Consul at Christiania.

It relates to a vessel found in a mound a few years ago in the parish of Tune, about three-quarters of a mile above the town of Fredrikstadt, which I myself saw at Christiania, in 1871, in a shed attached to the university.

"The vessel," says the translation, "stood in the mound on a level with the surrounding surface of the earth, in the direction of N. N. W. and S. S. E. a little lower in the southern than in the northern end. It is clinker built, with iron nails, and made almost exclusively of oak; only the ribs and wooden nails, which were found at some places, are made of fir.

The keel, which is made of a single piece of wood and quite undamaged, is 43½ feet in length.

The width of it can no longer be given with exactitude. as the upper boards have disappeared, but it has undoubtedly been more than 13 feet wide amidships.

The perpendicular height from the keel to the gunwale can not have exceeded four feet.

As will be seen from these measurements, the vessel has been very flat and low.

Both ends are almost alike and both very pointed, so that one can be in doubt, which is fore and which aft.

But several circumstances, especially the position of the mast, appear to indicate, that the northern end is the stern.

The pieces preserved of the ends of the vessel show that there must have been 10 or 11 boards in height on each side.

There are still remnants left of the tenth board amidships and there cannot have been more than eleven to judge from the height of the perfectly preserved ribs.

The boards are one inch thick, but of different widths, varying from 6 to 12 inches.

One board, the eighth from below, is much thicker than the others; viz, more than two inches, but only five inches wide.

The clinker nails have round heads outside and square ones inside; they are 6 to 9 inches apart.

The openings are tightened with tarred oakum of neat's hair.

Where the boards are joined together they are cut off obliquely and held together by three clinker nails.

As the gunwale was entirely destroyed, the thowls are also wanting.

It can however be taken for granted, that they have been of the same form as is still used in the boats on the Northern and Western coasts of Norway.

The ribs have been thirteen in number; of these, however, the outermost in the southern end has disappeared and several others have been badly damaged.

They are built of three different layers of wood one above

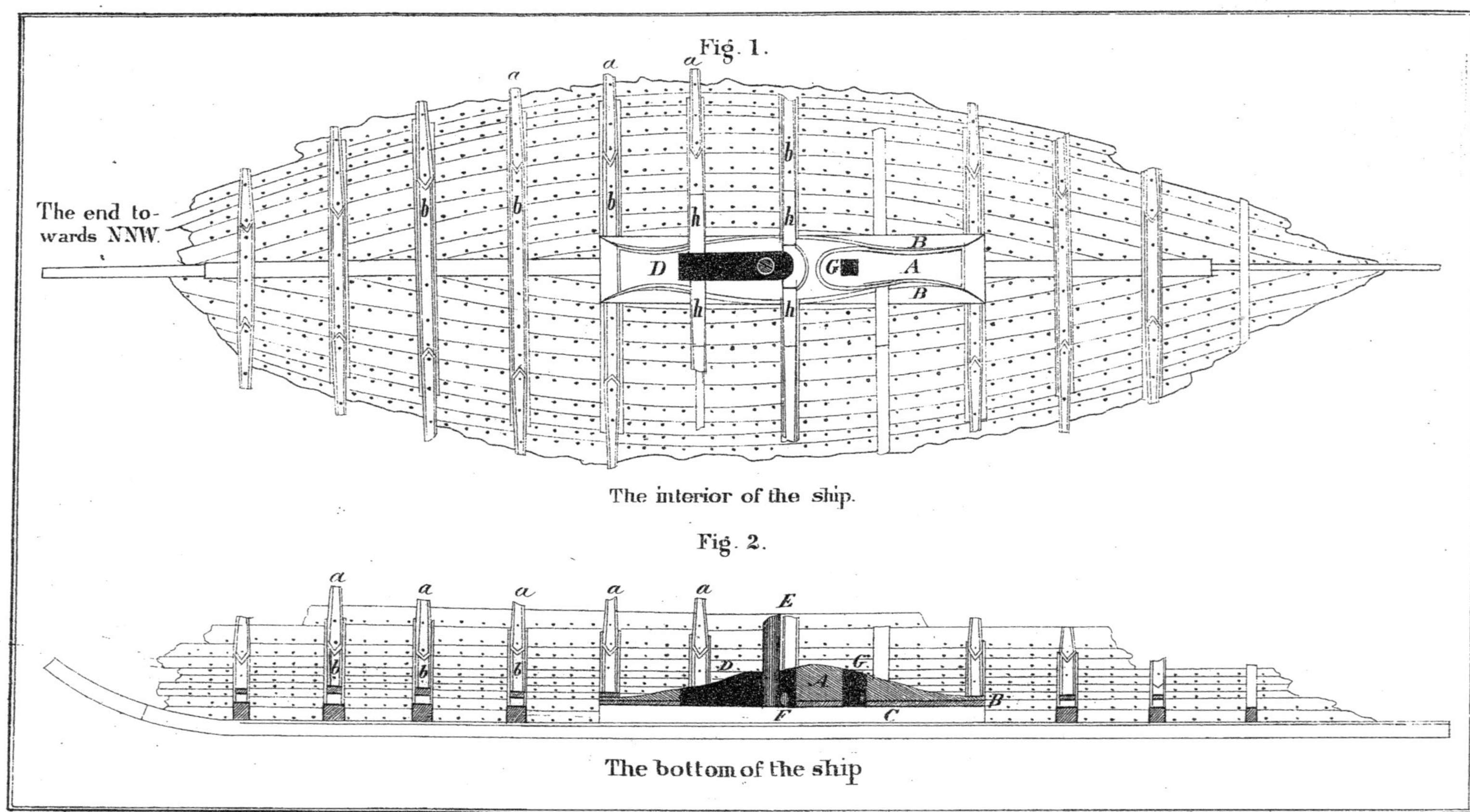

The interior of the ship.

The bottom of the ship

PLATE IV.

the other, joined together partly by oak and partly by iron nails.

The upper and the lower layers are made of oak, while the centre one, which is wider than the others and projects a little beyond them on both sides, is of fir.

The relative distance of the ribs is rather regular, 2 feet 7 inches; their width in the central layer is 7 or 8 inches.

The ribs have been tied to the boards with bast ropes.

On the inside of the boards, at every rib a long clamp is carved out of the wood; two holes have been made in the clamp and in the lower side of the rib a similar one, through which the rope has been run.

Fragments of bast were still found in several of the holes.

The uppermost boards, however, have been secured to the ribs by wooden nails.

The keel and the ribs are not joined in any way; the keel was consequently only secured by the nails, which fastened it to the boards in the bottom.

This peculiar mode of joining must undoubtedly have made the vessel rather weak, but it has, at the same time, given it more elasticity and augmented its speed.

There was no deck, but there have probably been thin planks between the ribs; they must have rested on the projecting edge of the central layer of the ribs.

There was no trace of thwarts to be seen; in consequence, the number of oars cannot be known.

To judge from the number of ribs it may, however, be concluded that there have been 10 on each side.

This vessel however has not been propelled by means of oars alone; it has also had a sail, and the way in which the mast was secured is one of the most peculiar points about it.

Along the bottom there lies a large square-hewn beam of oak, extending across five ribs in the middle.

A little behind the rib in the centre (supposing that the stern was pointing northwards) there is a square hole for the mast, and in front of it close by the rib, the stump of a thick branch in the wood has been left to support the mast.

Above the said beam there is a still larger log of oak, 6 ells long, a little over one ell wide and 1⅝ feet thick in the middle, but growing thinner towards the ends, which are carved in the shape of a fish-tail.

Right through the log is made a square hole, 3 feet 9 inches long and 11 inches wide, in the foremost part of which the mast and the stump supporting it are standing.

This hole has without doubt been made so large to facilitate the lowering of the mast.

When it was raised the hole must have been filled with plugs.

There was still a stump of the mast about one ell long found standing in its place; it is made of fir.

A little in front of the mast hole there is a square hole, descending in the upper beam about 6½ inches square ; it has perhaps served to fix some other instrument for the further support of the mast.

The undermost beam is lying quite loose on the keel and the two beams were not at all joined together, they are only fastened to the ribs.

The whole work is executed with evident care and elegance for that period.

All the boards are ornamented with mouldings on the edges both inside and outside; there are also mouldings and carved ornaments on the upper side of the ribs.

At many places in the ship traces were found on the wood of a conglomeration of light blue color which was at first thought to be paint.

On closer examination this supposition however proved to be erroneous, according to the opinion of persons qualified to judge.

It is an iron combination (phosphoric oxide of iron) deposited on the wood from the surrounding earth, which abounds in iron.

Fig. 4.

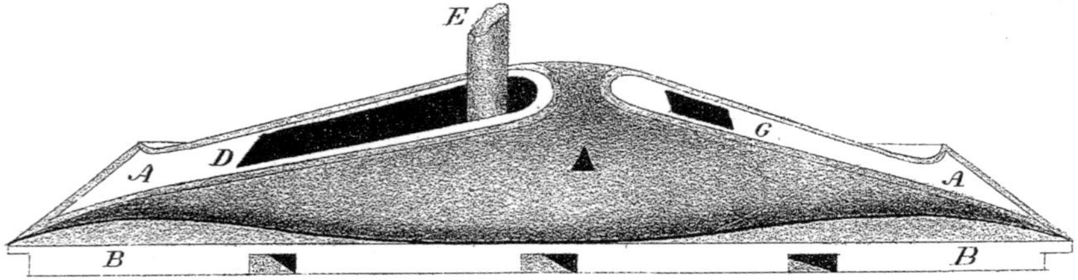

The mast-hole.

Fig. 6.

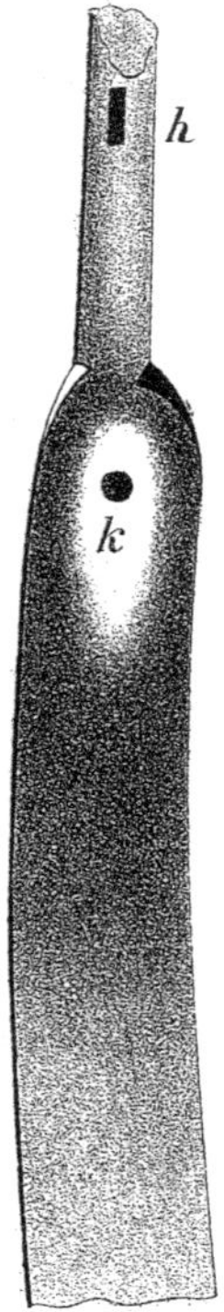

Fig. 7.

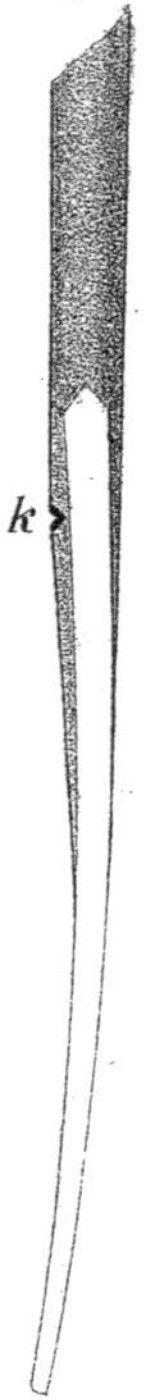

The rudder.

Fig. 8.

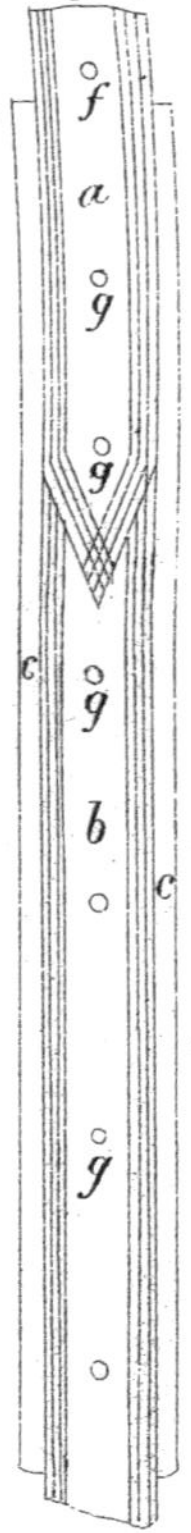

One of the ribs.

PLATE V.

FRAGMENTS OF A VESSEL OF THE VIKING PERIOD FOUND IN A TUMULUS NEAR FREDRIKSTADT NORWAY

No small implements, belonging to the vessel, were found with the exception of a rudder.

According to the account given by the owner of the farm, it was lying across the vessel a little behind the mast. It is made of fir.

The blade is 4 feet 7 inches long and 10½ inches wide.

The stem which begins at the central and widest part of the blade, has a length of 1 foot 10 inches.

At the very top of the stem is a square hole for the tiller; it stands perpendicularly on the flat side of the blade.

In the centre of the blade of the rudder itself and 7 inches from its upper edge is a round hole through which the rope was run which secured it to the side of the ship.

For it must have been a side rudder fixed to the side of the ship a little in front of the sternpost, where it can be seen on drawings of ancient ships from the earlier middle ages.

Some other implements have been previously discovered and carefully preserved by the proprietor of the farm.

Just behind the mast beam, the spot being indicated by small flat wooden blocks, sunk in the clay and laid in a square along the sides of the ship and right across it, lay some unburnt bones of a man and a horse.

There were also discovered two beads of colored glass, some cloth compactly rolled together and four small pieces of carved wood, which appear to be fragments of a saddle.

Close by, part of a snow-skate was found, viz; the middle piece on which the foot rests, with a hole for the strap.

At a later excavation it was observed that the inside of the vessel had been covered with a thin layer of moss before the earth was thrown over it.

According to report the same had been observed in the part earlier excavated.

In the southern end of the mound at the height of the vessel's gunwale and still higher, traces of iron utensils were seen at many places, but they were so rusted away, that there was hardly any thing left but some stripes of rust in the earth.

By the prow at the eastern gunwale of the vessel the handle of a sword of the form used in the Viking period was clearly distinguished; nearly opposite on the western side the point of a spear and the boss of a shield seem to have laid.

Just where the prow must have been, lay a long heavy lump of iron rust, apparently a fragment of a coat of mail.

On the western side of the gunwale about opposite the mast, there was a heap of horse-bones, but so decayed, that only the teeth could be exhumed in any way whole.

They were examined by a veterinary surgeon, who declared that there must have been the skeletons of at least two horses, viz; of an older and a younger animal.

In that part of the mound was also found a little round bung of oak, such as might be used for a barrel, and also several oaken sticks of different sizes, 1 or 2 ells long, somewhat pointed at one end, scattered here and there in the vessel.

At many places inside of the vessel, but not equally distributed throughout it, juniper bushes which had been pulled up by the roots were lying in the clay and still so well preserved, that the needles could be distinctly seen.

Finally under the vessel on its eastern side, were found an oaken spade or shovel and a handspike made of a young oak trunk, of which the bark was partially preserved.

The articles found in and near the vessel completely establish, what might also have been supposed without their testimony, viz; that one had come on a ship-tomb from the younger iron-age.

The ship was carefully drawn out of the river not far distant; it was placed on the ground, the turf and the earth having been previously removed.

The situation chosen was such as was generally preferred for interments in heathen times, as the mound could be seen at a great distance on all sides, and the deceased could thus

Fig. 5.
a
a
b
c
f
f
f
f
d
c
The joinings of the boards.
Fig. 3.
a
b
d
c
Fig. 9.
g
g
Clamp on the inside of the boards.
Fig. 10.
The boards outside.

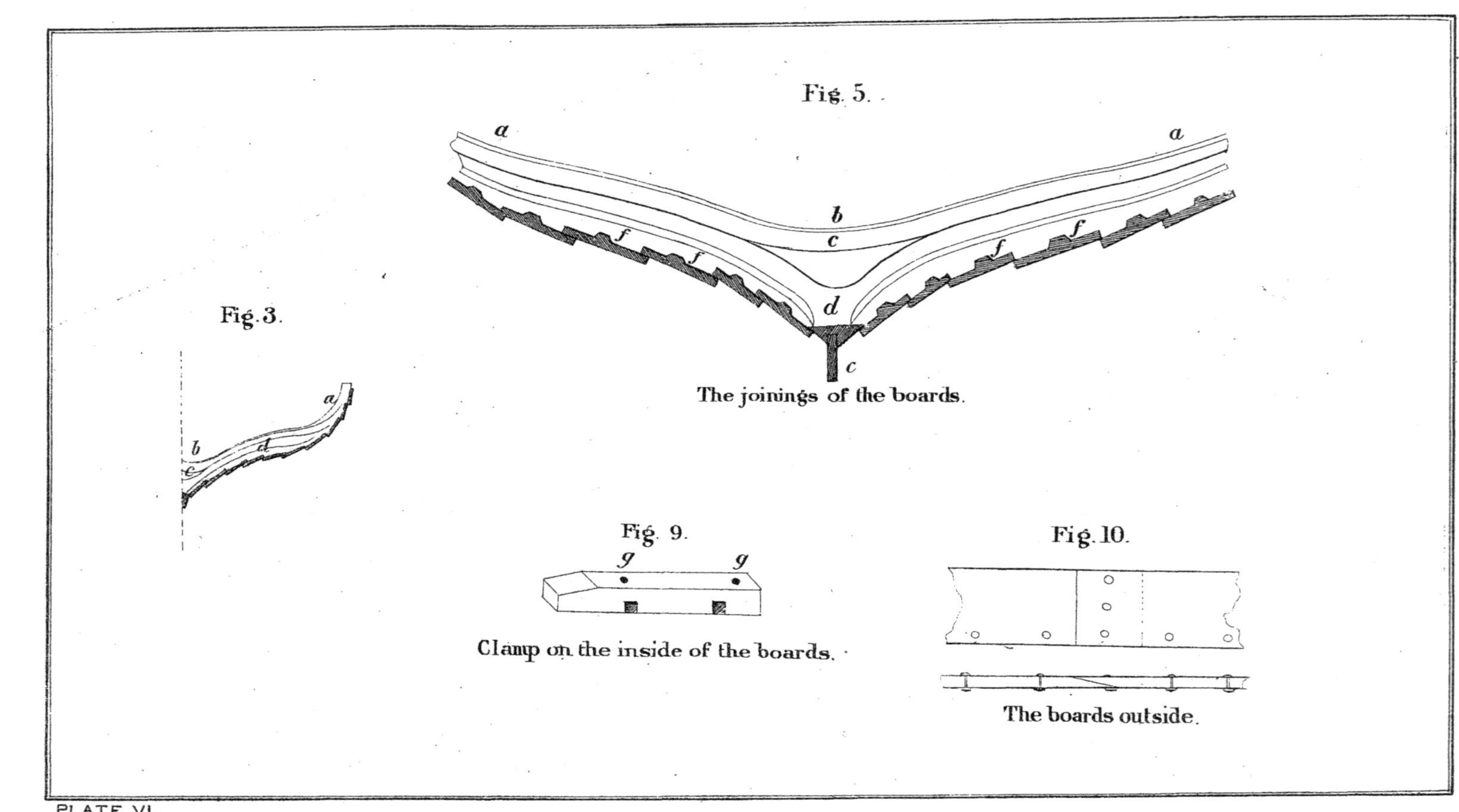

PLATE VI.

enjoy, from his last resting place, a fine view over the country, where he had lived and toiled.

After the space under the ship had been filled with earth, the body of the deceased was placed in its after part, where, as its captain, he had sat when alive.

The beads and the pieces of cloth indicate that the body was buried with clothes on.

By his side a horse and saddle, harness and snow-skates were laid.

Thus he had ship, horse and snow-skates with him in the sepulchral tumulus.

One involuntarily calls to mind the ancient account of the burial of Harald Hildetand, who fell at the battle of Braavalla.

Sigurd Ring ordered the body of the fallen King to be driven into the mound on the chariot he had used in battle.

The horse was killed, and Sigurd then had his own saddle buried in the mound, " that Harald might choose whether he would ride or drive to Valhalla."

A little farther out in the mound, and apparently without regard to order, the weapons and several of the horses of the deceased were buried.

With respect to several other articles discovered here, we can make the same remark, as with articles now and then found in other tumuli, that it is rather difficult to understand for what purpose they have been laid there.

We have then here considerable fragments of a vessel undoubtedly belonging to the Viking period.

It can hardly be supposed that this is one of the ships, on which the Norwegians of that period made their bold Viking-expeditions in the Baltic, the North Sea and the Atlantic.

A vessel so small in size, and built so low and flat, could not be adaptedto long voyages in the open sea ; it could only have been used for coasting trade and shorter expeditions."

Referring to the last paragraph quoted, it may be remarked that the Norsemen had large sailing transports for distant enterprises which are supposed to have been the archetypes of the modern Dutch galliot; and such doubtless were the vessels of Rolf Ganger, the conqueror of Normandy, whose dry-docks (certain rude excavations in the sand), are still pointed at by the inhabitants of Vigroe, an island in the bailiwick of Soud Möre, as the proudest monuments their country can exhibit.

OLAF TRYGGVESSON, NORWAY'S FIRST CHRISTIAN KING.

Next to Rolf Ganger, in the estimation of his countrymen, comes the Norse king whose life we are about to sketch: Olaf Tryggvesson was born on a small island in one of the lakes of Norway, three months after his mother, Astrid, had taken refuge there from the murderers of her husband, Tryggve Olafsson.

When the boy was but a few weeks old, Astrid took him to Sweden, where she resided two years; at the expiration of which, accompanied by her foster-father, Thoralf Luiskiog, and his son Thakil, she sailed with him for Russia, to seek the protection of her brother Sigrid, who held a high office under King Valdemar of Novogorod.

On the way thither, however, she and her party fell into the hands of Esthonian pirates and became slaves.

Olaf was now separated from his mother, and he and Thakil sold together for "a good and stout ram," while Thoralf was knocked in the head by his captor, Klerkon, as being too old to work.

Olaf was afterward sold separately, "for a new cloak," to a man named Reas, with whom he lived six years, when his uncle visiting Esthona on King Valdemar's business, found him out, and took him with him to Novogorod, when he soon gave evidence of the spirit that was in him, by driving a battle-axe, his favorite plaything, deep into the brain of the murderer of his foster-father, whom he saw one day seated in the market and immediately recognized.

For this offence he would have been put to death, but for the intervention of Valdemar's wife, Queen Allogia, who, with a sense of justice and the eternal fitness of things truly feminine, declared "that the boy was too good looking to lose his head," and thereupon paid over to the relatives of the deceased Esthonian, in "good gold," the price that was demanded for it.

Olaf remained in Novogorod, under the queen's protection, until his eighteenth birthday, when, being considered the handsomest man of his day, and very expert in the management of a boat and in all other manly exercises, it naturally suggested itself to his benefactress that the proper theatre for the display of himself and his accomplishments was the sea; so she at once fitted out a fine fleet for his command, in which he cruised for many years in the Baltic and North Seas, plundering everything he fell in with, in proper Viking fashion.

During this period he married Geyra, the daughter of King Burislaf of Vendland, with whom he lived very happily indeed; but one day Geyra was taken suddenly ill and the next she died; and then, Vendland becoming hateful to him —for every object there reminded him of happiness past—he shifted his cruising-ground to the British Channel, where his renown as an *impartial freebooter* reached its highest pitch.

It is true that in the Scilly islands he became converted to Christianity by a pious hermit, who was endowed with the gift of prophesy; but this converson abated not a whit his ardor in "gathering property," since nothing was held to be more Christian in that age than for a man, in humble imitation of the Church itself, to lay violent hands on whatever came in his way.

Stopping in Ireland, on his return voyage, Olaf's fighting propensities so endeared him to the men that great numbers of them enlisted under his banner, while his extraordinary personal beauty made him a universal favorite with the women, "one of whom," says the chronicle, "Gyda by name, the daughter of the King of Dublin, and widow of an English earl, chose him for her husband over a large number of well-dressed men, although he had nothing but his *bad-weather clothes on.*"

Setting out from Ireland, with a large force, for the recovery of the kingdom which was his by right of inheritance, he had the good fortune to reach Norway at a time when the whole body of the bonders were in arms against Earl Kakon, the usurper, who had insulted the wife of one of their number.

Olaf put himself at their head, and the usurper being slain, the Great Thing, assembled at Drontheim for the purpose of choosing his successor, declared Olaf Tryggvesson king of Norway.

All the Norwegians now embraced Christianity (except those of the province of Viken who under Earl Eric, son of the late king, betook themselves to their boats); and on the spot where Olaf first landed, opposite Moster Island, the first Christian Church erected in Norway was built.

From this time every thing went well with the king until he proposed marriage to queen Sigrid the Haughty, sister of Olaf, king of Sweden, and was accepted by her; when meeting her at the place appointed for the wedding, he pressed her, before becoming his wife to become a Christian, and upon her refusal, ungallantly threw his glove in her face, and called her "a faded heathen hag."

Being called a hag in a country where witchcraft was commonly practised could hardly be reckoned an insult, but *faded!* that word of fearful import to a woman, whether applied to her clothes or to her complexion, what female of any age could be expected to stand that!

Sigrid certainly was not of that complexion.

She neither started nor screamed, however, but merely remarked in a very low voice, as she turned from the king, "This will some day prove your death;" and as she had many years before this roasted alive Harald Granske, king of

Nestfold and Visaveld of Russia, while they were asleep in their beds, saying, "She would make these small kings tired of coming to see her," she seemed a dangerous woman to trifle with, as indeed the event proved.

Time passed, and Sigrid married Swend Forked Beard, king of Denmark, whose sister Thyri, bethrothed to Burislaf, the king of Vendland before spoken of in this narrative, had run away to Norway and married Olaf Tryggvesson, who at the time of which we speak, had demanded her dower of Burislaf, and was about fitting out a fleet to enforce his demand, in case it should not be promptly acceded to.

Sigrid now saw that the hour for wreaking the vengeance she had long meditated was at hand; and so she spoke constantly to her husband and brother of the great danger each of them ran, in permitting the king of Norway to maintain such a large navy as he was said to possess, at the same time depicting in glowing colors the excellent opportunity for destroying him, which would present itself upon his return from Vendland when, forced to pass close to the coast of Denmark, and with his vessels encumbered with spoils, he could undoubtedly, she declared, be taken by surprise.

The two kings, who both envied and feared Olaf Tryggvesson, were easily won over to Sigrid's way of thinking, and Earl Eric Kakonson uniting his fortunes with theirs, the three set vigorously to work preparing for their meditated attack.

OLAF TRYGGVESSON WITH A LARGE FLEET VISITS THE KING OF VENDLAND. A SCANDINAVIAN BANQUET.

The king of Norway, meanwhile, having assembled his forces, got underway for Vendland, and as he sailed out of the harbor of Sole with his fleet of sixty-one vessels, an old scald, standing upon a sea-girt cliff whence he could take in the whole grand spectacle at a glance, enthusiastically improvised of it as follows:—

"From Norway-fiord sailing free,
Our ships sweep o'er the dark blue sea,
Their sails well trimmed to catch the wind,
Their gunwales low with bright shields lin'd,
Their prows with dragons' heads adorned,
Or hissing shakes or bisons horn'd,
Or warrior grim, in mail-clad vest,
With visor closed and lance at rest.
Others again go dashing by
(Throwing the sea-foam bulwark-high),
With falcons bold, about to fly,
Forming their beaks ; and one draws nigh,
Bearing the name of Odin dread,
Upon whose gilded billet-head
A raven sits, with wings outspread :
Above that bird of evil mien,
A bold defiant cock is seen,
With neck outstretched and gaping mouth
(Turning his head now North, now South),
High perched upon the coal black mast,
To tell the veering of the blast.

Hurra! Hung out o'er every prow,
The war-flag red is flying now,
The *Dragon-flag* each Norseman knows—
To friends a shield, a scourge to foes!
A goodly sight it is to see
That banner waving fair and free !
A goodly sound it is to hear,
From Norsemen's throat, cheer after cheer,
As, gliding swiftly by the strand,
They bid farewell to father-land.

But now, the outer skerries past,
Lost to our sight is each tall mast ;
And chilly evening draweth nigh,
And thralls and bonders homeward hie.
In every house, from light to light,
The sparkling ale will pass to-night;
The *good-luck* ale, of strongest brew,
To Olaf and his gallant crew !

Arrived in Vendland, the warrior-king, instead of finding

an armed host drawn up along the shore to oppose his landing, was greeted with the utmost cordiality by his quondam father-in-law, who not only restored to Thyri her dowry, but made her rich presents beside, and then insisted upon Olaf's passing the summer with him, " that he might renew his acquaintance with his old friends."

So Olaf loitered many weeks there, little knowing that his enemies were all the while assembling their fleets, and, at the same time, keeping a watchful eye upon his every movement through a spy of theirs named Sigvald, who, having married Astrid, the youngest daughter of king Bursilaf, stood high in the esteem of this petty sovereign, and, of course, knew all that transpired at the court.

Now Sigvald, or Earl Sigvald, as he is styled in the Sagas, was a noted Viking, and, like the kings of Sweden and Denmark, jealous of the growing power and popularity of Olaf Tryggvesson, whose praises, at this epoch, resounded far and near.

"For he was," says Snorro, " handsomer and more expert in all exercises than any man whose memory is preserved to us in story, and he was stronger and more agile than most men.

" He could run across the oars outside of his vessel while his men were rowing, and could walk all around upon the rail.

" He could play with three daggers in the air, catching the one falling always by the handle ; could cut and strike equally well with both hands, and could cast two spears at once.

" He one day ascended the Smaller Horn and fixed his shield upon its very peak, where never man had been before nor has been since.

" He was, too, of a merry temperament, gay and social very, and had great taste in dress as in everything else.

" In battle he was the bravest of the brave, and a firm friend, though a bitter enemy."

But a day was now fixed for the king's return to Norway

and so Burislaf gave him a grand farewell supper, according to the fashion of that day, wherein, as the majority of the Vendlanders, Burislaf among the number, had not yet embraced Christianity, heathen and Christian ceremonies were strangely intermingled.

The supper table was spread in an old temple, whose walls and floor were liberally sprinkled with the blood (called *laut*) of the animals slaughtered for it, conspicuous among which, and right in the centre of the table, was a horse roasted whole even to the hoofs—a custom which had its origin among the ancient Scythians, and was retained by the Scandinavians, at first in commemoration of their ancestry, but finally as a religious rite, the horse being sacred to Odin.

The drinking-horns, which, at great feasts, were passed from hand to hand, were of large size, with rings, equidistant from and parallel to each other, inscribed on their inner sides; and each bonder, when his neighbor's horn was handed to him, was expected to drink down to the uppermost ring covered by the liquid.

When the banquet was ready, Burislaf, preceded by his harpers, fiddlers, and cup-bearers, conducted Olaf Tryggvesson to a seat on his right, after which he invoked a blessing upon the meat and drink, and then called upon his guests to do full justice to his cheer; whereupon, without further parlance or ceremony, the feasting began.

And first Odin's great goblet was drained for victory and power to the king, and next Niord's for health and a good season.

When these were emptied the Christians drank Christ's health and Saint Michael's, "and the strongest drink and the fullest measure were given to the Norsemen."

Then the full bowl called the *braga bowl*, over which vows were made, was drunk by all; after which King Olaf, rising from his seat, called, in a loud voice, for the *funeral ale*, and, filling his horn with it up to the brim, "This cup," he cried, "to the memory of Rolf Ganger!"—a toast that was received with acclamation; for all present had heard of the valiant deeds of the conqueror, and regarded him as the mightiest of Norsemen.

While the liquor was circulating thus, great slices of horse-flesh were handed round, which were eagerly devoured by the devout followers of Odin; but the Christians drew back with pious horror, as the dish was proffered to them, partaking instead of beef, or boar's flesh.

The regular toasts having been disposed of, "amidst much minstrelsy and shouting," the warriors now pledged each other, and as the drinking was *without measure*, the horns were filled and emptied so often that but few of the bonders were able to stand without support, when Burislaf, whose seasoned brain was proof against the strongest potations, rapping upon the table, called upon all to drink from the *remembrance* bowl to the health of absent friends, and next, as a signal that the feast was ended, ordered the *farewell ale* to be distributed.

This being done, the guests rose in a body and drank a bumper as a parting glass, the Vendlanders crying out with one accord, as they turned their horns bottom upward, "Good luck and a fair wind to Olaf Tryggvesson!"

Then the temple was left to its accustomed silence, and the Norsemen and Vendlanders, in every conceivable stage of intoxication, were seen staggering homeward,—some to their ships, some to the *tilts* stretched along the shore, and others to the lofts of neighboring houses.

When Olaf Tryggvesson awoke from a long and deep sleep, he found many of his principal officers stirring around his tent, for a vague rumor of what was going on in Denmark had reached them, and they were clamorous to get on board their vessels and fight their way, should it become necessary, to Norway; but Earl Sigvald, who took care to join them at this juncture, laughed aloud at the report, remarking, as was quite true, that King Swend would never dare with his force alone to meet the famous warriors of the North; and when, to this fine speech, he added, in an off-hand way, that he himself would lead the advance with eleven well-manned dragons, the fears of the most anxious among them faded away before his cheery words and presence, as night-shadows vanish at the coming of the orb of day.

OLAF TRYGGVESSON SAILS FROM VENDLAND FOR NORWAY, AND IS ATTACKED BY THE COMBINED NAVAL FORCES OF DENMARK AND SWEDEN AND A NORWEGIAN EARL NAMED ERIC. GREAT BATTLE OFF STRALSUND.

So another night was wasted in revelry; but on the morrow, the war-horns sounded the departure, and Earl Sigvald, who had now received notice from Swend that the combined fleets had sailed from Denmark and were lying, in ambush, as it were, in a sequestered harbor on the mainland, near the site of the present city of Stralsund, took the lead as he had promised, calling out merrily to the king of Norway, as he passed him, to be sure and sail in his "keel-track;" "for I know every foot of the way," said he, "and your big ship, like a huge whale, swims best in deep water."

Thus gayly they took the sea, and, as the breeze was light, the *snekars* greatly outsailed the rest of the fleet, so that when the confederates came out from their place of concealment, they had long been lost to the king's view.

At this critical moment, Earl Sigvald, lowering his sails, pulled in to join his friends, whereupon, with many maledictions upon the traitor, Olaf commenced making preparations for the impending conflict.

For hours before this, Earl Eric, standing on a high hill, had been watching for him.

He had counted carefully the vessels of his advance, as they sped swiftly by, and had discouraged any attack upon them on the part of the impatient Swedes and Danes, who were eager to begin the fray.

"Nay, nay," cried he, "let the young birds fly with their

white wings. We shall have work enough to capture the old eagle when he comes, even though he be alone."

At length Earl Sigvald's squadron was seen rounding the Southern point of Rugen Island, and immediately behind it, a fine large vessel, which the king of Sweden declared must be the flag-ship.

But Earl Eric informed him that it was the Crane, commanded by the king's uncle Thorkel Dyrdil.

"I know her," said he, "by the colored stripes in her sail, and by her high stem and stern.

"She is long and narrow and goes like the wind, for she pulls sixty oars, but she is not to be compared to the king's own vessel, The Long Serpent."

Soon after, they saw three ships sailing abreast, and one of them Eric pointed out as the Short Serpent, a vessel which had formerly belonged to Raud the idolater, and which, after he had captured her, the king offered to restore to Raud, provided he would embrace Christianity.

But this the idolater obstinately refused to do; so the king forced an adder into his mouth, which crept down his throat and gnawed its way out of his side; and Raud perished as Roderick, the last king of the Goths, had perished more than two centuries before.

Following the Short Serpent was the Odin, which Eric told the bystanders had been captured from a great sorcerer named Eyrind Kellda. "He had a fair wind with him," said he, "wherever he went; and, after he and his crew were taken, the king had them bound securely and then placed at low-water on a skerry which is always covered when the tide comes up. It stands near Kormt Island, and is now known as the *Skerry of Shrieks*."

Then came three more large ships, and king Swend was exceedingly anxious that the Earl should get afloat; but Eric still kept his place.

"They have many more biting dragons besides the Long Serpent," said he quietly, "let us wait awhile."

A few minutes later, however, a vessel hove in sight which was so much larger than any which had preceded or was following it that it needed not the Earl's affirmation of the fact, to convince his hearers that this indeed was The Long Serpent, that master-piece of the great *ship-volundar* Thorberg Skafting. For she loomed upon the water, like a great castle.

Her length was one hundred and fifty feet, and her breadth of beam, at the midship section, nineteen, while "her bulwarks were as high as those of a sea-going vessel."

Her hull represented the body of a dragon, whose head, projecting well beyond the bow, served as a *ram*, while its tail, twisted in many folds about the stern, ended in a thick coil just above the tiller-head, affording a protection for the helmsman in bad weather.

The richly-gilded carved-work on each side of the stem and stern commemorated various incidents in the life of the king, as, for instance, where, in the Saltenfiord, in a great tempest, after good bishop Sigurd had said mass, the water suddenly became smooth about the Crane, the king's ship, while at a little distance on either hand "the waves were lashing up so high that they hid the sight of the mountains."

And again where the king entered the great temple of Thor at Drontheim, regardless alike of the remonstrances and threats of the Diars, or priests, and in the presence of all the people, smote the image of the god with his battle-axe, so that it fell from its pedestal to the floor.

The broad blue sail of the mammoth vessel was so cut as to resemble a dragon's wings, while the shining shields, of various colors and devices, hung over the rail, from stem to stern, well simulated the scaly sides of the monster, whose slimy legs, represented by the dripping oars (which when Earl Eric first looked were still), were all in full motion now, as if the Dragon had become suddenly alarmed, or was about to dart upon its prey.

Now king Swend cried out to his men: "That dragon shall carry me this evening, and I will steer it."

But Earl Eric said, quietly, "If Olaf Tryggvesson had no other vessel but that, you could not take it from him with the Danish force alone."

Then the trumpeters sounded the call to arms, and the allies struck their tents, and, rushing on board their ships, commenced clearing them for action.

It may be remarked here, that the description given of the Long Serpent will serve generally for all the vessels arrayed against each other in this battle, the difference between them being only in their dimensions, the color and cut of their sails, and the fashion, quality and quantity of their ornamental work.

Earl Eric's vessel, which was to play so conspicuous a part in the battle and which he called the Avenger, was coal-black, even her masts and sails being of this dismal hue.

A hideous animal supposed to resemble the wolf Fenrir, which, according to the Scandinavian mythology, is destined at the last day to devour mankind, crouched upon her figure-head, while an ugly raven, Odin's favorite bird, and "the witch wife's horse," usurped the place of the cock, the ordinary weather vane, at her high mast-head.

Around the sides of the Avenger three iron bands were fastened, the upper two of which connected at the prow with the lowest and were there intertwined with it, so that the whole formed a short projecting spur designed to pierce an enemy at the water-line; and on the bulwarks, as a protection against boarders, was an iron comb with its teeth inverted, to which the Earl had more than once owed his exemption from death on his various Viking-expeditions.

As the confederate fleet drew clear of the land, and by its colors showed the nationality of the various vessels of which it was composed, the Norsemen began to comprehend the nature of the combination which had been formed against them, and as their present force of twenty vessels was outnumbered four to one, they strenuously urged upon the king the necessity of flight.

But from his childhood Olaf had delighted in strife; and, sooth to say, he had so often been a winner against fearful odds, that it was not strange he should be over confident now.

"I have never yet shown my back to an enemy," he cried indignantly, "and I never will!"

"Let God dispose of my life as best pleases Him. Strike the mast and sail and man the oars that the rest of the fleet may follow our example."

Then turning to the trumpeter, who stood by his left side, "Sound the *close up* and *form line*, Orm," said he, "and see thou blowest a lively blast and a strong, that our men may know we are in good heart."

Then Orm Stoganef raising his trumpet to his lips, blew so cheery a peal, that no man thereafter thought of flight; but all, bending to their oars, sought to gain their position in the line of battle, as speedily as possible.

After the ships had got abreast of each other, finding they were but poorly supplied with small, hard stones, which at that period under the name of *hardsteinagriot* formed so important a part of the ammunition of the Baltic mariners, the king changed front to the right, and threw Rugen Island directly in his rear, and then detached four of his smallest vessels—two from each wing—to bring to the fleet from the island, such stones as could be collected there while the action was going on.

The king's ship occupied the middle of the line between the Short Serpent and the Crane, and the other vessels were ranged to starboard and port, according to their size, the largest being nearest to the centre; and, as the men were about to lash their bows together, *Norse fashion*, the king ordered that the Long Serpent's stern should be on a line with the Short Serpent's and the Crane's. Then said Ulf Rode, the standard bearer:

"If the Long Serpent is to be as far ahead of the other vessels as she is longer then they, we shall have hard work of it on the forecastle."

But the king replied: "If I have willed that *my* dragon should be longer than any other, it is that all may see her foremost in the battle."

"That might do well enough in a fair fight," cried Kolbiorn, the marshal (who by virtue of his office had charge of that part of the ship, lying between the prow and the main-hold, which was called the *rausn*, or fore-defence), "but here where we are so greatly out-numbered we shall be beset on all sides and my gallant *berserkers*, invincible as they seem, can hardly be expected to defend themselves in front and flank at the same time."

"It were madness so to expose them!" exclaimed Rode.

"I did not know until now," retorted the king angrily, "that I had a coward among my men."

"A coward!" ejaculated Ulf. "It will be well for us this day if you defend the quarter-deck as I defend the fore-castle."

The king, without reply, seized a javelin and seemed about to cast it at the speaker's head; but the sturdy Rode moved not an inch aside: "It were better for you not to be so lavish with your weapons," said he calmly. "You will have need of them all ere long."

"True enough, Ulf," cried Olaf, throwing the javelin high in the air and catching it by its handle as it came down, "there will be a fine arrow-song in our ears by and by," and then, bursting into a hearty laugh, he continued. "It will be good fun, too, pricking the flesh of those soft Swedes and Danes; and as for our stem, Ulf, lash it as best pleases thee; for never had king a truer or braver banner-man than thou."

The call to quarters was now sounded, and as, contrary to the usual custom among the Norsemen, there was no special vessel with the fleet, for the purpose of taking from it such articles as would be an incumbrance to it in battle, each captain cleared ship for action by sending ashore in his boats everything that he did not actually require. Then the tents and awnings, "rolled up hard," were placed on the high forecastles, after the manner of the breastworks and épaulements of a shore battery, and inside of them the grappling-irons, whose long hauling lines, neatly coiled down alongside of them, were secured by their lower ends to stout staples in the deck.

Fore and aft, on the narrow platforms or gangways leading just inside of the bulwarks, from the poop to the forecastle decks, were ranged huge piles of stones, and great arm chests filled with weapons of every description, while along the rails were hung the shields, which being of metal, and each large enough to carry a warrior on it to his grave, afforded an excellent protection against an enemy's missiles.

Forward, the archers were drawn up in two ranks, and in their rear, three deep, the spearmen and halberdiers, while a select body of mail-clad men, stood around the commander of each vessel, completely covering him with their shields, and with swords drawn, menacing with instant death, any who should be bold enough to venture within their reach.

The king stood aft on the Long Serpent, eagerly watching the movements of his foes.

He was clad in full armor, over which he wore a short red cloak, and with his towering form and high plumed helmet formed the most conspicuous figure among all the famous warriors who surrounded him.

Glancing along the line, he observed that the fleet still had the banner of peace flying which it had worn in Vendland, a white flag with a lamb in the centre of it.

"Ulf," he cried, "this will never do, our enemies have made up their minds to attack us, and, by the Rood, they shall see that we are ready for them! Hoist the war standard!"

Then Ulf, seizing hold of the signal halliards, rove through a block at the top of an immense flag-pole on the starboard side of the forecastle where he stood, joyfully bent on a large red flag, and, in a moment after, the fiery, winged dragon which it bore, was soaring high above the prow, amid the prolonged cheering of the whole fleet.

The king rubbed his hands gleefully as the sound greeted his ears: "Those who came to shear," said he, "are likely to return shorn, for our dragon scratches terribly. Now let them come on!"

His order of battle was a strong one indeed; for his line was formed directly across the mouth of a little deep-water cove, so that his flanking vessels rested upon the land; and as there was a light wind and current setting directly into the cove, a single sweep from the stern of each vessel, easily kept the fleet in position.

The confederate fleet now formed in three lines, half a mile apart, and moved rapidly to the attack.

The first line, wearing the Danish colors, soon came within bow-shot of the Norsemen, who fairly covered it with arrows, killing and wounding many of its principal officers and men; yet it continued steadily onward, through this and the javelin tempest that followed, until it was stem to stem with the enemy, when a close hand-to-hand conflict ensued.

The second line following the first into action, under the leadership of the Swedish king, kept close in its rear, hastening to re-enforce it with vessels and men, whenever the exigencies of battle made it necessary.

The third line, led by Earl Eric, and carefully preserving its distance from the second, stopped short as the latter neared the enemy, and apparently took no further interest in the engagement, an occasional shaft discharged from the Avenger in the direction of the Long Serpent, being the only indication given of its hostility to the Norsemen.

By this time however, the battle was raging furiously in the front, and king Swend's vessel, a very large and fine one called the Royal Dane, had become directly engaged with the Long Serpent; but it was a common saying, among seamen, that the Long Serpent's crew as far excelled other men in bravery, strength, and daring, and the skilful use of arms, as their great ship excelled other ships in beauty and grandeur: so the Royal Dane was soon captured, scuttled and sunk, and king Swend had to fly for safety to the Big Dragon, Olaf, the Swede's flag-ship, which in her turn boldly engaging the Serpent, shared the fate of her consort; for Kolbiorn, the marshal throwing a grapnel aboard of her, and with the assistance of his gallant forecastlemen, dragging her close to, gave the word to board, and in a trice, her deck was cleared of defenders and a large hole bored in her bottom; whereupon the Danish king had again to seek protection in flight, this time accompanied by his royal brother.

In this way many more tall ships, both of the Swedes and the Danes were destroyed all along the line, and yet the array of the Norsemen had not been broken, nor a single vessel of theirs destroyed or captured, while their wild cheering gave evidence of their unflagging spirit and enthusiasm.

Then Earl Eric aroused from his apparent lethargy: "I thought those Danes and Swedes would find they had caught a vulture," said he to his brother, Swend, who was standing beside him. "It is high time for us to be moving, let the war horns signal to my division to move to the right!"

A single trumpet blast was now heard from the Avenger, followed by one from a vessel on each flank; and immediately the division swung to starboard, and, in the order which we now call "column of vessels," pulled to the right, about two or three miles, when it came to port again and entered a wide semi-circular inlet, whose bold water permitted it to lie alongside the shore.

The object of this movement became evident a few minutes thereafter, when a hundred stout fellows, carrying the banner of Earl Swend, were seen wending their way along a narrow, craggy road, toward a high cliff which overhung the closing vessel of the Norsemen's left; for a few big rocks, tumbled headlong from the height, must inevitably have fallen upon and crushed the vessel, and thus have opened a way for an attack upon Olaf's left flank and rear by Earl Eric, while his front was still hard pressed by the Swedes and Danes.

But Olaf Tryggvesson had fought too many times, both ashore and afloat, to be out-witted thus; and so the assailants, pressing forward in a confused mass, had no sooner got within fifty yards of the cliff, than some twenty of their number went down under the "arrow-rain" of a chosen body of archers who had been lying in wait for them in front, while a company of spearmen from the vessels detached by Olaf to gather stones, advanced upon them from the rear. Thus situated, there was no alternative but retreat, and with a loss of over half their number, they withdrew precipitately to their ships.

As the discomfited Swend went over the side of the Avenger, Earl Eric hastened to meet him at the gangway. "It was my fault, brother," said he, "I might have known that that famous old sea-dog would never have left one of his flanks unguarded. We must resort to another expedient."

He now took two of his oldest ships and filled them with all the combustible matter he could obtain, and, after towing them to a position opposite to the enemy, and warning the Swedes to clear the way, had them joined together by a long chain, fired and set adrift in the full expectation of seeing them borne by the wind and current directly against the particular dragons he aimed to destroy; but the Norsemen, manning their boats, towed the burning vessels clear of their line, and the Earl had the mortification of seeing them consumed to the water's edge, without damage to any but himself.

Baffled in this, he repeated the experiment with two fire-ships under full sail; but, the enemy boarding them, and lowering their sails, they too went wide of their mark, and drifted harmlessly away.

The confederates had now lost in all, twenty-three vessels, and their trumpeters, by king Swend's order, loudly sounding the retreat, they withdrew out of bowshot of the enemy. Then, after a short conference between their leaders, a new disposition of their forces was made, and the attack renewed, the Danes and Swedes being this time in three lines extending from the Norsemen's extreme right, to the fourth vessel from the left, opposite to which, at the distance of half a mile, Eric's division of sixteen dragons, was seen drawn up in double column, and midway between it and the enemy, the Earl's own vessel bearing "The Enchanted Banner," which with all its embroidered work, representing an erne with open beak and flapping wings—a year's full task for an ordinary needle—was made by king Swend's three sisters in a single night.

At a signal given by Eric, the two leading vessels of the column moved forward, and passing him at full speed, with their men at quarters, all loudly singing the *Biarkamal* (the ancient war-song of the Scandinavians), swept grandly toward the enemy; but so terrible was the storm of arrows, stones, javelins and darts that greeted them on their near approach, that their oarsmen, wounded and bleeding, were forced to relinquish their oars, and they must have fallen into the enemy's hands, had not the Avenger, hastening to their assistance, towed them out of action.

The next vessels, with an improvised mantelet of shields over the heads of their rowers, struck full and fair against the enemy, but lashed together, as his dragons were, it was like striking a granite rock, and the assailants with their bows stove in, foundered instantly with all on board; the carrying away of the ram of their flank-closer, a heavily built ship, called the Sea Horse, being the only injury sustained by the Norsemen in this rough encounter; yet, scanning closely the damaged vessel, Eric observed that she seemed to be down by the head. "She is leaking forward," said he, "now is our opportunity!" His horns sounded a charge as he spoke, and the next instant the Sea Horse, pierced by the Avenger's spur, commenced settling fast, and the "sun-dried ropes," which bound her to her next on the right, being cut by her crew, as they abandoned her, the king of Norway's left flank was at last exposed to his enemies.

It took but little time now for Eric to lead his division into the cove and capture the squadron there, after which he returned to his attack upon the end of the line, always engaging its outer vessel in front and flank, with the Avenger, and another dragon which he took with him for the purpose, while the rest of his division, remaining in the cove, attacked the Norsemen everywhere in rear.

One after another the vessels of the enemy's left wing fell into the Earl's hands, who, as fast as he got possession of them, cut their lashings and let them drive, while the Danes and Swedes, encouraged by his valor and following his example, met with equal success on the right, so that the allies gradually neared each other, and finally came together around the Long Serpent, which, left to its own resources for defense, resembled the citadel of a beleaguered fortress whose outer walls have all been carried by the foe. Yet all the mighty Norsemen who had not been laid low, were now gathered together on board the Serpent; so that her bulwarks were lined with mail-clad men, while in the "shield circle" about the king, there was not a single warrior whose name was unknown to fame. On the forecastle still stood Kolbiorn and sturdy Ulf Rode, while around them clustered that chosen body of men called Berserkers who were bound by an oath never to desert their chief. Disdaining the use of armor, these fierce barbarians bravely exposed their naked bodies to the foe, and, from their ferocity in battle, were said to be fed on wolves' hearts, torn from the animals while they yet lived, and eaten raw or seethed in human blood.

The kings of Denmark and Sweden and Earl Eric stood on the prows of their respective flag-ships, where covers of shields had been set up, and directed the movements of their men.

Some wielded swords, some spears, and others battle-axe or lance; others again used the bow or threw javelins or stones by hand.

The crew of the Serpent, on the other hand, from their height above their assailants, fairly rained down on them missiles of every kind, and occasionally, a caldron of some boiling liquid, poured upon their crowded decks, put many a brave fellow to flight.

The loss on both sides now was fearful, but with this difference in favor of the allies, that whenever a man was stricken down in one of their dragons nearest the enemy, another stepped into his station from an outside vessel, while there were none to supply the places of the killed and wounded on board the Serpent; until at last, her crew was reduced to such straits that the king himself had to keep guard at the gangway, "always throwing," says his chronicler, "two spears at once."

By his side stood the great bow-shooter, Einar Tamberskelver, and around him were the *scalds*, who were to record his heroism and his deeds of prowess in those rude rhymes, which, through nearly nine centuries, have come down to our times.

"Shoot me that tall soldier there, Finn," said Earl Eric, pointing to Einar Tamberskelver. "I know the fellow well, for he served under my father, and he is the best marksman in all Norway."

"I know him too," said the man addressed, a low, broad-shouldered Laplander, "and I will do my best to pierce his breastplate."

Finn shot, and the arrow, hitting the middle of Einar's bow, just as the famous archer was about drawing it, the bow split with a loud noise in two. "What is that?" cried Olaf, turning quickly in the direction of the sound.

"Norway king has parted from thy grasp!" was Einar's startling reply, as he gazed mournfully at the fragments of the weapon remaining in his hands.

"Nay, nay," cried the king, cheerily, "say not so, valiant Einar—Take my bow and try again."

Einar took the proffered bow, and carefully adjusting a shaft to it, discharged it at Earl Eric's breast; but although it struck full and fair upon the Earl's corslet it failed to penetrate it, and fell shattered to atoms at his feet.

"Too weak, too weak, king," cried the disappointed archer, flinging the bow contemptuously from him—"I will not shoot it again." Then, seizing lance and shield, he continued fighting bravely until he fell desperately wounded at Olaf's feet.

The king looked along the Serpent's rail and "saw that his men struck briskly with their swords yet wounded seldom." "Why do you strike so gently?" he asked. "Our blades are blunt and full of notches!" was the reply.

Then he had new arms taken from the arm-chest, and distributed fore and aft; but they cut no better than the others, for in truth, the men who were using them were entirely worn out; yet, attributing their failure not to their own exhaustion but to supernatural causes, they whispered darkly to one another—for they were but half Christianized after all—"that Odin was fighting with their enemies."

At the same time blood was observed to be dripping from the king's steel gauntlets, and the defence visibly relaxed.

Then Earl Eric ordered a couple of masts, with stout cleats nailed upon them, to be brought to him, and laying one of them from the poop of his vessel and the other from the prow upon the bulwarks of the Serpent, he attempted to board his enemy in two places, he leading one set of boarders and his brother the other.

Earl Swend's party were met by the king and quickly driven back to their ship; but Earl Eric with a half-dozen of his men gained the forecastle of the Long Serpent, and killing the few berserkers who yet remained alive there, rushed aft as far as the main-hold where he hoped to join forces with his brother; but being met instead by the king's brother-in-law, Thorolf Hyrming, and his uncle Thorkel Dyrdel, with other warriors of note, he was forced, after a desperate struggle, to fall back upon the deck of the Avenger. Boarding the second time, however, he was more successful, and after a brief but sharp encounter, found himself in full possession of the enemy's deck, while Olaf Tryggvesson, wounded to the death, Kolbiorn, and Ulf Rode with the king's standard wrapped around his body, were all that were left of the defenders of the Long Serpent.

"Now yield thee, king, my prisoner!" cried the Earl advancing upon him.

"To a traitor never!" shouted the dying hero, as, throwing his sword into the sea, he jumped after it, crimsoning the water with his blood, and followed by his banner-man and marshal.

The noise of the strife had ceased and Earl Eric was leaning wearily on his sword, by the side of the king of Denmark, when Earl Sigvald approached with his wife Astrid.

King Swend received the Viking most graciously, but Earl Eric refused his offered hand. "I fought against the king of Norway," said he, "because I had to avenge my father's death; but I fought openly. You, Earl Sigvald, ate of his bread and drank with him the good luck ale and then betrayed him; and I would rather this moment be that mainmast of battle, Olaf Tryggvesson, dead, than Earl Sigvald, his betrayer, alive."

Then Astrid's full heart welled up into her eyes, and her weeping was like the autumn rain.

"I thought it strange," said she, addressingher husband, "that you went not to the king of Norway's assistance, but I had no idea you had lured him into a snare. Nor did I know that a Viking, the descendant of Vikings, had fallen so low as to become a spy. "Hereafter you are dead to me, and I will live in my father's house a widow to my dying day." As she ceased speaking, the indignant woman jumped into a Vendland cutter and was soon far away. Her husband would have followed her, but was prevented by the warriors present; and it is recorded that he never saw her face again.

"Kolbiorn, the marshal, was captured in the water and his life spared, but Ulf Rode swam to the island, where he was warmly greeted by a handful of his comrades, who, like himself, had made their way in safety to the shore.

But the trusty banner-man was sorely wounded, and he knew that his last hour was at hand; so, when night had fairly set in, he induced his companions to step the mast of one of the vessels that had been cut adrift by Earl Eric and was floating about the cove, and to make a funeral pyre of tar-wood in its fore-hold; then, having the tiller lashed amidships and the great sail hoisted with its yard laid square, he jumped on board and bade them good-bye, and setting fire to the pyre in several places threw himself flat upon it.

The wind had changed since the morning, and was now blowing strongly off the land, and the ship fairly flew, burning in clear flame, out into the open sea. "Great was the fame of this deed in after times."

Of the lamented king of Norway many strange tales were told; the Christians asserting that he made his escape with Astrid in the Vendland cutter and died a palmer in the Holy Land, while the worshippers of Odin, singularly enough, declared he had been carried by the god in his good ship Skidbladnir (built by "the dwarfs" and so curiously constructed that it could be "rolled up like a cloth") straight to Asgaard the Scandinavian heaven.

The truth is, he sunk under the weight of his heavy armor in full five fathoms water and was drowned; and if his body was ever recovered it was privately interred, and no record of the fact kept for mankind.

When the news of his defeat and death reached Norway, there was a cry of anguish throughout the land; and all the women mourned for him as Freya in Asgaard mourns for the lost Odur; "for he was," says Carlyle, "the wildly beautifullest man, in body and in soul, that one has ever heard of in the North."

EARL ERIC USURPS THE SOVEREIGNTY OF NORWAY.

Norway was now held in fief for the crowns of Denmark and Sweden, respectively, by Earls Eric and Swend, "who allowed themselves to be baptized and took up the true faith; but held fast by the old laws and all the old rights and customs of the land, and were excellent men and good brothers;" but about 1014 A. D. Eric, whose wife was Gyda, daughter of Swend Forked Beard, and consequently sister of Canute, was summoned by this truly great monarch who had just ascended the throne of Denmark, to accompany him on an expedition westward to England, and as "the Earl would not sleep upon the message of the king, but sailed immediately out of the country," Norway was left in the keeping of his son Earl Hakon, a youth of but seventeen years of age, and was soon in the possession of one of the royal race of Haarfagers again, Olaf, Harald Grœnske's son, known in history as Olaf Haraldsson, the Saint.

OLAF HARALDSSON, THE SAINT.

Like Olaf Tryggvesson, Olaf Haraldsson went to sea at an early age, and, although he was but a "common rower" when he made his first cruise under "Rane, the far-travelled," he was addressed by his shipmates as king, since it was the custom to bestow this title upon all youths of kingly descent when they first went afloat, although they had no land or kingdom—a title, which, it may be remarked, they generally made good, by exercising a pretty rigid sovereignty over the seas which they scoured in their Viking enterprises.

Being of a warlike temper, it was not long before Olaf was in command of several vessels and he was spoken of as an expert seaman and able commander before he had attained his twentieth birthday.

Once, while cruising in the gulf of Finland, he was in a dreadful storm, "conjured up in the night by the heathens; but the king's seamanship prevailing more than the Finlanders' witchcraft he had the good fortune to beat round the Balagard's side and so got out to sea." On another occasion, he was running for Sotholm, Sweden, and had just got within the Skiergard or Skerry-gard, the name given to the belt of rocks and rocky islets which protect the shores of Norway and Sweden from the violence of the ocean, when he was confronted by a fleet much larger than his own, manned by Jomsburg Vikings, the most daring of all the many freebooters of the North, and commanded by Soto, a leader of fame and experience.

Of the fight that followed, we have no details, simply a disjointed account from which we are only able to gather that it was a very desperate one, lasting many hours, and that laying his ships between some "blind rocks," which made it difficult for the Vikings to get alongside, and throwing grappling irons into the vessels which came nearest to him, and clearing them of men, Olaf finally put his assailants to flight with a loss both of vessels and reputation. Shortly after this being "blocked up in lake Malære by the land and naval forces of the Swedish king, he cut a canal across the flat land Agnafet, out to the sea. "Now over all Swithiod," says the chronicle, the "running waters fall into the Malære lake; whose only outlet to the sea is so small that many rivers are wider; and when much rain or snow falls, the water rushes in a great cataract out by Stokesund, and the lake rises high and floods the land. It fell heavy rain just at this time, and, as the canal was dug out to the sea, the water and stream rushed into it. Then Olaf had all the rudders unshipped, and hoisted all sail aloft. It was blowing a strong breeze astern, and they steered with their oars, and the ships came in a rush over the shallows, and got into the sea without any damage, whereat the Swedish king was exceedingly enraged. This passage has since been called King's Sound, but large vessels cannot pass through it unless the waters are very high."

OLAF, THE SAINT, ASSAULTS AND DESTROYS LONDON BRIDGE WITH HIS FLEET.

But Olaf's greatest naval achievement, and the one for which he was most celebrated in after times, was the taking of London in 1014 A. D. from the Danes, whom he, not unnaturally, regarded as the born enemies of his family. This event happened just after the death of Swend Forked Beard, when Ethelred the Unready, upon the invitation of the English prelates and nobility, had returned to England from Norway and invited all men who would enter his pay to join him in recovering his country; "whereupon many people flocked to him, and among others king Olaf and his Marshal with a great troop of Northmen."

In a War Thing, it was determined that the allies should endeavor to get possession of London, as a preliminary step to further operations, and, for this purpose, the English and Norse fleets ascended the Thames together, while an English army marched along the left bank of the river, keeping the vessels always in view. So soon as the city was reached, an attack was made upon the castle, a stone fortification of considerable strength occupying the site of the present Tower, and this enterprise having failed, through the desperate valor of its Danish defenders, it was resolved to make an attempt on Sudrviki (Southwark) on the opposite side of the stream. But Southwark, besides being surrounded by a deep ditch and a high wall, was connected with the castle by a bridge ("so broad that two wagons could pass each other upon it"), having stone turrets erected at regular intervals across its entire length, between which were strong wooden parapets affording ample shelter to quite an army of men; and Olaf, in a council held in king Ethelred's tent, gave it as his opinion that no assault on the works on either side of the Thames could be successful, so long as the means of communication between their large garrisons were such that the one force could readily march to the assistance of the other. "And so the Great Bridge must come down!" he cried. "Easily said," remonstrated an English Earl, "but how are we to get at it?"

"With our fleets, was the bold response, and I myself will lead the way to it!" But at this proposition Ethelred the unready looked aghast, while even old Rane, Olaf's foster-father, who had been with him in many a desperate encounter, shook his head disapprovingly. Then Olaf drawing from its sheath his good sword Knikarr,[2] afterwards so famous in story, and reverently kissing the cross on its hilt, swore by Christ's blood either to destroy the bridge or perish in the attempt. Carried away by his heroism, all the Naval commanders vowed to follow him to the death, and when the assembly broke up at nightfall, repaired forthwith to their vessels, to make preparations for the meditated attack, which it was agreed should come off just before sunrise on the morrow. The intervening time was passed by the Anglo-Saxons, according to their custom before a battle, in revelry and feasting, but on board the Norse vessels, the sound of the hammer and hatchet was heard all the night through, and when morning came, there was not one of them but had a stout roof over it, whose sloping sides, well supported by huge upright timbers, nearly reached the water.

The Thames now presented an animated panorama, which to one ignorant of what was transpiring there, would have seemed a holiday spectacle, for everywhere along its banks, were to be discerned the banners of the opposing armies, and great bodies of horsemen and foot soldiers moving to and fro, while the river itself was alive with war-ships, having their largest ensigns hoisted, and sending forth, hither and thither across the stream, some for provisions, others for arms or ammunition, myriads of boats, gayly painted and ornamented with gilding, from whose tiny flag-poles drooped the miniature colors of the nation to which they belonged.

Just after daylight a great flourish of trumpets was heard from King Ethelred's tent, a signal for both fleets to get under way ; and shortly afterward, the English vessels, which had been anchored below the Norsemen, but were now to lead the advance, rowed by King Olaf's dragon, the Charlemagne, sounding their war-horns, and dipping their flags to her as they passed; and although their array was very irregular, for it was not until some centuries after this period, that the English acquired that reputation for superior seamanship, which they maintain in our day ; yet was it a gallant sight to behold these fiery Anglo-Saxons, who disdained even the cover of their shields, moving steadily forward, and, notwithstanding that they fell like November leaves before a storm, as they got within range of the enemy, still pressing onward until their ships actually touched the bridge with their prows. Then, however, great masses of rock, and limestone were rolled down upon them, breaking their decks, smashing their oars, and involving rowers and men-at-arms alike in one common ruin, from which no valor could extri, cate them, and the English fleet drifted helplessly down the river, until it was full a league below the castle, when, with- the assistance of reinforcements from the army, it reformed and pulled up in rear of the Norsemen. It was now the turn of these to attack, and they were not slow to avail themselves of the opportunity. Forming in line with their heads down stream, they backed directly towards the bridge, and, unhurt by missile weapons or falling stones, which either glanced from, or rolled harmlessly down the steep sides of their novel mantelets, succeeded in getting so far under it that their prows alone were visible. Then the harsh grating of many saws gave evidence to the Danes of their enemy's intention to so weaken the props of the bridge, as to cause it to fall by its own weight; yet they were not disheartened at the sound: On the contrary, some cut great holes in the bridge and poured boiling pitch down, in the vain hope that through cracks in the roofs, it would fall upon the Norsemen's heads; others, more daring, leaped from the bridge upon the roofs and endeavored to destroy them with pole-axe and pike, while others again, and these were the most renowned of the Danish warriors, putting off from the shore in small boats, actually made an attempt to carry the Charlemagne, sword in hand. But this attempt ending miserably, with the utter annihilation of the boats and their crews, and the axe-men and pike-men being driven to take shelter behind their bridge intrenchments, by the shafts of the famous archers on board the English fleet, some of whom, perhaps, lived long enough to "draw a good bow" at Hastings,* the Norsemen continued their work of demolition for several hours, almost unmolested, at the expiration of which their great dragons shot out from between the piers of the bridge, with all the velocity that doubly-manned oars and a six knot current could give them, to a distance of perhaps two hundred yards, when they brought up with a sudden jerk, and a noise like that of falling timber,—and behold the piles of the bridge, broken asunder or torn from their river bed by the momentum of the vessels, to whose sterns by stout hawsers they had been attached, were drifting off in detached masses down stream, while a cry of horror from the Danish women, who, on both banks of the river, had long been anxious spectators of the strife, gave warning that the bridge was tottering to its fall. A second afterwards, and it went down with a fearful crash, carrying with it turrets, breast-works and battlements, and burying one-half of its defenders under their *debris;* of the others, a few got into Southwark, a few into the castle,

* As the bow was used in Denmark from the earliest times, I cannot but think it was introduced into England by the Danes, long before the time of the Norman Conquest, although there is no mention of *English* archers at the battle of Hastings.

but by far the greater number fell into the Thames, and were drowned. On the next day, amid the fierce shouts of the Saxons of "Down with the invaders! Death to the Danes!" and the stern commands of the Norse chieftains to their followers: "Close up Christ-men! Forward Cross-men! Follow your leaders, and defend your banners!" Southwark was stormed and carried almost without resistance, seeing which the castle capitulated, and London was restored to its rightful owners.

Of the many lines written by the *Scalds* in commemoration of the fall of the bridge, these, by Ottar Swarte, seem to have been the most popular.

"London bridge is broken down,
Gold is won and bright renown!
Shields resounding,
War horns sounding,
Hildur shouting in the din!
Arrows singing,
Mail coats ringing,
Odin makes our Olaf win!"

It was not long after this great event, however, when Olaf Haraldson heard of Eric Hakonson's departure from Norway and sailed for home, and, about the same time, Canute arrived in England with a large re-inforcement of Danes, whereupon things went from bad to worse with the English, until finally, as we know, they were forced to submit to Danish rule.

OLAF THE SAINT BECOMES KING OF NORWAY AND REIGNS THIRTEEN YEARS, WHEN HE FALLS AT THE BATTLE OF STIKLESTAD, AND IS SUCCEEDED BY SWEND, A SON OF CANUTE THE GREAT.

Olaf reached Norway in due season, and, as he jumped ashore on Sælo island, one of his feet slipped, but the other sunk deep in the mud. Then said he to his foster-father,

"The king falls!" "Nay," was the ready response, "thou didst not fall, king, but set fast foot in the soil." And so, indeed, it turned out; for it was not long after this, when Earl Hakon being his prisoner, and Earl Swend forced to fly to Sweden, he was acknowledged by the bonders as their king. He had reigned over Norway but thirteen years, however, when he was obliged to retire from the country before the overwhelming forces of Canute, to whose demand that he should hold the kingdom as his tributary, he had returned the spirited reply: "Now ye shall tell king Canute these, my words: I will defend Norway with battle-axe and sword as long as life is given me." And it was in an effort to recover his crown, that he fell in the great fight of Stiklestad, August 31st, 1030. The battle-axe, called Hell or Death, which he wielded with such effect on that bloody day, descended to his son, Magnus, but his sword Knikarr was picked up by a Swede on the field of battle, and kept as a precious heir-loom in his family for several generations. "Now it fell out," says the saga, "more than a century after the engagement at Stiklestad, that a young Swede, belonging to the body-guard of Kyrialax, emperor of Constantinople, found, on awakening one morning, that his sword, which he had placed under his head on going to bed, was missing. He looked after it, and saw it lying on the flat plain at a distance from him. He got up and recovered the sword, thinking that his comrades had taken it from him in a joke, but they all denied it. The same thing happened three nights. Then he wondered at it, as well as they who saw or heard of it; and people began to ask him how it could have happened. He said that this sword was called Knikarr, and had belonged to king Olaf the Saint, who had himself carried it in the battle of Stiklestad; and he also related how the sword since that time, had gone from one to another, and had done great service against the *heathen*. This was told to the emperor who called the man before him, and giving him three times as much gold as the sword was worth, had it laid in St. Olaf's Church." Now the truth of this story is well attested, "for there was a lenderman of Norway in Constantinople when the sword was placed in the church, and he saw it there on the altar." And somewhere in that vicinity it will doubtless be found, and, in the hands of a devout Russian, again do great service against the "heathen" when the Czar not long hence drives the Turk from the city of Saint Constantine.

THE NORSEMEN "CHASE SWEND BACK TO DENMARK," AND PLACE OLAF THE SAINT'S SON, MAGNUS THE GOOD, ON THE THRONE, WHO REIGNS MANY YEARS, AND IS SUCCEEDED BY HIS UNCLE HARALD HARDRADA.

After Olaf's death, Canute placed his son Swend over Norway: "but when by the law every ship that sailed from the land had to reserve stowage for the king, and the testimony of one Dane invalided that of ten Norsemen, the bonders chased him back to Denmark, and remembering the freedom they had enjoyed under king Olaf, they placed his son Magnus the Good on the throne." Magnus reigned many years over Norway and added Denmark to his dominions. He was a great warrior, but is most famous in history "for the law-book he had composed in writing," which was in use in the Drontheim district as late as the fourteenth century. It was called the *Gray Goose*, from the color of the parchment on which it was written, and "embraced subjects," says Laing, "not dealt with probably at that period by any other code in Europe."

After Magnus, came his uncle Harald Hardrada, a half-brother of Olaf the Saint, who, when he was but three years old, Olaf predicted would some day become a king, because upon being asked what he would like to have, just after his brother Halfdan had wished for a large herd of cows and oxen, he answered quickly, "O! as many house servants as would eat up Halfdan's cattle at a single meal!" A reply which, coupled with Olaf's prediction, proves that the divine right of kings, in the eleventh century, to eat up the substance of their loyal subjects was as fully recognized in Norway as in other countries. Harald commenced his career as a "helm striker" in his fifteenth year at Stiklestad, where, in his brother's defense, he was desperately wounded. Carried from the battle-field, by a faithful follower, he lay concealed in the house of a poor peasant until his wounds were healed, when, guided by the peasant's son, he made his escape to Sweden. His bold, hopeful and aspiring spirit was never more conspicuous than upon a certain occasion during this journey, when forced to betake himself to a thick wood, for concealment from pursuers, he burst forth, to the wonderment of his guide, with:

"My wounds were bleeding as I rode :
And down below the bonders strode,
Killing the wounded with the sword,
The followers of their rightful lord.
From wood to wood I crept along,
Unnoticed by the bonder-throng ;
Who knows I thought, a day may come,
My name will yet be great at home."

Harald's contempt of danger was afterwards displayed in many countries, and his knowledge of *scald-craft*, in the sea of Azof, when he composed sixteen songs for amusement, all ending with the same words; yet, as there can be no reasonable doubt but that *his* quill was an exception to the rule that the pen is mightier than the sword, I shall transfer him at once from his *wanderings* among the muses to his *home* on the field of Mars, and end my account of the battles of the Baltic with the great sea fight off Nisaa, which, with the engagements already described, will, it is hoped, give the reader a just idea of the naval tactics and strategy of the Scandinavians.

The cause which led to the battle was the unjust claim of Harald to the crown of Denmark, which Magnus had given on his death-bed to Swend Ulfsson; Harald declaring that, through Magnus himself, he had an inalienable hereditary right to the whole Danish dominions. "So he went South, and plundered in Denmark all one summer, but as he could gain no foothold on the land he returned to Norway and wintered there." His raid seems to have been very unexpected; for the Danish girls, on being told the winter before that Harald might be looked for with his fleet as soon as warm weather set in, cut their cheeses into the shape of anchors, laughingly declaring "that with such killicks they would undertake to hold all king Harald's vessels." Theodolf makes mention of the matter in the following lines, which show how deeply Harald resented the jest, and what unlimited license he gave his men on their landing in Denmark:

"The island girls, we were told,
Made anchors all our fleets to hold;
Their Danish gibe, cut out in cheese,
Did not our stern king's fancy please.
Now many a maiden fair, may be,
Sees iron anchors splash the sea,
Who will not wake a maid next morn,
To laugh at Norway's ships in scorn."

The next summer Harald plundered in Denmark a second time; but, as he was returning to Norway with his sixty vessels burdened with spoil, he came near falling into a snare prepared for him by Swend, who, with over a hundred vessels, was lying in wait for him somewhere in the vicinity of Lesso. But, as the Norsemen drew near to Lesso, the lookout men on the king's ship cried out, lustily, "Lights ahead! Lights on the starboard bow! Lights on the port bow!" The vessel was enveloped in a fog at the time, yet, quick as lightning, the thought flashed across Harald's brain that it had cleared up along shore, and that the lights reported were the gilded figure heads of Swend's dragons, upon which the rays of the rising sun were shining. "Go about and pull for your lives!" was the order quickly passed from vessel to vessel and as quickly obeyed. "But the Northmen's ships," according to Snorro, "were both soaked with water and heavily laden; so that the Danes approached nearer and nearer. Then Harald, whose own dragon-ship was the last of the fleet, saw that he could not get away; so he ordered his men to throw overboard some wood, and to lay upon it clothes and other good and valuable articles; and it was so perfectly calm, that these drove about with the tide. Now when the Danes saw their own goods floating about on the sea, they who were in advance turned about to collect them; for they thought it was easier to take what was floating about, than to go on board the Northmen to take it. But when king Swend came up to them, he urged them on; saying 'it would be a great shame if they, with so great a force, could not overtake and master so small a number!' The Danes then began again to stretch out at their oars. When king Harald saw that the Danish ships were faster, he ordered his men to lighten their ships, and cast overboard malt, wheat and bacon, and to let their liquor run out, which helped a little. Then Harald ordered the bulwark-screens, the empty casks and puncheons, and the prisoners to be thrown overboard; and, when all these were driving about on the sea, Swend ordered help to be given to save the men; in doing which so much time was lost that the Norse fleet got away."

It was not to be supposed that a warrior like Harald would soon forgive his rival for putting him to flight, and, accordingly, we find him, a few years later, sending a message to king Swend, "that he should come northward in spring, and fight him on the river Gotha, and so settle the division of the countries, that the one who gained the victory should have both kingdoms." He then sailed from Nidaros with four hundred vessels, large and small, whose rowers were so well drilled that their oars all touched the water at the same instant, and of Harald's ship in particular, on board of which he served, Theodolf sings:

"Our blades together rose and fell,
One stroke was all the eye could tell,
And, when at Drontheim's holy stream
Our seventy oars in distance gleam,
We seem, while rowing in from sea,
An erne with wooden wings to be."

GREAT SEA-FIGHT OFF NISAA, BETWEEN THE NORSEMEN AND THE DANES.

After cruising in the vicinity of the Gotha several weeks, finding the Danish king did not make his appearance, Harald concluded he had declined his challenge, and, therefore, sent home all but one hundred and fifty of his vessels, with which he repaired to Lofo fiord, where he employed his men wasting the country, driving off cattle and collecting grain. While thus engaged, a fisherman, coming from sea, reported to him, one morning, that Swend's fleet was near at hand; and he was still questioning the man as to its size and equipment, when it entered the fiord, presenting a naval spectacle, such as has been rarely seen; for the whole power of Denmark was there, in three hundred ships, commanded by the king in person, and divided into six squadrons, each of which was lead by an Earl.

When this vast armament first hove in view, the Norse vessels were scattered in all directions, and the crews of many of them had landed in search of plunder; but, as trumpet answered trumpet, from cliff to cliff and from ship to shore, they hurriedly got together, and, in small detachments, were soon seen issuing from cove, creek and inlet to the support of their flag-ship, the old Charlemagne, which had won such renown in England, as we have seen, under Olaf the Saint. Earl Hakon, who was Harald's second in command, had *his* flag hoisted on a large dragon called the Bison, built by Olaf, and long used as the ocean-home of his son Magnus. "It had a great bison's head on the bow," says Arnor, "and aft on the sternpost was its tail, and both its head and tail and the sides of the ship were gilded over." Beside the Charlemagne and the Bison, there was another famous dragon with the fleet, whose real name was the Sea Wolf, but which was commonly known to seamen as the Dane-Cheater, from the following circumstance:

When Saint Olaf made his escape from Canute's great fleet, he made his way to Sweden, where he ordered his vessels to be hauled up on shore, proposing to abandon them, and march across the country to Norway; but Harek of Thiotto, a very wealthy bonder who owned the Sea Wolf, declared he was "too old and heavy to travel on foot and that he would make his way home in his ship, even if he should find Denmark itself underway and cruising in the Baltic." Accordingly, he took his departure, with a fair wind, and as soon as he came near the Danish fleet he un-shipped his mast and stowed it away, and after covering his gilt-work with cloth, smeared his vessel all over with mud. Next he nailed strips of wood to her rail, at right angles to it and about ten feet apart, over which he stretched grey tilt-canvass, so that she seemed to have very high bulwarks like a merchantman. Then putting out a few old oars on either side, manned by not more than a dozen men, he steered unmolested through the enemy's line, Canute's watchmen merely reporting to the king that an old *buss*[3] loaded with salt or herrings was passing through the fleet, steering to the northward. After he had got a couple of miles beyond the enemy, however, Harek raised his mast, hoisted sail and sent up his gilded vane; whereupon the mortified Danes, realizing the trick that had been played upon them, spread all their canvass in pursuit; but, the Sea Wolf going two feet to their one, the wily old Norseman was soon far away, and singing gaily, after the manner of his countrymen,

"A young man who is hale and sound
May leave his ship and walk the ground;
But Harek, with his gouty feet,

Prefers to sail with flowing sheet:
So, ere I take to shore, I'll see
What my good ship will do for me."

Many of the dragons of king Swend's fleet were of great size, and the one carrying his royal standard had also worn that of Canute, whose name she bore. Her sail was entirely blue, while the sails of the other vessels were painted in stripes of blue, white and red; the hulls and masts of all being black, differing in this from the Norse vessels, whose masts were scraped, while their hulls were of various hues.

After Harald had formed his fleet in line, he took his station in the centre of it, and lashed the vessels together, with his right resting on the land, near the village of Nisaa, from which this battle takes its name, and his left stretching toward the opposite shore, but at some distance from it (for the fiord is very wide at this point), so that there was room enough for many vessels abreast to pass between him and it; and, fearing lest the Danes should take advantage of this pass to get in his rear, he kept a strong reserve for its guard just astern of his left flank, which he confided to Earl Hakon.

On the right of the king, Ulf Ospaksson, the marshal, laid his ship, "ordering his men to bring her well forward;" and on the left was Guttorm Kalfsson, a famous seaman whom the Norsemen supposed to be under the especial protection of Saint Olaf; "for once, when attacked by King Margad, of Dublin, with sixteen ships, while he himself had but five, he called upon God and his uncle, Saint Olaf, to aid him, and won the battle, King Margad and every man who followed him, old and young, being slain. Then Guttorm had an image of the Saint, seven feet high, made from the silver which he found in the king's ships, and set up in the temple of Drontheim."

Swend, the Danish king, also drew up his fleet in order of battle, and "laid his ship forward in the centre, opposite to Harald's ship." On his right was the great Earl of Halland, Finn Arneson, and on his left a warrior noted for his strength, called Thorkel, *the helm-splitter*, from the many casques he had cut through with his ponderous battle-axe, "which no other man in the fleet could wield, and but few men lift."

"As the Danes began to bind their ships together, King Swend called out that a third of them must remain loose, and pull around outside of the battle, attacking the Norsemen wherever they were found to be vulnerable. Then King Harald, ordering a war-blast to sound, his vessels moved forward to the attack, and the strife began and became very sharp, both kings urging on their men." But so much time had been consumed, in making the necessary dispositions for battle, that darkness had now set in; so that, although the fight continued through the whole night, it was simply a *mêlée*, there being no resort to strategy or stratagem, nor attempt at manœuvring on either side. The obstinacy with which it had been maintained by both parties was made apparent, however, at the dawn of day, by "the vast number of dead men floating all around the ships," and yet it continued with unremitting fury, and, so far as the eye could judge, without advantage to either side—the black raven of Odin on Denmark's national ensign, still confronting, as boldly as on the previous evening, the green dragon of Norway, said to have been brought originally from the remote province of Toorkestan.

The steel-clad men of the Charlemagne, but one of whom—not yet distinguished for heroic valor—was forced by military law to carry the "shield of expectation,"[4]—white when he left his home, but now stained red with blood,—were engaged in an almost hand to hand conflict with the crew of the Canute, "armed in foreign helmets and coats of stout ring-mail." On the forecastle of their respective flag-ships stood the contesting chiefs, each "with a gold-mounted helmet on his head and a lance in his hand," and surrounded by the warriors of his shield-circle, who were ever ready to give up their lives in his behalf. In front of Harald was the flag he had long carried, appropriately called *The Land Ravager*, and opposite to it, on the Canute's prow, the *Enchanted banner*, borne, as we have seen, by Earl Eric, in the battle of Rugen, and thereafter adopted as the royal standard of Denmark, with which the fate of the country was believed by the superstitious to be inseparably connected.

As soon as it was fairly light, an attempt was made, by full fifty vessels of the Danish reserve, to turn King Harald's left; but, in a trice, Earl Hakon swooped upon them with his division, and sinking some and disabling others, he struck the remainder with such panic terror that they turned and fled, not stopping, it was jeeringly said of them, for many years afterward, "until they had reached their mother Denmark." As the Earl was engaged in towing off his prizes, "a boat came rowing to him, and, hailing him, said that the other wing of Harald's fleet had given way, and many of their people had fallen. Then Hakon hastened thither, and gave so severe an assault that the Danes had to retreat in a hurry. The Earl went on in this way, as he had been doing all the night, coming forward wherever he was most wanted, and always driving the enemy before him."

While the fierce Earl was thus retrieving the fortune of the day on the right, the warriors who yet remained alive in the centre of the Norse fleet were battling stoutly for the honor of their flag, while many who had fought their last fight, were sleeping peacefully, side by side with the dead heroes of King Swend. But now a stalwart Dane, named Hildur, who had long been battling bravely in the foremost ranks of his friends, sprung from the prow of the Canute upon the deck of the Charlemagne, and calling upon Odin to aid him, endeavored to make his way to the Norwegian king. He had approached, indeed, within a few feet of Harald, when a giant among the *berserkers*, noted throughout all Norway for his herculean strength, devoted himself to death in his sovereign's defense. Rushing upon Hildur and clasping him in his iron embrace, even while his life's blood was ebbing away from the wound inflicted by Hildur's sword, which had passed through and through his naked breast, this noble barbarian with one bound cleared the bulwarks of the Charlemagne and leaped with his adversary into the sea! As the waves closed over Hildur, his comrades were seized with a sudden fright, taking advantage of which Harald gave the order, Board! An instant thereafter the Land Ravager was advanced to the forecastle of the Canute, "followed by the king himself, and all his valiant men," and a fierce hand to hand conflict ensued with the immediate supporters of King Swend, to whose assistance now rushed Finn Arneson and the Helm-splitter, at the head of a select body of veterans, "who had seen much service in England," while the number of Harald's followers was augmented by the arrival of Guttorm Kalfsson, Ulf Ospaksson, and their shield-circle men. Each instant the strife waxed hotter and hotter, and the air resounded with the clashing of swords, the war-cries of the combatants, and the groans of the wounded and dying, to which was added an occasional splash in the water, as a corpse was thrown overboard that chanced to be in the way of friend or foe.

Suddenly Guttorm Kalfsson, rushing in front of his men, and laying a foeman low with every stroke of his good sword, succeeded in reaching the enchanted banner and wresting it from the bannerman's hands; but at this critical instant a voice was heard calling out, in stentorian tones, "Halland to the rescue!" and Guttorm falling to the deck, with his right arm severed from the shoulder, the Danes recovered their standard. Ere Finn Arneson could repeat his blow, however, he was confronted by King Harald, who, in the excitement of the moment, had leaped over the shields by which he was encompassed; "and by Harald's side was his marshal, and at his back stood Rolf the courageous, and many other distinguished men." On the other side Swend was not less prompt than Harald in getting to the front, nor were the Danish warriors one whit behind the Norsemen in rallying to the support of their king.

The fight on the Canute now took the form of a series of single combats, which the rival armies—their weapons for the moment laid aside—regarded with breathless interest, each army feeling that on their result depended the fate of its king and country.

Cutting down all who beset his path, King Harald at last reached the King of Denmark, and the two were soon fiercely engaged, foot to foot, and blade to blade; but Swend, although of great personal bravery, was no match in arms for one who had gained eighteen battles in Africa and the East, and who had commanded for many years the *Vairingers*[5] of the Greek Emperor; and, in less time than it takes to tell it, his sword went whirling from his grasp into the sea, leaving him at the mercy of his antagonist. King Harald was about to follow up his advantage, when a blow on his helmet, from behind, brought him to his knee; yet, quick as thought, he sprang to his feet, and, although his brain was reeling, and his cloven casque fell to the deck, he turned, with the ferocity of a tiger, upon his assailant, the redoubtable Thorkel, who was now obliged to cover his helm with his ponderous battle-axe, so fast and furious were the blows rained upon it by the enraged monarch with his Damascus steel. Tired at length of acting on the defensive, Thorkel ventured to draw back his weapon to the length of his right arm, with the intent of bringing it down upon the king's defenceless skull; but ere the axe descended, his own head was fairly cleft in twain by Harald's blade, and he fell forward on his face, dead. As his body struck the deck, the gauntlet of his right hand fell off, exposing to view his unpared nails, which were of such extraordinary length as to make his fingers resemble the talons of a bird of prey. King Harald had been baptized a Christian, yet all his early Pagan superstition came back to him at the sight. "Wretch" cried he, spurning the corpse with his foot, "get thee to Hell with thy raven claws, thou accursed of gods and men, who hast thus furnished a plank for the ship[6] Naglfar; and may the great serpent gnaw upon thy soul until the universe is consumed by Surtur's flame!"

While the king was yet speaking, Guttorm Kalfsson, whom all had supposed to be dead, rose to his feet, and seizing the enchanted banner[7] from the terrified standard-bearer, bore it to the rear; then, clambering on board the Charlemagne and leaning against the bulwarks, he held it with his left arm rigidly in air. His companions hastened to him with shouts of approbation; but their plaudits fell upon heedless ears—the mail-clad warrior, so proudly holding the captured flag on high, had struck his own flag to the Conqueror Death!

"A miracle! a miracle!" now cried the crew of the Charlemagne—a cry that was taken up by ship after ship all along the line, as, with one accord, resuming their arms, the Norsemen charged upon their foe; but the awe-struck Danes awaited not their approach, but—some by swimming, others in their boats—betook themselves to the reserve, which now fled amain, hotly pursued by King Harald, leaving the abandoned vessels, more than seventy in number, to fall into Earl Hakon's hands.

While Harald was absent in pursuit of the fugitives, "a man came rowing in a boat to the Earl's ship and lay at the bulwarks. The man was stout, and had on a white hat. He hailed the ship. 'Where is the earl?'" said he.

The earl was in the fore-hold stopping a man's blood. He cast a look at the man in the hat and asked him his name. He answered "here is Vandraade, speak to me earl!"

The earl leant over the ship's side to him. Then the man in the boat said, "Earl, I will accept of my life from thee, if thou will give it."

Then the earl raised himself up, called two men who were friends dear to him, and said to them, "go into the boat; bring Vandraade to the land, attend him to my friend's, Karl the bonder, and tell Karl to let him have the horse which I gave to him yesterday, and also his saddle, and his son to attend him."

This is the Vandraade of whom we have made mention as having been reproved by the house-frau (Karl's wife), for presuming to wipe his face in the middle of a towel; and he was no less a personage than Swend, king of Denmark.

The king's reply was: "I may yet come so far forward in the world as to dry myself with the middle of a cloth," and he seems never to have forgiven the woman for her churlishness; for many years afterward, upon his bestowing a fine farm upon Karl as a reward for his services, he expressly stipulated that Karl should put away his wife before taking possession of it. He, however, gave him a new wife, showing from his conversation with the bonder about the matter, that his opinions in relation to the female sex harmonized entirely with those of the immediate successor of the Prophet. "Women," said Abu Beker, "are a great evil, and the worst of it is they are a necessary evil!"

King Harold was much displeased with Earl Hakon for his magnanimity in sparing Swend's life, and would have put him to death, had not the earl fled to Sweden.

Of the many monkish legends relating to the engagement off Nisaa, which were current in Norway in Harald's day, there was one that gave as great offence to the Norse warriors as that told by Gomara, five centuries later, of the battle of Santa Maria de la Vittoria in Mexico gave to Bernal Diaz and the other old soldiers of Cortez.[8]

It was to this effect, that when Guttorm was about being struck the second time by the Earl of Holland, Olaf the Saint made his appearance on the forecastle of the Canute, clad in full armor, and that it was he who seized the magic banner and waved it from the Charlemagne. This, the heroes who had taken part in the fight, indignantly denied, stoutly averring that it was the king's and their own good swords that defended the prostrate form of Kalfsson, and that if Olaf were present they did not see him, but that they did see Guttorm seize and carry off the Danish standard and with his remaining strength display it above his head, and that in the heroic act he expired.

HARALD HARDRADA SAILS FOR ENGLAND AS THE ALLY OF EARL TOSTI, AND IS SLAIN AT STANDFORD BRIDGE.

About five years after the battle of Nisaa, king Harald sailed for England as the ally of Earl Tosti in his quarrel with his brother Harold. Before leaving Norway, several men in his fleet had dreams portending his death, of which the most remarkable narrated in the sagas are these.

"While they lay in Solundir a man called Gyrder, on board the king's ship, had a dream. He thought he was on the forecastle, and saw a great witch-wife standing on the island, with a fork in one hand, and a trough in the other. He thought also that he saw all over the fleet, and that a fowl was sitting upon every ship's stern, and that these fowls were all ravens or ernes; and the witch-wife sang this song:

"From the East I'll lure the King,
To the West the King I'll bring;
Many a noble one will be
In English meadows left for me.
Ravens o'er Harald's ship are flitting,
Falcons on her high stern sitting,
Eyeing their prey.
The King is fey, the King is fey!"

"There was also a man called Thora, in a ship which lay not far from the king's. He dreamt one night that he saw king Harald's fleet coming to land, and he knew the land to be England. He saw a great battle array on the land, and he thought both sides began to fight, and had many banners flapping in the air. And before the army of the people of the country was riding a huge witch-wife upon a wolf; and the wolf had a man's carcass in his mouth, and the blood was dropping from his jaws; and when he had eaten up one body she threw another into his mouth, and so, one after another, he swallowed them all. It was said, too, that Harald's brother Olaf appeared to him and told him if he went to England he would serve as food for the witch-wife's steed."

But Harald Hardrada was not a man to be deterred from the prosecution of any object he had set his heart upon, by idle dreams or imaginary apparitions; and so he set sail, as we have said, and landing in England, lost his life, fighting gallantly, in the battle of Standford bridge, Sept. 25th, 1066. His body was carried to Norway and buried at Nidaros where it still lies. But when, at the last day, the Gjallar horn shall sound and Odin rides forth with his heroes, through one of the five hundred doors of Valhalla, to contend with the wolf, the dog, and the serpent, backed by the monster "Lodi, the caluminator of the gods," and all the other inmates of Hell, Harald, if old Norse prophecies may be relied on, will not be far from the warrior-god's right hand.

King Harald is described as "a handsome man of noble appearance; his hair and beard yellow. He had short whiskers and long mustaches and one eye-brow somewhat higher than the other, and was in height five ells."

With him ends our connection with the romantic land of Scandinavia, whose sea-kings, according to Mallet, "fought equally well on foot, on horse-back, and on board a vessel."

Lest the reader should suppose that the binding together of vessels, when acting on the defensive, was peculiar to the Norsemen, it may be well here to mention that it was resorted to before their day, on the Indian Ocean and the Red and Mediterranean Seas. So common, indeed, was this order with the Arabs, that they gave to it, says Jal, "the distinctive name of *maremme;*" and Polybius calls two vessels bound together a *sambuca*, whether from the resemblance of the formation to a harp, or to a kind of craft known in India as a *zambuca*, is a mooted question.

According to Livy, Publius Scipio, when attacked by the

Carthaginian fleet off Utica, formed his "round ships" into four lines, the ships of each line being at such distances from each other as would permit of the passage of a galley between them. These *intervals* were bridged over with masts and spars, placed from rail to rail, with thick planks laid upon and securely fastened to them, upon which were stationed large bodies of slingers and pikemen, and various engines of war then in use; and from under these bridges the galleys pulled to the attack, falling back upon them, and taking advantage of their cover, when hard pressed by the enemy.

The Venetians, Genoese and Spaniards also adopted this order of battle on some occasions.

In attacking fortified places, vessels were not unfrequently lashed together to afford a secure platform for artillery. Great results were obtained from this by Alexander the Great, at Tyre, and by many other celebrated commanders, at later periods.

RISE OF THE BRITISH NAVY. BATTLE BETWEEN THE ENGLISH AND FRENCH OFF SLUYS.

Having now traced the galley of the Baltic to the end of the eleventh century, after which period there was no improvement in its construction, and the Norman war vessel, so famous in the twelfth and thirteenth centuries, being built like it, with some slight modifications borrowed from the Greeks and Venetians, whose fleets, as well as those of other Mediterranean peoples, we have several times seen arrayed in order of battle, it would be unprofitable to pursue the subject of galley fighting further; I shall therefore take leave of it with an account of the Invincible Armada, wherein galleys were used for the last time on the high seas as vessels of war.*

Before proceeding however, to chronicle the advent to the

* Small row-galleys were used with effect by us against the enemy on our rivers, during "the revolutionary war." See Cooper's Naval History.

British channel of that vast armament "under whose weight the very sea appeared to groan," it becomes necessary to sketch briefly the rise of the Naval Power, against which its efforts were directed.

The opinion of several eminent writers that the Britons were masters of a considerable sea force before the time of Julius Cæsar, is based upon the supposition that when the Veneti implored their aid against the Romans, they sent them their whole fleet, and that every vessel of it perished in the memorable combat that ensued.

Passing over such an absurd conjecture as unworthy of serious consideration, I would remind the reader that when the old standard-bearer of the 10th legion, calling upon his fellow-soldiers "to follow him or see their Eagle fall into the hands of the enemy," leaped into the sea near Deal, there was nothing in the shape of a fleet belonging to the British Isles, according to Cæsar himself, but an inconsiderable number of fishing boats, "made of wicker and hides." It was not indeed until nine centuries later, and after Britain had been the prey successively of the Roman, the Saxon and the Dane, that anything deserving the name of a naval organization was attempted by its rulers.

To Alfred the Great belongs the honor of being the founder of the British Navy, and as he took command of his first fleet in person, Mr. Southey very properly regards him as the first English Admiral. British vessels were built by his order of twice the length of those they were to engage, and were less unsteady and higher, and far swifter than the enemy's galleys. England's first naval victory was probably gained during his reign, when the Danes were defeated in a sea-fight off Essex.

Athelstan, Alfred's grandson, so well understood the necessity of encouraging commerce as the only sure foundation of naval power, as to decree that any merchant who had made three voyages over the high seas in his own ship, freighted at his own expense, should have the rank of *thane*, "a title," says Yonge, "previously confined to men of noble rank and extensive landed possessions." It is recorded that the king of Norway held Athelstan in such esteem, that he sent him "a goodly dragon with a golden beak and purple sails."

The monastic writers assert that Edwy the All Fair, had "four fleets of twelve hundred vessels each, stationed in the four seas for the defence of the whole island." But as the sea-coast of Britain was repeatedly ravaged during his reign by "the Danes and Vikings," we may well doubt the truth of the story. It is certain, however, that, through his marine he had considerable intercourse with the continent, to the great detriment of his subjects, "who learnt drunkenness from the Danes, effeminacy from the Flemings, and from the Saxons a disordered fierceness of mind."

From this period we hear but little of English vessels until the reign of Canute the Great, under whose wise rule, commerce had assumed such prominence, that, upon his decease, the merchants of London decided by their voice, the question of the succession in favor of Harold Harefoot, against Hardicanute, whom Earl Godwin and the people of Wessex would have preferred, "because Queen Emma, a favorite with the English, was his mother." In the time of Henry II. a law was passed requiring the justices of every county "to prohibit any one from buying or selling any ship to be carried out of England, or from sending or causing to be sent any mariner into foreign service," and, a few years later, Richard Cœur de Lion set sail for the Holy land, with a large fleet of war-vessels and transports which excited the admiration of all the crusaders, "for the completeness of its armament and the excellence of its mariners." That these marienrs were rather a turbulent set, however, is proved by the stringent laws found necessary for their government. "If any man killed another on board ship he was to be fastened to the dead body and thrown into the sea; if the crime were committed on shore, to be bound to the corpse and buried with it." The first case of tar and feathering, in the world's history, probably occurred during this expedition; for by the law, "a thief was to have his head shaved and covered with hot pitch, after which a bag filled with feathers was to be emptied over it." During the reign of John, it was decreed "that any ships of other nations, though at peace and in amity with England, should be made lawful prizes, if they refused to strike to the royal flag;" and a naval victory over the French was gained by John's fleet in the harbor of Damme. For a century after this a sort of piratical war raged between England and France, during which the coasts of both countries were continually pillaged by freebooters; but in 1340 a great naval battle was fought between the contending parties off Sluys, on the Flemish coast, in which the English, led by their Sovereign, Edward the Third, came off victorious, though with the loss of 6,000 men; the French loss in killed, wounded and prisoners being over twenty thousand, and nearly their whole force of three hundred vessels falling into the enemy's hands. This engagement, according to Charnock, was "the first wherein galleys and beaked vessels were totally laid aside, since, though the use of ships, as vessels of a different construction from galleys and depending mainly on sails for their propulsion, were then called, had been partially adopted for many years, yet in every preceding action which had taken place, they had been intermixed with the loftier vessels, built according to the newly introduced system. On board the latter the archers and slingers, supplying the place of the modern marines, were stationed near the prow and stern, the centre or midship was filled with the various engines then in use, contrived for the purpose of throwing darts and stones, which were not long afterwards supplanted by cannon."

In these vessels, oars were only used in calm weather or to assist the sails in turning to windward, yet the French, for many years after the battle of Sluys, continued to build galleys for particular service, such as the protection of their harbors, etc. The great victory gained by the English king was long the boast of his subjects, and it is said that when news of it reached the French Court, none of the courtiers of the reigning king, Philip of Valois, dared to tell him of it. "At length, however, Philip's jester, upon being informed that many of the French seamen had leaped overboard to avoid the arrows of the English, rushed into the presence crying out, 'Oh, the cowardly English! the faint-hearted English!' Whereupon the king enquiring, 'Why such cowards; what have they done?' 'Why?' replied he, 'for not daring to jump into the sea, as your Majesty's brave Frenchmen have done!'"

From this time there seems to have been no improvement in the British marine until the accession of Henry VII. to the kingdom in 1485, who saw the importance of having some ships of his own to be used solely as men-of-war, the vessels hitherto made use of by the sovereigns of England being a mere volunteer force, contributed by the various seaport towns of the kingdom, when an emergency made it necessary, and laid up, or employed in trade, as soon as the emergency was over.

Henry's largest vessel was the *Henri Grace a Dieu,* better known as the *Great Harry,* "which," says Charnock, "may without impropriety be termed the parent of the present British Navy, and, taking this view of it, it may perhaps prove interesting to seamen to have a full account of the ship in Charnock's own language.

"The representation of the Henry Grace a Dieu is preserved and transmitted to us by an original drawing in the Pepysian library at Magdalen college. This celebrated floating structure, the existence of which is recorded in many of the ancient chronicles, cost the King, by report, nearly fourteen thousand pounds, this will be found a very considerable sum, when we recollect the very high value money bore in those days. Very little description of its particular form is necessary, the singularity of it being sufficiently apparent in the annexed representation. From that we may learn the derivation of many terms preserved even to the present hour, though the parts consonant to those on which the names were first bestowed, have long since become so materially altered in their form, that without this, or some similar clue, we might be at a loss to trace the true cause of its first application, among these we may number the round-top, the yard-arm, and, rude as its form is in the painted record, and also perhaps in the original itself, the forecastle.

The invention of port-holes for cannon of the largest size then mounted on board ships was extremely recent; and the first use made of the contrivance was the introduction of a double tier. The same kind of attention was paid to the disposition of them that has ever since that time been uniformly practised, a circumstance which affords an undeniable proof that however improvement is admissible on most occasions, there are some inventions which defy the further power of human ingenuity, and burst forth, even at their very birth, in all the splendor of consummate perfection. Those guns which appear on the quarter and forecastle, were either sakers (five pounders) minions (four pounders) or falcons (two pounders) all which appear to have been mounted in a very different manner from those on the lower decks. Their ports were circular holes cut through the sides of the vessel, so small as scarcely to admit the guns being traversed in the smallest degree, or fired otherwise than straight forward. This fashion of circular ports prevailed in Britain, and other countries, till after the revolution; but they were latterly enlarged so as to obviate the principal inconvenience which at first attended the use of them. The same practice was observed with regard to such other small cannon as were intended for the defence of the ship's deck, in case the enemy proved successful in an attempt to board, and for that reason were mounted on the aftermost part of the forecastle. The two pieces of ordnance which appear one on each side of the rudder, being meant solely for de-

PLATE VII.

TAKEN FROM CHARNOCK

fence in case of pursuit from a superior foe, were very properly styled the stern-chase; these were of greater calibre and weight than any others in the ship, being either demi-cannon, nearly of the same bore with a modern thirty-two pounder, or cannon petronels, which were twenty-four pounders.

The masts were five in number, a usage which continued in the first-rates, without alteration till nearly the end of the reign of King Charles the First; thev were without division, in conformity with those which had been in unimproved use from the earliest ages. This inconvenience it was very soon found indispensably necessary to remedy, by the introduction of separate joints, or topmasts, which could be lowered in case of need, an improvement that tended to the safety of the vessel, which might very frequently, but for that prudent precaution, have been much endangered by the violence of the wind. The rigging was simple, and at first somewhat inadequate, even to those humble wants of our ancestors, which a comparison with the present state of naval tactics fairly permits us to call them; but the defects were gradually remedied as experience progressively pointed them out. Of the ornaments it is not necessary to say much, they being immaterial to those grander purposes which that wonderful piece of mechanism, called a ship, was intended to answer; they consisted of a multitude of small flags, disposed almost at random on different parts of the deck, or gunwale of the vessel, and one at the head of each mast. The standard of England was hoisted on that which occupied the center of the vessel; enormous pendants, or streamers were added, though an ornament which must have been very often extremely inconvenient. This mode of decoration was evidently borrowed and transferred from the galley.

Henry VIII. has the credit of having been the first sovereign in Europe to establish an order of officers who should be confined to the sea-service, without which there could be no real or lasting efficiency in his marine, and he built several "goodly ships." His first admiral was Sir Edward Howard with whom he made a written contract drawn up in due form and commencing thus:

"Henry VIII. anno regni tercis, anno Dom. 1512, sudentura inter Dominum Regem et Edwardum Howard, capitaneum generalem armatæ super mare, witnesseth, that the said Sir Edward is retained towards our said sovereign lord, to be his admiral in chief, and general captain of the army, which his highness hath proposed and ordained, and now setteth to the sea, for the safeguard and sure passage of his subjects, friends, allies, and confederates."

Sir Edward Howard is said to have been a brave soldier and skilful seaman, who held it as a maxim that "no sailor could be good for anything, unless he were resolute to a degree of madness."

He lost his life in an attempt to cut out six gallies and four foists in the bay of Conquet near Brest, and when he saw it was impossible to escape he took the whistle (the badge of his degree) from his neck and threw it into the sea, before he himself was borne overboard by the Frenchmen's pikes. And it is gratifying to know that Henry was "right sorry for his admiral's death."

Henry's own death took place in 1553, and more had been done for the improvement of the Navy in his than in any former reign. In this reign it was that a Navy office was formed, and that regular arsenals were established at Portsmouth, Woolwich, and Deptford. Henry is said to have greatly improved the models of his vessels, employing many Italian shipwrights in his service, and to have left to his successor, Edward the Sixth, a force of seventy-one vessels, thirty of which were ships, and the remainder small barks and row-barges of from one hundred to fifteen tons measurement. He had also two row-galleys. A few years after his death this force was greatly reduced, and the navy languished until the time of Queen Elizabeth, "who began to provide against war that she might the more quietly enjoy peace,—and was called the restorer of the glory of shipping, and queen of the North sea. And now the wealthier inhabitants of the sea-coast, in imitation of their princess, built ships of war, striving who should excel, insomuch that the queen's navy, joined with her subjects' shipping, was in a short time so puissant, that it was able to bring forth 20,000 fighting men for sea-service."

THE INVINCIBLE ARMADA !

Such, then, was the condition of British Naval affairs when the *Demon of the South*, as the Flemings not unnaturally styled Philip the Second, the man who from his closet in Madrid aspired to govern the world, and whose abhorrence of Protestantism was so intense, that he declared "if his own son were a heretic he would carry wood to burn him," projected the invasion of Protestant England. Secretly at first, but finally with the publicity which could no longer be avoided, "the patient letter-writer" set about providing the means necessary for the accomplishment of his purpose until every dockyard and arsenal of Spain resounded with the hum of a busy multitude laboring incessantly by night and by day. New ships were built and old ones repaired, and immense quantities of naval and military stores forwarded to the Netherlands, which was to serve as the base of supplies for the invaders; and the enormous wealth accruing to Philip, from the enthrálment of the New World, was poured out, like water, for the subjection of all that was free in the old. Rendezvous for the shipment of seamen were opened in every sea-board town, while throughout Philip's vast domain, there was not a hamlet so insignificant, nor a cottage so lonely but that the recruiting-sergeant made his way to it, in his eagerness to raise troops for the grand army, which, blessed by the Pope, and led by the famous Duke of Parma, was destined, it was confidently believed, to march in triumph through the streets of London, and, by one sweeping *auto da fe*, extirpate heresy from that accursed land, which every Spanish Catholic was taught to regard as the Devil's stronghold.

Volunteers, too, of every degree, and from every corner of Europe hastened to enlist under the banner of Castile. Of these many were religious bigots, impelled to this crusade against the English by fanatic zeal; a few, men of exalted character not unknown to fame; but by far the greater number needy adventurers seeking for spoil. At length, in April, 1588, after nearly three years of preparation, the army of invasion, 60,000 strong, was concentrated at Dunkirk and Newport, where flat-bottomed transports were made ready for its reception; but still the Armada, that was to convoy the transports, and cover the landing of the troops, on their arrival in England, loitered in Lisbon, waiting for a favorable wind. Toward the end of May, however, it moved out of the Tagus, by detachments, and passing the dangerous shoals called the Cachopos in safety, took its departure from Cape Roca, the Westernmost point of Portugal and of the continent of Europe, on the 1st of June, sailing with a light Southwesterly breeze due North. The fleet consisted in all of one hundred and thirty-two vessels, carrying 3165 guns, 21,639 soldiers, 8,745 seamen, and 2,088 galley-slaves; and its aggregate burden was not less than 65,000 tons.

The Saint Martin, a vessel of 50 guns belonging to the squadron furnished by Portugal, had the honor of wearing the flag of the Commander-in-Chief, the Duke of Medina Sidonia, a powerful and gallant nobleman, but one who had had no experience at sea, and, unfortunately for his country the Duke had surrounded himself with a staff of military men as utterly ignorant of naval affairs as their Chief. Making its way at an average rate of but about thirteen miles a day the unwieldy armada passed the Berlingas and Farilhoës islets, crept by Figuera, Oporto, and Vigo, and, finally, on the morning of the 19th of May, lay becalmed off Cape Finisterre. Up to this time, although the winds had been baffling, the weather had been pleasant and the sea as smooth as glass, but now the Spaniards were assailed by a tempest which might be called fearful even in the stormy bay of Biscay, and which, blowing fitfully, in heavy squalls, all day long, had by nightfall settled into a steady gale from W. N. W., driving before it a tremendous sea, whose surges broke with a roar distinctly heard above the fierce howling of the wind. Yet, though the sea ran high, it was not irregular, and the armada, on the port tack and under snug canvass, was still making good weather of it, when, a little after midnight, the wind suddenly shifted to Northeast, taking every ship under square sail flat aback, and blowing with the violence of a tornado. Some of the vessels, gathering sternboard, lost their rudders, some, thrown on their beam-ends, were forced to cut away their masts and throw overboard their batteries, while all lost their sails and top-hamper, and not a few even their upper deck cabins; so that when day dawned the melancholy spectacle presented itself of a whole fleet *adrift* on the ocean, many of whose noblest vessels were lying in the trough of the sea, which ever and anon made a clean breach over them, carrying many a poor fellow to his final home. But worst of all was the condition of the Diana, a huge Portuguese galley, which, knocked down at the first shift of wind, and with everything gone by the board, had not righted, but gradually filled with water, and was now fast settling by the stern. As the officers and men of the rest of the armada, forgetful of their own danger in their sympathy for their distressed comrades, gazed upon her, with throbbing hearts, she went down, with a great groan, like a living creature, carrying with her every soul on board. And next, as if to add to the horrors of the storm and shipwreck, a mutiny broke out among the rowers of the galley Vasana (a motley crew of Turks, Moors, and Christians), who had long been watching an opportunity to strike for freedom, and who now seeing their vessel to windward of all the armada with the exception of the Capitana, also a galley, which was more than a mile away from them, judged the occasion favorable for the accomplishment of their purpose. Led by a Welshman named David Gwynn, the mutineers attacked the sailors and soldiers of the Vasana whom they somewhat outnumbered, and who, taken by surprise, had no time to seize their arms, while each assailant snatched from his bosom, where it had long lain hid, a trusty stiletto. While this strife was going on, the commander of the Capitana had not been idle, but running as close to his consort as the heavy sea would permit, and finding her already in the hands of the intrepid Welshman, he poured a broadside into her, which made her very timbers quake, and filled her decks with dead and wounded men. At this moment, however, while engaged with the enemy from without, the crew of the Capitana found themselves threatened with a greater danger from within; for their own slaves (whether or not they had had previous notice of what was about to transpire aboard the Vasana, I have not been able to ascertain) now took a part in the engagement, and rushing upon their late masters and oppressors, with such weapons as they had beforehand provided or could seize at the moment, they attacked them with a fury and resolution that could not be withstood. The struggle for the mastery of the Capitana's deck was furious but brief, ending in the complete triumph of the galley-slaves, who, like their brothers of the Vasana, gave quarter neither to beardless youth nor hoary old age. After the massacre was over, the bodies of the unfortunates were consigned to the deep, and, the gale soon after abating, the Vasana and Capitana were run into Bayonne, France, where Gwynn, according to Motley, was graciously received by Henry of Navarre, while the crippled armada, despoiled of three of its finest galleys, made its way, as best it could, to the various sea-ports distributed along the northern coast of Spain. Corunna having been named, however, in the sailing directions of its squadron commanders, as the rendez-

PLATE VIII.

TAKEN FROM CHARNOCK

vous in case of separation, it soon concentrated there, whence, after a month spent in repairing damages, it sailed on the 22d of July for Calais.

Favored with fair winds and fine weather, the Spaniards struck soundings in the English channel, on the 28th, and on the afternoon of the following day, sighted and were seen from the Lizard, when all England became aware that the danger which had long threatened was at hand, and prepared resolutely to meet it. The British fleet was lying off Plymouth at the time, and the wind was blowing directly into the harbor; but its commander-in-chief, Lord Howard of Effingham, the Lord High Admiral of England, was equal to the emergency, and before day dawned on the following morning, sixty-seven of his best ships had been kedged into deep water, and, led by such men as Drake, Frobisher and Hawkins, were keeping a sharp lookout for the Spaniards off the Eddystone rock, while every hour a half dozen or more vessels were added to the number. All the forenoon the wind was light and the weather thick; but towards evening, a fine southwesterly breeze lifting the misty curtain that lay between them, the hostile fleets had a full view of each other.

The Armada, in splendid battle array, in the form of a half moon, and in such compact order that its flanking vessels were separated by a distance of but seven miles, was steering steadily up the channel and with its frowning cannon of much heavier calibre than anything the English carried, presented so formidable an appearance that the Lord Admiral at once saw that he could not successfully confront it. He, therefore, permitted it to pass him without firing a shot, but hung upon its rear, watching an opportunity to cut off any of its vessels which should chance to drop astern of the others. It was not until the next day, however, Sunday, July 31st, that an opportunity offered for attacking to advantage. Then "sending a pinnace before him, called the Defiance to denounce war against the enemy by the discharge of all her guns," Howard immediately opened fire from his own ship, the Ark-Royal, on a large galleon, commanded by Don Alphonso de Leyva which he took to be the Admiral's ship, while the combined squadrons of Drake, Frobisher and Hawkins cannonaded furiously the fleet of Biscay, which, consisting of fourteen vessels, carrying 302 guns, and commanded by Vice Admiral Recalde, an officer of great experience, had been formed into a rear guard, in anticipation of an attack from that quarter. Recalde maintained the unequal fight with great obstinacy for some hours, all the while endeavoring to get within small arm range of the English, which he knew would be fatal to them, since he had a large force of arquebusiers in his division; but his wary antagonists whose vessels "light, weatherly and nimble, sailed six feet to the Spaniards two and tacked twice to their once" evaded every effort to close, and keeping at "long taw," inflicted much injury on their enemy without receiving the slightest themselves. At length, however, the Duke of Medina Sidonia signalled to Recalde to join the main body of the fleet, and hoisting the royal standard of Spain at his main, drew out his whole force in order of battle, and endeavored to bring on a general engagement; but this Howard prudently avoided; and so the Spaniards had to keep on their course again up channel, and "maintain a running fight of it," the English now, as before, hanging on their rear, and receiving re-enforcements every hour from their sea-port towns, in full view of which, as the Armada hugged the English shore, Howard and his gallant men were passing.

But the night that followed was one fraught with disaster to the Spaniards; for the gunner of the Santa Ana, a Fleming by birth, who had been reprimanded by his captain for neglect of duty, in revenge, laid a train to the magazine, and blew the whole of the after part of the ship up, with more than half her officers and crew. The vessels nearest to the Santa Ana hurried to the assistance of the survivors, and, in the confusion that ensued, a couple of galleys fell foul of the flag-ship of the Andalusian squadron, and carried away her foremast close to the deck, so that she dropped astern of the Armada, and, the night being dark, was soon lost sight of by her friends and assailed by her enemies. Being well manned and carrying 50 guns she was enabled to maintain the defensive until day dawned, when, finding the English hemming her in on all sides, Don Pedro de Valdez, whose flag she carried, gave orders to her commander to strike to Drake in the Revenge, which was presently done, much to the chagrin of Frobisher and Hawkins, who had hoped to make prize of her themselves. Drake received Don Pedro very courteously, and kept him with him until the 10th of August, so that the Spaniard was an eye-witness of all the subsequent operations of the hostile fleets and of the final discomfiture of his countrymen; but the immediate commander of the surrendered vessel, was spared this humiliation, since Drake "sent him prisoner to Dartmouth and left the money on board the prize to be plundered by his men."

All the next day was spent by the Duke in re-arranging his fleet, and, after its various vessels had taken the places assigned them, each captain was strictly enjoined in written orders, not to leave his station under penalty of death. In this new order the rear-guard was increased to forty-three vessels, and placed under Don Alfonso de Leyva, who had orders to avoid skirmishing as much as possible, but not to lose any opportunity that might offer for bringing on a decisive battle.

On the 2d of August, at daylight, the wind shifted to the northeast, whereupon the Spaniards, being to windward, bore down upon the English under full sail; but the latter, squaring away and refusing, as before, to let their assailants close with them, the engagement was without result, there being but little loss on the side of the Spaniards, and "one Mr. Cock," according to Burchett, "being the only

15

Englishman who fell, whilst he was bravely fighting against the enemy in a small vessel of his own."

Towards evening the wind backed to west, and the Armada continued its course for Calais. On the 3d of August there was a cessation of hostility on both sides, and the Lord High Admiral received a supply of powder and ball, and a re-enforcement of ships, " whereupon he determined to attack the enemy in the dead of the ensuing night; but was prevented by a calm."

On the 4th of August, however, one of the Spanish ships not being able to keep up with the rest was made a prize of by the English. This brought on a sharp engagement between the Spanish rear-guard and the English advance, under Frobisher, which would have resulted in Frobisher's capture had not Howard himself gone to the rescue, in the Ark-Royal, "followed by the Lion, the Bear, the Bull and the Elizabeth, and a great number of smaller vessels."

The fighting for a while was severe; but as soon as Frobisher was relieved, Howard, observing that the Duke was approaching with the main body of the Spanish fleet, prudently gave the order to retire. It was indeed high time, for his own vessel was so badly crippled that she had to be towed out of action; and, although he took occasion afterward to knight the Lord Thomas Howard, the Lord Sheffield, Roger Townsend, Hawkins and Frobisher, for their gallantry on this occasion, it was determined at a Council of War "not to make any further attempt upon the enemy until they should be arrived in the Straits of Dover, where the Lord Henry Seymour and Sir William Winter were lying in wait for them,"—a very convincing proof that the English were worsted in the encounter.

So the Armada kept on its way unmolested, before " an easy gale at S.W. by S.," past Hastings and Dungeness, until it got to the north of the Varne, when, leaving the English coast, it hauled up for Calais Roads, where it anchored on the afternoon of Saturday, August 6th, close in to shore, with the castle of the town bearing from its centre due east; and not two miles away was the English fleet, which now came to anchor also, and, strengthened by the accession of Seymour's and Winter's squadrons, numbered not less than a hundred and forty sail, "all stout ships, though the main stress of battle lay not upon more than fifteen of them."

Since his arrival in English waters the Duke had not suffered a day to pass without despatching a messenger across the Channel to France, and thence by land, to the Duke of Parma, to advise him of the Armada's approach and to impress upon him the necessity of his being ready to make his descent upon England the moment it reached Calais, and, especially, he desired him to send to him with all despatch pilots for the French and Flemish coasts, which no one in the fleet, he declared, had the slightest knowledge of.

It was, then, with a feeling of bitter disappointment that, upon reaching Calais, he found not a single transport awaiting his arrival.

All that night and the following day, Aug. 7th, the vast fleet lay idly at anchor, vainly watching for the coming of Parma's army, whose egress from Newport and Dunkirk was simply an impossibility, since the fleets of Holland and Zealand were in full possession of all the narrow channels between Newport and Hils Banks and the Flemish shore, and Parma had not a single vessel of war to oppose to them.

As the sun went down on the evening of the 7th, behind a thick bank of clouds, the anxiety of the *seamen* of the fleet grew more and more intense: for they, at least, recognized fully the insecurity of their anchorage,, whence a northwesterly gale, such as then might be looked for at any instant, would be sure to drive them pell-mell upon the treacherous quick-sands under their lee.

While such was the state of mind of the watchers on board the Armada, the English themselves were full of apprehensions lest Parma's transports, eluding the vigilance of the

Dutch cruisers, should, at any moment, heave in view, but noticing the threatening appearance of the sky, and listening to the surf on the shore, which to their experienced eyes and ears forboded a storm, they became reassured, and, a little before midnight of the 7th,—the weather being so thick that objects could not be discerned at any distance, and the current then setting towards their enemies,—they prepared to send into their midst eight fire-ships which they had all day long been preparing. The honor of having originated this project has been assigned to various persons, but, in truth, there was but little honor to be derived from it, since from the earliest antiquity it had been the custom among seamen to send fire-ships and fire-rafts among the enemy's vessels whenever they found them, as in this instance, huddled closely together. The coolness of Young and Prouse, however, in towing them into position is, certainly, worthy of all admiration, and contrasts strongly enough with the Spaniard's want of pluck on this occasion, whose panic terror must, however, be ascribed to the presence among them of certain artillerymen who, at Antwerp, three years before, had witnessed the explosion of a floating mine, constructed by an Italian engineer named Giannibelli, "which had seemed to rend asunder both the earth and the air," and doomed to instant destruction more than a thousand veterans, among whom, was "that much lamented cavalry general, the Marquis of Rouvaise." These soldiers knowing that the man of "diabolical imagination" was then in the service of England, no sooner saw the fire-ships, "all alight with flame from their kelsons to their mast-heads," drifting down upon them, than they imagined that Giannibelli himself was in their midst; and wringing their hands and shouting wildly each to the other, "Giannibelli! Giannibelli! we are lost! we are lost!" they distributed the contagion of their fear throughout the fleet. Amid this "hideous clamor" the Duke of Medina Sidonia, who had been warned by Philip to be on his guard against any attempt "on the part of *Drake* to burn his vessels," with perfect self-possession made the signal agreed upon, "to cut cables and stand clear of the danger," and in a few minutes the Armada was under sail and out of harm's way; but the "confusion and fright" among its various vessels continued all night through, so that when about 4 A. M., the Duke fired a gun for the fleet to rally, and return to its anchorage, "its report was not heard by many, their fears having so dispersed them that some had got a considerable distance out to sea, and others among the shoals on the coast of Flanders."

When the day "dawned with fresh southwesterly squalls," some of the Spanish vessels were observed by the English to be in a crippled condition and drifting to leeward, while the St. Lawrence, flag-ship of the squadron of galleasses—a class of vessels that had contributed so powerfully to the glories of Lepanto—was endeavoring to get into the harbor of Calais. Her rudder was gone, and notwithstanding that her rowers were doing their utmost to keep her in the narrow channel leading to the town, she yawed wildly across it, from time to time, and finally grounded on a sand bank within a few hundred yards of the castle. In this helpless condition she was attacked by the boats of the British fleet, and after a brave resistance, during which many fell on both sides, boarded and carried. As she was directly under the guns of the castle, however, the governor of Calais claimed her "as of right pertaining to him," and so, the English contenting themselves with such plunder as they could obtain on board of her, and mindful of the good political and military maxim "not to carry on two wars at once," wisely withdrew to their ships. They were no sooner returned, than Howard bore up for the Armada, which was overtaken off Gravelines, sailing in double echelon with its flanks protected "by the three remaining galleasses and by the great galleons of Portugal."

The Duke at once came by the wind with the signal for close action—the royal standard flying at his fore;

but the English having *handiness*, speed, and the weather-gage in their favor were enabled, as on former occasions, to choose their own distance for engaging, and after a desultory but hot fight of six hours, the Duke, finding that a large number of his men were slain, three of his best ships sunk, and many more placed *hors de combat*, while there was not a single shot left in his locker, nor the slightest chance of his bringing his wary antagonist Howard within boarding distance "or of Parma's coming out to join him," reluctantly telegraphed to the fleet "to make its way to Spain, north about the British isles," and kept away for the North sea. With the sands of Zealand threatening him on the one hand, and on the other the legitimate sons of Neptune, the odds, indeed, were too greatly against him, and the chivalrous Spaniard had no resource left to him but retreat. That night "a double-reefed topsail breeze" came out from the north, and the next day some of the Spanish vessels were in such close proximity to a dangerous shoal called the Oovst bank that their enemies, who were still following them, each instant expected to see them take the ground; but a favorable change of wind extricating them from their perilous position, they once more steered for the open sea, with squared yards and all their canvas spread. The English kept after them until Friday, August 12th, when being themselves out of ammunition and their provisions falling short besides, they determined "to wrestle no further pull," and coming by the wind, stood back to the land, which, when it received the glad tidings brought by the Lord High Admiral might truly be called "merry England."

It has been asserted "on the authority of certain Dutch fishermen," that Medina Sidonia so much dreaded the passage, "around the grim Hebrides," that he was on the point of surrender to Howard when he approached him last, but was dissuaded from doing so by the ecclesiastics on board his vessel; but this story, as well as the one told by the Spanish soldiers, who were taken prisoners in the fight of

August 8th, and who wished to curry favor with their captors, that this fight "far exceeded the battle of Lepanto," may safely be classed with the marvellous narrations of the "intelligent contraband" and "the reliable gentleman just from Richmond," so often brought to the front during the great civil war in America.

Why indeed should the Duke have surrendered to a force unable to fire a shot at him, and which, had it ventured within boarding distance of the Armada, must inevitably have fallen into his hands? Was not the St. Matthew, when assailed in a sorely crippled condition by the squadron under Van des-Dus, defended by her commander for two long hours, and did not several Spanish vessels, refusing to strike when they were in a sinking condition, go down with their colors flying? Was then the commander-in-chief less courageous, than his subordinates? Let the truth be told. Medina Sidonia, from his want of experience at sea, was utterly disqualified to command the great fleet intrusted to his care; but Spain possessed no braver man than he.

The history of the Armada, after Howard parted company with it, is one of shipwreck and disaster,* many of its vessels being lost on the coasts of Scotland and Ireland, and many foundering at sea, while of its squadron leaders—men of high rank and reputation—but few lived to return to their native land; so that when the Duke reached Santander in October, with all that was left of his command, less than half of its original strength, and the whole measure of the calamity that had befallen the nation became known throughout Spain, there was hardly a family in the land but went into mourning for the loss of one or more of its members, "insomuch that king Philip was forced by proclamation to shorten the usual time for the same as the Romans of old, upon their great defeat at Canna, found it necessary to limit the public grief to thirty days."

* For a full and circumstantial account of the frightful sufferings of the Spaniards on their homeward bound voyage, see Froude, vol. xii. ch. xxxvi.

A merchant of Lisbon, however, who was imprudent enough to express some joy at the misfortunes of the conquerors of his people, was immediately hanged by Philip's order. "Thus," says Motley, "men remarked that one could neither cry nor laugh within the Spanish domains."

The Catholic world was much puzzled to know how a fleet, which had been blessed by the Pope, could have so signally failed of accomplishing its object; but the Spanish priests solved the enigma, when they discovered that it was all owing to Drake, who had sold himself to the devil on condition of being allowed to triumph over the Spaniards; and it was a source of infinite satisfaction to all pious Catholics, when, upon Drake's departing this life, a few years later (1596), off Porto Bello, they were assured that his soul, without stopping at purgatory, had taken the most direct route to hell. Their pleasure was still further enhanced when in 1602, Lope de Vega, who had served in the Armada, published his poem called *La Dragontea*, wherein Christianity, in the form of a beautiful woman, prays to God to protect Spain, Italy and America from he reticsin general, and from, "that Protestant Scotch pirate," * in particular. But a more reasonable explanation of the cause of the Pope's failure in this instance, would seem to a Protestant mind to be in the fact that His Holiness had altogether forgotten when he so liberally bestowed, the British channel upon his favorites, that the refractory Howard was *bishop of that diocese.* The *Saints*, it is true, were all on the side of the Spaniards, and the greater part of them were actually in the Armada; but it is not to be presumed that they were then, more than now, a match for the ungodly Bulls and Bears of England.

It was without doubt most unfortunate for those who sailed in the luckless Armada, that its first commander-in-chief, the celebrated Don Alvaro de Bazan, one of the most famous seamen of his day, should have died just before it was

* History of Spanish Literature, vol. ii., p. 141. Ticknor—Southey.

ready to sail fron Lisbon, for he certainly could have taken better care of it in storm and in battle than the inexperienced Duke of Medina Sidonia, who had nothing but his rank and riches to recommend him ; and if, as is reported, a fisherman informed the Duke as he approached Plymouth, that more than one half of Howard's fleet was then lying wind-bound in that harbor, he certainly lost a chance of destroying that part of it, through a too strict adherence to Philip's orders, which it is not probable the great Marquis of Santa Cruz would have thrown away. It was, then, most unfortunate, I repeat, that the Armada should have exchanged "for an iron admiral" a "general of gold;" but the man whom impartial history will ever hold responsible for the greatest naval *fiasco* of modern times, is Philip the Second, the bigot, who, rejecting the sage advice of the Duke of Parma and the Marquis of Santa Cruz, "to get possession of some secure port in North Flanders before attempting to cross to England," took it upon himself to arrange the minutest details of the expedition, trusting, perhaps, to his patron saint to guide him concerning naval and military matters, of which he seems to have known as little as a child ; and, worst of all, he, the author of the national humiliation, either was, or affected to be, entirely indifferent to it, dismissing it from his mind with the puerile remark, "I sent my ships to strive with men, not with the elements."

And well might "all England rejoice" when the full news of the series of disasters which had befallen the Armada at last reached her shores ; for through the obstinacy of Philip, England had escaped a great danger ; and wisely she profited by the lesson it had taught her, "to set to work vigorously to build up a potent navy," since her safety from aggression must ever mainly depend upon the superiority of her fleet over that of any other power. But should the day ever come, as seems not unlikely, when, through a coalition of unfriendly states, another armada more powerful than her own shall be assembled in British waters, while a great army, such as but lately reduced France, in a few weeks, almost to the condition of a German province, shall be ready, under its protection, to embark for *anxious* England, let us hope that we, the people of the United States, will not remain neutral in the strife; but that, casting aside all petty jealousies, and remembering only the priceless boon of civil and religious liberty which has come to us from the "mother country"—our common language and our common freedom,—we may hasten to her in her hour of need, and that "the gorgeous ensign of the republic, with not a stripe erased, nor a single star obscured, will then be found *not* as a British writer has chosen to picture it, in such an emergency, arrayed against the banner of Saint George, but, in friendly greeting, waving side by side with it—its stars for England, its stripes for England's foes!

Through steam and the *weather reports*, the transportation of a large army across the British channel would now be a *certain* matter of a few hours.

APPENDIX.

Illi robur et aes triplex
Circa pectus erat, qui fragilem truci
Commisit pelago ratem
Primus, etc., etc.

Hor. Ode iii.

[2] A la sixième année (sin mao) avant J. C., des personnes de Touet-chang, un royaume maritime du sud, vinrent apporter des faisans blancs. Tcheon Koung leur fit présent de chars qui montraient le sud. On sera peut-être surpris de voir que le *Char Magnétique* des Chinois et leur boussole marine montrent le sud tandis que la propriété de l'Aiguille aimantée est de se tourner vers le *Nord* avec plus ou moins de déclinaison ; mais on cessera de l'être si l'on refléchit que les premières applications qui furent faites par les Chinois de cette attraction incompréhensible, étaient pour indiquer le sud ; on trouvera tout simple que, tout en reconnaissant que l'Aiguille aimantée était attirée vers le pôle *Nord*, ils aient affecté au pôle opposé, qui n'est que la continuation de l'axe, une figure saillante pour indiquer le pôle *sud*, et le nom *d'indiquant le sud* (*tchi nan*), sera resté à toutes les applications du principe une fois reconnu, avec le signe indicatif affecté à l'extrémité sud de l'aiguille.—*Pauthier.*

[3] This shield, according to Wilkinson, also served as an *umbrella.*

[4] Jal is of the opinion that instead of reefing, the Egyptians substituted a small sail for a large one, in heavy weather.

[5] An amusing instance of the folly of men, however learned, attempting to describe naval manœuvres, without ever having trod the deck of a vessel at sea, is given us in Dr. Smith's translation of the Peloponnesian war, where after stating that the Corinthians "slackened their course" etc., etc., he adds, in a note: "The original is *πρυμναν εκρουοντο,* they knocked the hind deck, a phrase elegantly applied by Thucydides, to those that retreat fighting, and still facing their enemies. It was done by running their ships backwards upon their hind decks, in order to tack about." In support of this nonsense, he refers to the archæology of Archbishop Potter, who it is safe to say, knew no more of the matter than he did.

Another translator, according to Charnock, misinterpreting the meaning of the words *quatuor foros* (four decks), has gravely informed us that Ptolemy's great ship had four *Markets!*

[6] Translation of J. Talboys Wheeler, in his interesting work *entitled The Geography of Herodotus.*

[7] Les anciens avaient des navires dédiés aux dieux, et que les Grecs nommaient Théogides.—En Egypte, c'était le vaisseau consacré à Isis. Des figures emblématiques ornaient les côtés de ce bâtiment qu'avaient construit les plus habiles ouvriers ; sur la voile étaient écrits en gros caractères les vœux qu'on renouvelait chaque année pour les navigateurs. Lorsqu'on l'avait purifié avec une torche ardente, des œufs et du soufre, les prêtres et le peuple, dit Apulée, allaient y déposer des corbeilles remplies de fleurs, et tout ce qui servait aux sacrifices. Puis on levait l'ancre, et l'on abandonnait le navire, qu'on laissait voguer au gré du vent et des flots, pour aller dans le temple d'Isis conjurer la déesse d'être propice aux marins. Les Egyptiens considéraient aussi comme sacré le navire sur lequel on nourrissait, pendant quarante jours, le bœuf Apis, avant de le conduire à Memphis dans le temple de Vulcain.—En Grèce, les navires sacrés les plus renommés furent : l'Argo, qui fut même déifié et placé au nombre des constellations; la Salaminienne, galère de trente rames que montait Thésée lorsqu'il se rendit en Crète, et qui prit ensuite le nom de Déliarque, parce qu'elle allait porter tous les ans à Délos les offrandes des Athéniens ; le Parale, dont l'origine est inconnue ; l'Antigone, le Démétrius et le navire de Minerve. Ce dernier ne prenait jamais la mer ; on le conservait religieusement près du lieu où l'Aréopage tenait ses séances; il ne paraissait qu'à la fête des grandes Panathénées, qui se célébrait tous les cinq ans, et servait à porter en grande pompe au temple de Minerve le peplum de la déesse (Suidas). Mais ce qu'on admirait le plus, selon Pausanias, c'est que ce navire était mis en mouvement par certains ressorts cachés dans ses flancs. Les Romains avaient la plus grande vénération pour les navires qui avaient transporté dans leur ville la Bonne Déesse et le dieu Esculape. On célébrait aussi à Rome la fête du vaisseau d'Isis ; "Certus dies habetus in fastis, quo Isidis navigium celebratur" (Lactance). Ciceron parle d'une autre fête du même genre, qu'il nomme la première navigation ; Vegèce en fait mention, sous le nom de la naissance de la navigation. Histoire de la marine, par A. Du Sein.

[8] Mnesephilus, a man of "strong common sense," was a professor of wisdom at Athens before the Persian war, and Plutarch says Themistocles attended his lectures and entertained a great regard for him.

[9] I use the beautiful, spirited translation of Plumptre.

[10] It is difficult to arrive at any definite conclusion as to what the intentions of Themistocles really were. It is not impossible, indeed, that

he may himself have thought the Grecian cause lost, and have wished to ingratiate himself with Xerxes, by actually delivering the Greeks into his hands. His ruling passion, it must be remembered, was avarice, which, when it gets entire possession of a man, becomes a vice that will lead him to sacrifice any and everything to its gratification. His sophistry did not clear him in the opinion of his contemporaries from all complicity with Pausanias in his treasonable designs; and, certainly the man who, after Salamis, could propose to the Athenians the aggrandizement of their state by burning the Confederate fleet at Pagasæ, had a despicably mean *heart*, however great his brain. Herodotus accuses him of duplicity in his speech to the Athenians, after the battle of Salamis, dissuading them from sailing at once to the Hellespont to intercept Xerxes in his retreat. "He spoke thus," says the historian, "to secure favor with the Persians, that, if any misfortune should overtake him from the Athenians, he might have a place of refuge," etc., etc.

[11] Nothing is more to be regretted than the loss of the Persian account of the battle of Salamis, which, creditable as it was to the Greeks, was not, we may reasonably suppose, quite as one-sided an affair as they would have us believe.

[12] That the Romans had turned their attention to naval affairs before this is well known, however; for during their second war with the Samnites, 300 B.C., two commissioners for naval affairs were appointed, and twenty-two years afterward, a Roman squadron presuming to enter the Gulf of Tarentum, was attacked by the Tarentines and defeated, with a loss of four ships taken and one sunk. Polybius, in his anxiety to impress his readers with the greatness of the Roman people in overcoming obstacles, has certainly given an exaggerated picture of their maritime weakness at the breaking out of the first Punic war.

[13] "To the Romans," says Gibbon, "the ocean remained an object of horror rather than of curiosity, and they tried to disguise, by the pretence of religious awe, their ignorance and terror." See Tacitus, Germania 34.

[14] The Triarii, according to Livy, formed, as their name would imply, the third rank of an army; but Polybius states that they were embarked on this occasion with the fourth naval division, and remarks: *Triarii is the name which is appropriated to the last division of the armies upon land.*

[15] Cæsar, when he left his tent before day, to review his fleet, met a man who was driving an ass. Upon asking his name, the man answered: "My name is *Eutychus* (Good Fortune), and the name of my ass is *Nicon*" (Victory). The place where he met him was afterward adorned with trophies of the beaks of ships, and there Augustus placed the statue of the ass and his driver in brass.—*Plutarch.*

[16] According to Pliny, Terentius Varro, who served under Pompey

against the pirates, was the first Roman who received a rostral crown. It was of gold, and ornamented with figures resembling the beaks of ships.

NOTES TO THE BATTLE OF LEPANTO.

[1] "In his maris angustiis, postquam binœ classes ex improviso sese conspexissent, pugnam devitare nequaquam potuerunt. Quamobrem Joannes Austriacus, Imperator, cum prius consultandum quam in certamen descenderent quidam ex suis afferet, prudentissimæ respondit: Jam ne que tempus, neque locum nobis consiliis superesse," etc.—*Contareni.* (Latin version of Joan Nicolao Stupano, published in 1573.)

[2] Neither La Fuente nor Prescott make the slightest mention of this important division, while Rosell (Combate Naval de Lepanto, p. 101) says it hardly deserved the name of a reserve, and yet Stupano's translation, under the heading *Subsidiorum Agmen*, gives the name of each of the captains of its *thirty* vessels.

[3] La Fuente, vol. vii., p. 278.

[4] Preble.

[5] Bouet. Willaumez, *Batailles de terre et de mer.*

[6] "Christus enim e cœlis descensurum quod pro ipsius nomine pugnarent."—*Contareni.*

Among the many miraculous occurrences of the battle of Lepanto, that of the crucifix, as gravely narrated by Rosell, *on the authority of pious tradition*, is the most remarkable. In the heat of the action, a ball was flying right at the image of Christ, when the image avoided it, by inclining to one side, as if in the act of leaving the cross (*come en actitud de apartarse de la cruz*), and in this position it is still to be seen, behind the great altar of the cathedral of Barcelona.

[7] Prescott, following Herrera, says: "Barbarigo, who was still lingering in agony, heard the tidings of the enemy's defeat, and uttering a few words expressive of his gratitude to Heaven, which had permitted him to see this hour, he breathed his last."

This is surely an error; for Contareni, being a Venetian senator, must have had access to all the official reports, and have enjoyed, beside, a personal acquaintance with the Barbarigo family, and he says expressly that when Barbarigo was wounded he at once lost the use of speech. "Augustinus Barbadicus autem sagitta oculo infixa, lœtale vulnus accepit *quo loquendi usum statim* amisit."

[8] Contareni.

[9] Prescott evidently attaches but little importance to the possession by the Christians of these mammoth war vessels; for, after speaking of their first fire upon the *passing* fleet, he says: "they were, however, but un-

wieldy craft, and having accomplished their object seem to have taken no further part in the combat." Without a Turkish reserve to look after these troublesome ships, this was probably the best way to get rid of them; but that not *all* of them were "towed into action," as he supposes, is shown by Rosell, p. 97, and that they were not "unwieldy" is clearly proved by Contareni, page 134 of the translation, where, after a graphic description of the *terrific effect* of their fire upon the Turks, we read: "Eoque res maximé admiratione digna fuit quod sola sex magna illæ triremes, quarum usus in hujusmodi navalibus præliis compertus minimé fuerat, *sese* in *orbem vertentes*, et tela modò ex prora modò ex puppi et lateribus vibrantes, tautam hostium stratagem edere potuerint." Summing up the causes which led to the utter defeat of the Turks at Lepanto, Rosell concludes with: "Por ultimo, los Turcos ninguna especie de embarcacion podian oponer a la furia destructora de las *galeazas de Venecia*," etc.

From Pantero-Pantera we learn that the galeasses had a large oar or sweep on each quarter to assist their rudders in turning. *Hanno il timone alla navaresca, cioè ad uso de nave, e ai fianchi del timone portano due gran remi che aiutano a fargirare il vascello piu presto.—Armata navale.*

Burchett, in his "Complete History of the most Remarkable Transactions at Sea," remarks, "At the first discharge of the galeasses several of the Turkish galleys quitted the line; nevertheless they kept on their way, but in passing between them, were cruelly battered from their broadsides, etc. Some ships were shot through and through, others had their rudders struck off, several were seen in flames, and some deserted by their companies, who, in despair leaped into the sea, which was covered with floating oars, masts, yards, casks, and men. Such great execution did these galeasses do among the enemy, which was a contrivance as successful as it was new."

And as a further proof of the great service rendered by the galeasses at Lepanto, we may quote La Fuente, the greatest of Spanish historians (vol. vii., p. 416), who, although he makes but slight mention of them in his account of that battle, afterward in speaking of the fitting out of the Invincible Armada, says: *En los puertos de Amberes, de Nieuport etc., se habian construido y aperejado navios de varias formas y tamaños, galeones y galeazas, al modo de aquellas que en Lepanto contribuyeron tau poderosamente a la victoria de la Santa Liga.*

Charnock (vol. ii., p. 23) says there were four galeasses in the Armada—a pretty good proof that the Spaniards thought well of them—and Paul Hoste chronicles the performance of one of them thus: "Moncade fut jeté avec sa Galère sur les côtes de Calais, où ayant été attaqué par un grand nombre de frégates Anglaises, il se défendit comme un lion, etc."

For a full account of the construction, armament, etc., of these vessels, which were *marvels* in their day, see Jal Archeologie Navale, vol. i., pp. 385–396.

[10] Uluch Ali ayant laissé Doria au large, s'était jeté sur notre corps de bataille et y avait fait en peu de temps un grand ravage ; mais, craignant que Doria ne le prît par derrière, il se retira de la mêlée avec trente galères, qui seules échappèrent d'une défaite si générale. (Paul Hoste, p. 23.)

[11] Portandolo a' don Giovanni, con pensiero di portar alcuna cosa, gratissima dalchele con dispiacere glifia risposto—" Che voni ch' io faccia di cotesto capo? horgettalo in mare !" con tutto cio per ispatio d' un hora stalle fisso in una punta di picca alla poppa.

Caraccioli-Comentarii delle guerre fatte con Turchi.

[12] Paul Hoste.

[13] La Fuente.

[14] Ib.

[15] " The present which you sent me," says Don Juan, in his reply to Fatima, which is worthy of being printed in letters of gold, " I return with your brother. Not because I do not prize it as coming from your hands, but because it does not comport with the greatness of my ancestry (*la grandeza de mis antecesores*) to receive gifts of one who asks a favor at my hands." See Rosell and La Fuente.

[16] Asi supo ilustrar el hijo de Carlos V. un nombre que, sin la batalla de Lepanto, solo viviria en la historia para prueba de la debilidad de aquel monarca. Su triunfo no fué obra del acaso ; lo solicitó con vivo anhelo, lo intentó contra la opinion de capitanes experimentados, lo previnó con acertadas disposiciones lo obtuvó en fin combatiendo como candillo prudente y valereso. Rosell, p. 125.

In the Church of Our Lady of Pilau, at Barcelona, is the staff of command (*baston de mando*) which Don Juan carried in his hand on the memorable 7th of October. On it in letters of silver are these inscriptions: *Act Godt ongestvort geeft den prince dat hemto ebenvort* (keep God on your side and you will do great deeds.) *Versmaet suget trement soe Wesdy vanden heerenyet de kent.* (Fear the power of God and you will avoid his judgments.)

NOTES TO SCANDINAVIA.

In referring to Snorro Sturleson's work, I have used almost exclusively the fine translation of Laing.

[1] The " long-ships " of the Baltic were evidently only intended for rowing along shore. That they were not intended for sea voyages is shown by Snorro, who, in describing the Long Serpent, says, " she had

sides as high as a *sea-going* ship's. Snorro says, too, that when Olaf the saint found it necessary to return to Norway from England, in the fall of the year, he "made ready *two ships of burden* and left *his long ships behind.*

[2] Knikarr—Conqueror or hard-hitter.

[3] Buss—A vessel built for the herring or salt trade exclusively.

[4] Shield of expectation. When a young warrior was first enlisted they gave him a white and smooth buckler which was called "the shield of expectation." this he carried till by some signal exploit he had obtained leave to have proofs of his valor engraven on it etc.

Northern Antiquities, translated from the French of M. Mallet, by Bishop Percy.

[5] The Væringers (defenders) were the body-guard of the Greek emperors, and were composed mostly of Norsemen "With their broad and double battle-axes on their shoulders," says Gibbon, "they attended the emperor to the temple, the senate, and the hippodrome; and the keys of the palace, the treasury, and the capitol, were held by their firm and faithful hands."

[6] At the last day the sea rushes over the earth and in this flood floats the ship Naglfar, constructed of the nails of dead men. For which reason great care should be taken to die with pared nails ; for he who dies with his nails unpared supplies materials for the building of this vessel, which both gods and men wish may be finished as late as possible.

Prose Edda.

[7] The Danes had a famous enchanted standard, in the 9th century also, according to Hume, in which they placed great confidence. "It contained the figure of a raven, which had been inwoven by the three sisters of Hingvard and Hubba, with many magical incantations," etc. It was called *Reafen*, and captured at the battle of Kinwith Castle, by Alfred the Great, the Danes flying in the utmost consternation when they beheld their banner in the possession of the English.

[8] Y si fuera asi, como lo dice Gomara, harto malos cristianos fuéramos, enviandonos nuestro Señor Dios sus Santos Apóstoles, no reconocer la gran merced que uos hacia y reverenciar cada dia aquella iglesia; y pluguiera á Dios que asi fuera como elee coronista dice, y hasta que lei su Corónica, nunca entre conquistadores que alli se hallaron tal se oyó. Verdadera Historia, etc.

[9] The Gjallar-horn was the *last trumpet* of the Scandinavians.

Jeffers' Nautical Surveying.

Illustrated with 9 Copperplates and 31 Wood-cut Illustrations. 8vo. Cloth. $5.00.

NAUTICAL SURVEYING. By WILLIAM N. JEFFERS, Captain U. S. Navy.

Many books have been written on each of the subjects treated of in the sixteen chapters of this work; and, to obtain a complete knowledge of geodetic surveying requires a profound study of the whole range of mathematical and physical sciences; but a year of preparation should render any intelligent officer competent to conduct a nautical survey.

CONTENTS.—Chapter I. Formulæ and Constants Useful in Surveying II. Distinctive Character of Surveys. III. Hydrographic Surveying under Sail; or, Running Survey. IV. Hydrographic Surveying of Boats; or, Harbor Survey. V. Tides—Definition of Tidal Phenomena—Tidal Observations. VI. Measurement of Bases—Appropriate and Direct. VII. Measurement of the Angles of Triangles—Azimuths—Astronomical Bearings. VIII. Corrections to be Applied to the Observed Angles. IX. Levelling—Difference of Level. X. Computation of the Sides of the Triangulation—The Three-point Problem. XI. Determination of the Geodetic Latitudes, Longitudes, and Azimuths, of Points of a Triangulation. XII. Summary of Subjects treated of in preceding Chapters—Examples of Computation by various Formulæ. XIII. Projection of Charts and Plans. XIV. Astronomical Determination of Latitude and Longitude. XV. Magnetic Observations. XVI. Deep Sea Soundings. XVII. Tables for Ascertaining Distances at Sea, and a full Index.

List of Plates.

Plate I. Diagram Illustrative of the Triangulation. II. Specimen Page of Field Book. III. Running Survey of a Coast. IV. Example of a Running Survey from Belcher. V. Flying Survey of an Island. VI. Survey of a Shoal. VII. Boat Survey of a River. VIII. Three-Point Problem. IX. Triangulation.

Coffin's Navigation.

Fifth Edition.

12mo. Cloth. $3.50.

NAVIGATION AND NAUTICAL ASTRONOMY. Prepared for the use of the U. S. Naval Academy. By J. H. C. COFFIN, Prof. of Astronomy, Navigation and Surveying, with 52 wood-cut illustrations.

Clark's Navigation.

Illustrated. 8vo. Cloth. $3.00.

THEORETICAL NAVIGATION AND NAUTICAL ASTRONOMY. By LEWIS CLARK, Lieut.-Commander, U. S. Navy.

Simpson's Ordnance and Naval Gunnery.

Fifth Edition, Revised and Enlarged.

Illustrated with 185 Engravings. 8vo. Cloth. $5.00.

A TREATISE ON ORDNANCE AND NAVAL GUNNERY. Compiled and arranged as a Text-Book for the U. S. Naval Academy, by Commander EDWARD SIMPSON, U. S. N.

Young Seaman's Manual.

8vo. Half Roan. $3.00.

THE YOUNG SEAMAN'S MANUAL. Compiled from various authorities, and illustrated with numerous original and select Designs. For the use of the U. S. Training Ships and the Marine Schools.

Harwood's Naval Courts-Martial.

8vo. Law-sheep. $4.00.

LAW AND PRACTICE OF UNITED STATES NAVAL COURTS-MARTIAL. By A. A. HARWOOD, U. S. N. Adopted as a Text-Book at the U. S. Naval Academy.

Parker's Squadron Tactics.

Illustrated by 77 Plates. 8vo. Cloth. $5.00.

SQUADRON TACTICS UNDER STEAM. By FOXHALL A. PARKER, Captain U. S. Navy. Published by authority of the Navy Department.

Parker's Fleet Tactics.

18mo. Cloth. $2.50.

FLEET TACTICS UNDER STEAM. By FOXHALL A. PARKER, Captain U. S. Navy. Illustrated by 140 wood-cuts.

Parker's Naval Howitzer Ashore.

26 Plates. 8vo. Cloth. $4.00.

THE NAVAL HOWITZER ASHORE. By FOXHALL A. PARKER, Captain U. S. Navy. With plates. Approved by the Navy Department.

Parker's Naval Howitzer Afloat.

32 Plates. 8vo. Cloth. $4.00.

THE NAVAL HOWITZER AFLOAT. By FOXHALL A. PARKER, Captain U. S. Navy. With plates. Approved by the Navy Department.

Brandt's Gunnery Catechism.

Revised Edition. Illustrated.

18mo. Cloth. $1.50.

GUNNERY CATECHISM. As applied to the service of Naval Ordnance. Adapted to the latest Official Regulations, and approved by the Bureau of Ordnance, Navy Department. By J. D. BRANDT, formerly of the U. S. Navy.

"BUREAU OF ORDNANCE, NAVY DEPARTMENT,
WASHINGTON CITY, July 30, 1864.

"MR. J. D. BRANDT,—

"SIR,—Your 'CATECHISM OF GUNNERY, as applied to the service of Naval Ordnance,' having been submitted to the examination of ordnance officers, and favorably recommended by them, is approved by this Bureau.

I am, Sir, Your obedient servant,

"H. A. WISE, *Chief of Bureau.*"

Osbon's Hand-Book of the United States Navy.

12mo. Cloth. $1.50.

HAND-BOOK OF THE UNITED STATES NAVY. Being a compilation of all the principal events in the history of every vessel of the United States Navy from April, 1861, to May, 1864. Compiled and arranged by B. S. OSBON.

Totten's Naval Text-Book.

Second and Revised Edition.

12mo. Cloth. $3.00.

NAVAL TEXT-BOOK. Naval Text-Book and Dictionary, compiled for the use of Midshipmen of the U. S. Navy. By Commander B. J. TOTTEN, U. S. N.

"This work is prepared for the Midshipmen of the United States Navy. It is a complete manual of instructions as to the duties which pertain to their office, and appears to have been prepared with great care, avoiding errors and inaccuracies which had crept into a former edition of the work, and embracing valuable additional matter. It is a book which should be in the hands of every midshipman, and every officer of high rank in the navy would often find it a useful companion."—*Boston Journal.*

Roe's Naval Duties.

12mo. Cloth. $1.50.

NAVAL DUTIES AND DISCIPLINE: With the Policy and Principles of Naval Organization. By F. A. ROE, late Commander U. S. Navy.

"The author's design was undoubtedly to furnish young officers some general instruction drawn from long experience, to aid in the better discharge of their official duties, and, at the same time, to furnish other people with a book which is not technical, and yet thoroughly professional. It throws light upon the Navy—its organization, its achievements, its interior life. Everything is stated as tersely as possible, and this is one of the advantages of the book, considering that the experience and professional knowledge of twenty-five years' service, are crowded somewhere into its pages."—*Army and Navy Journal.*

SCIENTIFIC BOOKS

PUBLISHED BY

D. VAN NOSTRAND,

23 Murray Street and 27 Warren Street,

NEW YORK.

Any Book in this Catalogue, sent free by mail on receipt of price.

Weisbach's Mechanics.

Fourth Edition, Revised. 8vo. Cloth. $10.00.

A MANUAL OF THEORETICAL MECHANICS. By Julius Weisbach, Ph. D. Translated from the fourth augmented and improved German edition, with an introduction to the Calculus, by Eckley B. Coxe, A. M., Mining Engineer. 1100 pages and 902 wood-cut illustrations.

Francis' Lowell Hydraulics.

Third Edition. 4to. Cloth. $15.00.

LOWELL HYDRAULIC EXPERIMENTS—being a Selection from Experiments on Hydraulic Motors, on the Flow of Water over Weirs, and in open Canals of Uniform Rectangular Section, made at Lowell, Mass. By J. B. Francis, Civil Engineer. Third edition, revised and enlarged, including many New Experiments on Gauging Water in Open Canals, and on the Flow through Submerged Orifices and Diverging Tubes. With 23 copperplates, beautifully engraved, and about 100 new pages of text.

Kirkwood on Filtration.

4to. Cloth. $15.00.

REPORT ON THE FILTRATION OF RIVER WATERS, for the Supply of Cities, as practised in Europe, made to the Board of Water Commissioners of the City of St. Louis. By JAMES P. KIRKWOOD. Illustrated by 30 double-plate engravings.

Rogers' Geology of Pennsylvania.

3 Vols. 4to, with Portfolio of Maps. Cloth. $30.00.

THE GEOLOGY OF PENNSYLVANIA. A Government Survey. With a general view of the Geology of the United States, Essays on the Coal Formation and its Fossils, and a description of the Coal Fields of North America and Great Britain. By HENRY DARWIN ROGERS, Late State Geologist of Pennsylvania. Splendidly illustrated with Plates and Engravings in the Text

Merrill's Iron Truss Bridges.

Third Edition. 4to. Cloth. $5.00.

IRON TRUSS BRIDGES FOR RAILROADS. The Method of Calculating Strains in Trusses, with a careful comparison of the most prominent Trusses, in reference to economy in combination, etc., etc. By Bvt. Col. WILLIAM E. MERRILL, U.S.A., Corps of Engineers. Nine lithographed plates of illustrations.

Shreve on Bridges and Roofs.

8vo, 87 wood-cut illustrations. Cloth. $5.00.

A TREATISE ON THE STRENGTH OF BRIDGES AND ROOFS—comprising the determination of Algebraic formulas for Strains in Horizontal, Inclined or Rafter, Triangular, Bowstring, Lenticular and other Trusses, from fixed and moving loads, with practical applications and examples, for the use of Students and Engineers. By Samuel H. Shreve, A. M., Civil Engineer.

The Kansas City Bridge.

4to. Cloth. $6.00

WITH AN ACCOUNT OF THE REGIMEN OF THE MISSOURI RIVER,—and a description of the Methods used for Founding in that River. By O. Chanute, Chief Engineer, and George Morison, Assistant Engineer. Illustrated with five lithographic views and twelve plates of plans.

Clarke's Quincy Bridge.

4to. Cloth. $7.50.

DESCRIPTION OF THE IRON RAILWAY. Bridge across the Mississippi River at Quincy, Illinois. By Thomas Curtis Clarke, Chief Engineer. With twenty-one lithographed plans.

Whipple on Bridge Building.

New edition. 8vo. Illustrated. Cloth. $4.

An Elementary and Practical Treatise on Bridge Building. By S. Whipple, C. E.

Roebling's Bridges.

Imperial folio. Cloth. $25.00.

Long and Short Span Railway Bridges. By John A. Roebling, C. E. With large copperplate engravings of plans and views.

Dubois' Graphical Statics.

8vo. 60 Illustrations. Cloth. $2.00.

The New Method of Graphical Statics. By A. J. Dubois, C. E., Ph. D.

Greene's Bridge Trusses.

8vo. Illustrated. Cloth. $2.00.

Graphical Method for the Analysis of Bridge Trusses,—extended to Continuous Girders and Draw Spans. By Charles E. Greene, A. M., Professor of Civil Engineering, University of Michigan. Illustrated by three folding plates.

Bow on Bracing.

156 Illustrations on Stone. 8vo. Cloth. $1.50.

A Treatise on Bracing,—with its application to Bridges and other Structures of Wood or Iron. By Robert Henry Bow, C. E.

Stoney on Strains.

New and Revised Edition, with numerous illustrations. Royal 8vo, 664 pp. Cloth. $12.50.

The Theory of Strains in Girders—and Similar Structures, with Observations on the Application of Theory to Practice, and Tables of Strength and other Properties of Materials. By Bindon B. Stoney, B. A.

Henrici's Skeleton Structures.

8vo. Cloth. $1.50.

Skeleton Structures, especially in their Application to the building of Steel and Iron Bridges. By Olaus Henrici.

Burgh's Modern Marine Engineering.

One thick 4to vol. Cloth. $25.00. Half morocco. $30.00.

MODERN MARINE ENGINEERING, applied to Paddle and Screw Propulsion. Consisting of 36 Colored Plates, 259 Practical Wood-cut Illustrations, and 403 pages of Descriptive Matter, the whole being an exposition of the present practice of the following firms: Messrs. J. Penn & Sons; Messrs. Maudslay, Sons & Field ; Messrs. James Watt & Co. ; Messrs. J. & G. Rennie; Messrs. R. Napier & Sons; Messrs. J. & W. Dudgeon ; Messrs. Ravenhill & Hodgson; Messrs. Humphreys & Tenant; Mr. J. T. Spencer, and Messrs. Forrester & Co. By N. P. BURGH, Engineer.

King's Notes on Steam.

Nineteenth Edition. 8vo. $2.00.

LESSONS AND PRACTICAL NOTES ON STEAM,—the Steam Engine, Propellers, &c., &c., for Young Engineers. By the late W. R. KING, U. S. N. Revised by Chief-Engineer J. W. KING, U. S. Navy.

Link and Valve Motions, by W. S. Auchincloss.

Sixth Edition. 8vo. Cloth. $3.00.

APPLICATION OF THE SLIDE VALVE and Link Motion to Stationary, Portable, Locomotive and Marine Engines. By WILLIAM S. AUCHINCLOSS. Designed as a hand-book for Mechanical Engineers. Dimensions of the valve are found by means of a Printed Scale, and proportions of the link determined *without* the assistance of a model. With 37 wood-cuts and 21 lithographic plates, with copperplate engraving of the Travel Scale.

Bacon's Steam-Engine Indicator.

12mo. Cloth. $1.00 Mor. $1.50.

A TREATISE ON THE RICHARDS STEAM-ENGINE INDICATOR,—with directions for its use. By CHARLES T. PORTER. Revised, with notes and large additions as developed by American Practice, with an Appendix containing useful formulæ and rules for Engineers. By F. W. BACON, M. E., Illustrated. Second Edition.

Isherwood's Engineering Precedents.

Two Vols. in One. 8vo. Cloth. $2.50.

ENGINEERING PRECEDENTS FOR STEAM MACHINERY.—By B. F. ISHERWOOD, Chief Engineer, U. S. Navy. With illustrations.

Slide Valve by Eccentrics, by Prof. C. W. MacCord.

4to. Illustrated. Cloth, $3.00

A Practical Treatise on the Slide Valve by Eccentrics,—examining by methods the action of the Eccentric upon the Slide Valve, and explaining the practical processes of laying out the movements, adapting the valve for its various duties in the steam-engine. For the use of Engineers, Draughtsmen, Machinists, and Students of valve motions in general. By C. W. MacCord, A. M., Professor of Mechanical Drawing, Stevens' Institute of Technology, Hoboken, N. J.

Stillman's Steam-Engine Indicator.

12mo. Cloth. $1.00

The Steam-Engine Indicator,—and the Improved Manometer Steam and Vacuum Gauges; their utility and application. By Paul Stillman. New edition.

Porter's Steam-Engine Indicator.

Third Edition. Revised and Enlarged. 8vo. Illustrated. Cloth. $3.50.

A Treatise on the Richards Steam-Engine Indicator,—and the Development and Application of Force in the Steam-Engine. By Charles T. Porter.

McCulloch's Theory of Heat.

8vo. Cloth. 3.50.

A Treatise on the Mechanical Theory of Heat, and its Applications to the Steam-Engine. By Prof. R. S. McCulloch, of the Washington and Lee University, Lexington, Va.

Van Buren's Formulas.

8vo. Cloth. $2.00.

Investigations of Formulas,—for the Strength of the Iron parts of Steam Machinery. By J. D. Van Buren, Jr., C. E. Illustrated.

Stuart's Successful Engineer.

18mo. Boards. 50 cents.

How to Become a Successful Engineer. Being Hints to Youths intending to adopt the Profession. By Bernard Stuart, Engineer. Sixth Edition.

Stuart's Naval Dry Docks.

Twenty-four engravings on steel. Fourth edition. 4to. Cloth. $6.00.

THE NAVAL DRY DOCKS OF THE UNITED STATES. By CHARLES B. STUART, Engineer in Chief U. S. Navy.

Ward's Steam for the Million.

8vo. Cloth. $1.00.

STEAM FOR THE MILLION. A Popular Treatise on Steam and its Application to the Useful Arts, especially to Navigation. By J. H. WARD, Commander U. S. Navy.

Tunner on Roll-Turning.

1 vol. 8vo. and 1 vol. folio plates. $10.00.

A TREATISE ON ROLL-TURNING FOR THE MANUFACTURE OF IRON, by PETER TUNNER. Translated by JOHN B. PEARSE, of the Pennsylvania Steel Works. With numerous wood-cuts, 8vo., together with a folio atlas of 10 lithographed plates of Rolls, Measurements, &c.

Grüner on Steel.

8vo. Cloth. $3.50.

THE MANUFACTURE OF STEEL. By M. L. GRÜNER ; translated from the French. By LENOX SMITH, A.M., E.M. ; with an Appendix on the Bessemer Process in the United States, by the translator. Illustrated by lithographed drawings and wood-cuts.

Barba on the Use of Steel.

12mo. Illustrated. Cloth. $1.50.

THE USE OF STEEL IN CONSTRUCTION. Methods of Working, Applying, and Testing Plates and Bars. By J. BARBA, Chief Naval Constructor. Translated from the French, with a Preface, by A. L. HOLLEY, P.B.

Bell on Iron Smelting.

8vo. Cloth. $6.00.

CHEMICAL PHENOMENA OF IRON SMELTING. An experimental and practical examination of the circumstances which determine the capacity of the Blast Furnace, the Temperature of the Air, and the Proper Condition of the Materials to be operated upon. By I. LOWTHIAN BELL.

The Useful Metals and their Alloys; Scoffren, Truran, and others.

Fifth Edition. 8vo. Half calf. $3.75

THE USEFUL METALS AND THEIR ALLOYS, employed in the conversion of IRON, COPPER, TIN, ZINC, ANTIMONY, AND LEAD ORES, with their applications to the INDUSTRIAL ARTS. By JOHN SCOFFREN, WILLIAM TRURAN, WILLIAM CLAY, ROBERT OXLAND, WILLIAM FAIRBAIRN, W. C. AITKIN, and WILLIAM VOSE PICKETT.

Collins' Useful Alloys.

18mo. Flexible. 75 cents.

THE PRIVATE BOOK OF USEFUL ALLOYS and Memoranda for Goldsmiths, Jewellers, etc. By JAMES E. COLLINS.

Joynson's Metal Used in Construction.

12mo. Cloth. 75 cents.

THE METALS USED IN CONSTRUCTION: Iron, Steel, Bessemer Metal, etc., etc. By FRANCIS H. JOYNSON. Illustrated.

Dodd's Dictionary of Manufactures, etc.

12mo. Cloth. $1.50.

DICTIONARY OF MANUFACTURES, MINING, MACHINERY, AND THE INDUSTRIAL ARTS. By GEORGE DODD.

Von Cotta's Ore Deposits.

8vo. Cloth. $4.00.

TREATISE ON ORE DEPOSITS. By BERNHARD VON COTTA, Professor of Geology in the Royal School of Mines, Freidburg, Saxony. Translated from the second German edition, by FREDERICK PRIME, Jr., Mining Engineer, and revised by the author; with numerous illustrations.

Plattner's Blow-Pipe Analysis.

Third Edition. Revised. 568 pages. 8vo. Cloth. $5.00.

PLATTNER'S MANUAL OF QUALITATIVE AND QUANTITATIVE ANALYSIS WITH THE BLOW-PIPE. From the last German edition, Revised and enlarged. By Prof. TH. RICHTER, of the Royal Saxon Mining Academy. Translated by Professor H. B. CORNWALL; assisted by JOHN H. CASWELL. With eighty-seven wood-cuts and Lithographic Plate.

Plympton's Blow-Pipe Analysis.

12mo. Cloth. $1.50.

THE BLOW-PIPE: A Guide to its Use in the Determination of Salts and Minerals. Compiled from various sources, by GEORGE W. PLYMPTON, C.E., A.M., Professor of Physical Science in the Polytechnic Institute, Brooklyn, N.Y.

Pynchon's Chemical Physics.

New Edition. Revised and enlarged. Crown 8vo. Cloth. $3.00.

INTRODUCTION TO CHEMICAL PHYSICS; Designed for the Use of Academies, Colleges, and High Schools. Illustrated with numerous engravings, and containing copious experiments, with directions for preparing them. By THOMAS RUGGLES PYNCHON, M.A., President of Trinity College, Hartford.

Eliot and Storer's Qualitative Chemical Analysis.

New Edition. Revised. 12mo. Illustrated. Cloth. $1.50.

A COMPENDIOUS MANUAL OF QUALITATIVE CHEMICAL ANALYSIS. By CHARLES W. ELIOT and FRANK H. STORER. Revised, with the coöperation of the Authors, by WILLIAM RIPLEY NICHOLS, Professor of Chemistry in the Massachusetts Institute of Technology.

Rammelsberg's Chemical Analysis.

8vo. Cloth. $2.25.

GUIDE TO A COURSE OF QUANTITATIVE CHEMICAL ANALYSIS, ESPECIALLY OF MINERALS AND FURNACE PRODUCTS. Illustrated by Examples. By C. F. RAMMELSBERG. Translated by J. TOWLER, M.D.

Naquet's Legal Chemistry.

Illustrated. 12mo. Cloth. $2.00.

LEGAL CHEMISTRY. A Guide to the Detection of Poisons, Falsification of Writings, Adulteration of Alimentary and Pharmaceutical Substances; Analysis of Ashes, and Examination of Hair, Coins, Fire-arms, and Stains, as Applied to Chemical Jurisprudence. For the Use of Chemists, Physicians, Lawyers, Pharmacists, and Experts. Translated, with additions, including a List of Books and Memoirs on Toxicology, etc., from the French of A. NAQUET. By J. P. BATTERSHALL, Ph. D., with a Preface by C. F. CHANDLER, Ph. D., M.D., LL.D.

Prescott's Proximate Organic Analysis.

12mo. Cloth. $1.75.

OUTLINES OF PROXIMATE ORGANIC ANALYSIS, for the Identification, Separation, and Quantitative Determination of the more commonly occurring Organic Compounds. By ALBERT B. PRESCOTT, Professor of Organic and Applied Chemistry in the University of Michigan.

Prescott's Alcoholic Liquors.

12mo. Cloth. $1.50.

CHEMICAL EXAMINATION OF ALCOHOLIC LIQUORS.—A Manual of the Constituents of the Distilled Spirits and Fermented Liquors of Commerce, and their Qualitative and Quantitative Determinations. By ALBERT B. PRESCOTT, Professor of Organic and Applied Chemistry in the University of Michigan.

Pope's Modern Practice of the Electric Telegraph.

Ninth Edition. 8vo. Cloth. $2.00.

A Hand-book for Electricians and Operators. By FRANK L. POPE. Ninth edition. Revised and enlarged, and fully illustrated.

Sabine's History of the Telegraph.

Second Edition. 12mo. Cloth. $1.25.

HISTORY AND PROGRESS OF THE ELECTRIC TELEGRAPH, with Descriptions of some of the Apparatus. By ROBERT SABINE, C.E.

Haskins' Galvanometer.

Pocket form. Illustrated. Morocco tucks. $2.00.

THE GALVANOMETER, AND ITS USES;—A Manual for Electricians and Students. By C. H. HASKINS.

Myer's Manual of Signals.

New Edition. Enlarged. 12mo. 48 Plates, full Roan. $5.00.

MANUAL OF SIGNALS, for the Use of Signal Officers in the Field. By Brig.-Gen. ALBERT J. MYER, Chief Signal Officer of the Army.

Larrabee's Secret Letter and Telegraph

18mo. Cloth. $1.00.

CIPHER AND SECRET LETTER AND TELEGRAPHIC CODE, with Hogg's Improvements. By C. S LARRABEE.

Gillmore's Limes and Cements.

Fifth Edition. Revised and Enlarged. 8vo. Cloth. $4.00.

PRACTICAL TREATISE ON LIMES, HYDRAULIC CEMENTS, AND MORTARS. By Q. A. GILLMORE, Lt.-Col. U. S. Corps of Engineers. Brevet Major-General U. S. Army.

Gillmore's Coignet Beton.

Nine Plates, Views, etc. 8vo. Cloth. $2.50.

COIGNET BETON AND OTHER ARTIFICIAL STONE.—By Q. A. GILLMORE, Lt.-Col. U. S. Corps of Engineers, Brevet Major-General U.S. Army.

Gillmore on Roads.

Seventy Illustrations. 12mo. Cloth. $2.00.

A PRACTICAL TREATISE ON THE CONSTRUCTION OF ROADS, STREETS, AND PAVEMENTS. By Q. A. GILLMORE, Lt.-Col. U. S. Corps of Engineers, Brevet Major-General U. S. Army.

Gillmore's Building Stones.

8vo. Cloth. $1.50.

REPORT ON STRENGTH OF THE BUILDING STONES IN THE UNITED STATES, etc.

Holley's Railway Practice.

1 vol. folio. Cloth. $12.00.

AMERICAN AND EUROPEAN RAILWAY PRACTICE, in the Economical Generation of Steam, including the materials and construction of Coal-burning Boilers, Combustion, the Variable Blast, Vaporization, Circulation, Super-heating, Supplying and Heating Feed-water, &c., and the adaptation of Wood and Coke-burning Engines to Coal-burning; and in Permanent Way, including Road-bed, Sleepers, Rails, Joint Fastenings, Street Railways, etc., etc. By ALEXANDER L. HOLLEY, B.P. With 77 lithographed plates.

Useful Information for Railway Men.

Pocket form. Morocco, gilt. $2.00.

Compiled by W. G. HAMILTON, Engineer. Sixth Edition, Revised and Enlarged. 570 pages.

Stuart's Civil and Military Engineering of America.

8vo. Illustrated. Cloth. $5.00.

THE CIVIL AND MILITARY ENGINEERS OF AMERICA. By General CHARLES B. STUART, Author of "Naval Dry Docks of the United States," etc., etc. Embellished with nine finely-executed Portraits on steel of eminent Engineers, and illustrated by Engravings of some of the most important and original works constructed in America.

Ernst's Manual of Military Engineering.

193 Wood-cuts and 3 Lithographed Plates. 12mo. Cloth. $5.00.

A MANUAL OF PRACTICAL MILITARY ENGINEERING. Prepared for the use of the Cadets of the U. S. Military Academy, and for Engineer Troops. By Capt. O. H. ERNST, Corps of Engineers, Instructor in Practical Military Engineering, U. S. Military Academy.

Simms' Levelling.

12mo. Cloth. $2.50.

A TREATISE ON THE PRINCIPLES AND PRACTICE OF LEVELLING, showing its application to purposes of Railway Engineering and the Construction of Roads, etc. By FREDERICK W. SIMMS, C.E. From the fifth London edition, Revised and Corrected, with the addition of Mr. Law's Practical Examples for Setting-out Railway Curves. Illustrated with three lithographic plates and numerous wood-cuts.

Jeffers' Nautical Surveying.

Illustrated with 9 Copperplates and 31 Wood-cut Illustrations. 8vo. Cloth. $5.00.

NAUTICAL SURVEYING. By WILLIAM N. JEFFERS, Captain U. S. Navy.

Brunnow's Spherical Astronomy.

Illustrated. 8vo. Cloth. $6.50.

SPHERICAL ASTRONOMY. By F. BRUNNOW, Ph. Dr. Translated by the Author from the second German edition.

The Plane Table.

8vo. Cloth. $2.00.

ITS USES IN TOPOGRAPHICAL SURVEYING. From the papers of the U. S. Coast Survey.

Chauvenet's Lunar Distances.

8vo. Cloth. $2.00.

NEW METHOD OF CORRECTING LUNAR DISTANCES, and Improved Method of Finding the Error and Rate of a Chronometer, by equal altitudes. By WM. CHAUVENET, LL.D., Chancellor of Washington University of St. Louis.

Burt's Key to Solar Compass.

Second Edition. Pocket-book form. Tuck. $2.50.

KEY TO THE SOLAR COMPASS, and Surveyor's Companion; comprising all the Rules necessary for use in the Field; also Description of the Linear Surveys and Public Land System of the United States, Notes on the Barometer, Suggestions for an Outfit for a Survey of Four Months, etc. By W. A. BURT, U. S. Deputy Surveyor.

Howard's Earthwork Mensuration.

8vo. Illustrated. Cloth. $1.50.

EARTHWORK MENSURATION ON THE BASIS OF THE PRISMOIDAL FORMULÆ. Containing simple and labor-saving method of obtaining Prismoidal Contents directly from End Areas. Illustrated by Examples, and accompanied by Plain Rules for practical uses. By CONWAY R. HOWARD, Civil Engineer, Richmond, Va.

Morris' Easy Rules.

78 Illustrations. 8vo. Cloth. $1.50.

EASY RULES FOR THE MEASUREMENT OF EARTHWORKS, by means of the Prismoidal Formula. By ELWOOD MORRIS, Civil Engineer.

Clevenger's Surveying.

Illustrated Pocket Form. Morocco, gilt. $2.50.

A TREATISE ON THE METHOD OF GOVERNMENT SURVEYING, as prescribed by the U. S. Congress and Commissioner of the General Land Office. With complete Mathematical, Astronomical, and Practical Instructions for the use of the U. S. Surveyors in the Field, and Students who contemplate engaging in the business of Public Land Surveying. By S. V. CLEVENGER, U. S. Deputy Surveyor.

Hewson on Embankments.

8vo. Cloth. $2.00.

PRINCIPLES AND PRACTICE OF EMBANKING LANDS from River Floods, as applied to the Levees of the Mississippi. By WILLIAM HEWSON, Civil Engineer.

Minifie's Mechanical Drawing.

Ninth Edition. Royal 8vo. Cloth. $4.00.

A TEXT-BOOK OF GEOMETRICAL DRAWING, for the use of Mechanics and Schools. With illustrations for Drawing Plans, Sections, and Elevations of Buildings and Machinery; an Introduction to Isometrical Drawing, and an Essay on Linear Perspective and Shadows. With over 200 diagrams on steel. By WILLIAM MINIFIE, Architect. With an Appendix on the Theory and Application of Colors.

Minifie's Geometrical Drawing.

New Edition. Enlarged. 12mo. Cloth. $2.00.

GEOMETRICAL DRAWING. Abridged from the octavo edition, for the use of Schools. Illustrated with 48 steel plates.

Free Hand Drawing.

Profusely Illustrated. 18mo. Boards. 50 cents.

A GUIDE TO ORNAMENTAL, Figure, and Landscape Drawing. By an Art Student.

The Mechanic's Friend.

12mo. Cloth. 300 Illustrations. $1.50.

THE MECHANIC'S FRIEND. A Collection of Receipts and Practical Suggestions, relating to Aquaria—Bronzing—Cements—Drawing—Dyes—Electricity—Gilding—Glass-working—Glues—Horology—Lacquers—Locomotives—Magnetism—Metal-working—Modelling—Photography—Pyrotechny—Railways — Solders — Steam-Engine — Telegraphy—Taxidermy—Varnishes—Waterproofing—and Miscellaneous Tools, Instruments, Machines, and Processes connected with the Chemical and Mechanical Arts. By WILLIAM E. AXON, M.R.S.L.

Harrison's Mechanic's Tool-Book.

44 Illustrations. 12mo. Cloth. $1.50.

MECHANICS' TOOL BOOK, with Practical Rules and Suggestions, for the use of Machinists, Iron Workers, and others. By W. B. HARRISON.

Randall's Quartz Operator's Hand-Book.

12mo. Cloth. $2 00.

QUARTZ OPERATOR'S HAND-BOOK. By P. M. RANDALL. New edition, Revised and Enlarged. Fully illustrated.

Joynson on Machine Gearing.

8vo. Cloth. $2.00.

THE MECHANIC'S AND STUDENT'S GUIDE in the designing and Construction of General Machine Gearing, as Eccentrics, Screws, Toothed Wheels, etc., and the Drawing of Rectilineal and Curved Surfaces. Edited by FRANCIS H. JOYNSON. With 18 folded plates.

Silversmith's Hand-Book.

Fourth Edition. Illustrated. 12mo. Cloth. $3.00.

A PRACTICAL HAND-BOOK FOR MINERS, Metallurgists, and Assayers. By JULIUS SILVERSMITH. Illustrated.

Barnes' Submarine Warfare.

8vo. Cloth. $5.00.

SUBMARINE WARFARE, DEFENSIVE AND OFFENSIVE. Descriptions of the various forms of Torpedoes, Submarine Batteries and Torpedo Boats actually used in War. Methods of Ignition by Machinery, Contact Fuzes, and Electricity, and a full account of experiments made to determine the Explosive Force of Gunpowder under Water. Also a discussion of the Offensive Torpedo system, its effect upon Iron-clad Ship systems, and influence upon future Naval Wars. By Lieut.-Com. JOHN S. BARNES, U.S.N. With twenty lithographic plates and many wood-cuts.

Foster's Submarine Blasting.

4to. Cloth. $3.50.

SUBMARINE BLASTING, in Boston Harbor, Massachusetts—Removal of Tower and Corwin Rocks. By JOHN G. FOSTER, U. S. Eng. and Bvt. Major-General U. S. Army. With seven plates.

Mowbray's Tri-Nitro-Glycerine.

8vo. Cloth. Illustrated. $3.00.

TRI-NITRO-GLYCERINE, as applied in the Hoosac Tunnel, and to Submarine Blasting, Torpedoes, Quarrying, etc.

Williamson on the Barometer.

4to. Cloth. $15.00.

ON THE USE OF THE BAROMETER ON SURVEYS AND RECONNAISSANCES. Part I.—Meteorology in its Connection with Hypsometry. Part II.—Barometric Hypsometry. By R. S. WILLIAMSON, Bvt. Lt.-Col. U. S. A., Major Corps of Engineers. With illustrative tables and engravings.

Williamson's Meteorological Tables.

4to. Flexible Cloth. $2.50.

PRACTICAL TABLES IN METEOROLOGY AND HYPSOMETRY, in connection with the use of the Barometer. By Col. R. S. WILLIAMSON, U.S.A.

Butler's Projectiles and Rifled Cannon.

4to. 36 Plates. Cloth. $7.50.

PROJECTILES AND RIFLED CANNON. A Critical Discussion of the Principal Systems of Rifling and Projectiles, with Practical Suggestions for their Improvement. By Capt. JOHN S. BUTLER, Ordnance Corps, U. S. A.

Benét's Chronoscope.

Second Edition. Illustrated. 4to. Cloth. $3.00.

ELECTRO-BALLISTIC MACHINES, and the Schultz Chronoscope. By Lt.-Col. S. V. BENÉT, Chief of Ordnance U. S. A.

Michaelis' Chronograph

4to. Illustrated. Cloth. $3.00.

THE LE BOULENGÉ CHRONOGRAPH. With three lithographed folding plates of illustrations. By Bvt. Captain O. E. MICHAELIS, Ordnance Corps, U. S. A.

Nugent on Optics.

12mo. Cloth. $1.50.

TREATISE ON OPTICS; or, Light and Sight, theoretically and practically treated; with the application to Fine Art and Industrial Pursuits. By E. NUGENT. With 103 illustrations.

Peirce's Analytic Mechanics.

4to. Cloth. $10.00.

SYSTEM OF ANALYTIC MECHANICS. By BENJAMIN PEIRCE, Professor of Astronomy and Mathematics in Harvard University.

Craig's Decimal System.

Square 32mo. Limp. 50c.

WEIGHTS AND MEASURES. An Account of the Decimal System, with Tables of Conversion for Commercial and Scientific Uses. By B. F. CRAIG, M.D.

Alexander's Dictionary of Weights and Measures.

New Edition. 8vo. Cloth. $3.50.

UNIVERSAL DICTIONARY OF WEIGHTS AND MEASURES, Ancient and Modern, reduced to the standards of the United States of America. By J. H. ALEXANDER.

Elliot's European Light-Houses.

51 Engravings and 21 Wood-cuts. 8vo. Cloth. $5.00.

EUROPEAN LIGHT-HOUSE SYSTEMS. Being a Report of a Tour of Inspection made in 1873. By Major GEORGE H. ELLIOT, U. S. Engineers.

Sweet's Report on Coal.

With Maps. 8vo. Cloth. $3.00.

SPECIAL REPORT ON COAL. By S. H. SWEET.

Colburn's Gas Works of London.

12mo. Boards. 60 cents.

GAS WORKS OF LONDON. By ZERAH COLBURN.

Walker's Screw Propulsion.

8vo. Cloth. 75 cents.

NOTES ON SCREW PROPULSION, its Rise and History. By Capt. W. H WALKER, U. S. Navy.

Pook on Shipbuilding.

8vo. Cloth. Illustrated. $5.00.

METHOD OF PREPARING THE LINES AND DRAUGHTING VESSELS PROPELLED BY SAIL OR STEAM, including a Chapter on Laying-off on the Mould-loft Floor. By SAMUEL M. POOK, Naval Constructor.

Saeltzer's Acoustics.

12mo. Cloth. $2.00.

TREATISE ON ACOUSTICS in connection with Ventilation. By ALEXANDER SAELTZER.

Pickert and Metcalf's Art of Graining.

1 vol. 4to. Tinted Paper. Cloth. $10.00.

THE ART OF GRAINING, with description of Colors and their Application. By CHARLES PICKERT and ABRAHAM METCALF. With 42 tinted plates of the various woods used in interior finishing.

Wanklyn's Milk Analysis.

12mo. Cloth. $1.00.

MILK ANALYSIS. A Practical Treatise on the Examination of Milk, and its Derivatives, Cream, Butter, and Cheese. By J. ALFRED WANKLYN, M.R.C.S.

Rice & Johnson's Differential Functions.

Paper, 12mo. 50 cents.

ON A NEW METHOD OF OBTAINING THE DIFFERENTIALS OF FUNCTIONS, with especial reference to the Newtonian Conception of Rates or Velocities. By J. MINOT RICE, Prof. of Mathematics, U. S. Navy, and W. WOOLSEY JOHNSON, Prof. of Mathematics, St. John's College, Annapolis.

Coffin's Navigation.

Fifth Edition. 12mo. Cloth. $3.50.

NAVIGATION AND NAUTICAL ASTRONOMY. Prepared for the use of the U. S. Naval Academy. By J. H. C. COFFIN, Professor of Astronomy, Navigation and Surveying; with 52 wood-cut illustrations.

Clark's Theoretical Navigation,

8vo. Cloth. $3.00.

THEORETICAL NAVIGATION AND NAUTICAL ASTRONOMY. By LEWIS CLARK, Lieut.-Commander, U. S. Navy. Illustrated with 41 woodcuts, including the Vernier.

Toner's Dictionary of Elevations.

8vo. Paper, $3.00 Cloth, $3,75.

DICTIONARY OF ELEVATIONS AND CLIMATIC REGISTER OF THE UNITED STATES. Containing, in addition to Elevations, the Latitude, Mean Annual Temperature, and the total Annual Rain Fall of many Localities; with a brief introduction on the Orographic and Physical Peculiarities of North America. By J. M. TONER, M.D.

VAN NOSTRAND'S SCIENCE SERIES.

It is the intention of the Publisher of this Series to issue them at intervals of about a month. They will be put up in a uniform, neat, and attractive form, 18mo, fancy boards. The subjects will be of an eminently scientific character, and embrace as wide a range of topics as possible, all of the highest character.

Price, 50 Cents Each.

I. CHIMNEYS FOR FURNACES, FIRE-PLACES, AND STEAM BOILERS. By R. ARMSTRONG, C.E.

II. STEAM BOILER EXPLOSIONS. By ZERAH COLBURN.

III. PRACTICAL DESIGNING OF RETAINING WALLS. By ARTHUR JACOB, A.B. With Illustrations.

IV. PROPORTIONS OF PINS USED IN BRIDGES. By CHARLES E. BENDER, C.E. With Illustrations.

V. VENTILATION OF BUILDINGS. By W. F. BUTLER. With Illustrations.

VI. ON THE DESIGNING AND CONSTRUCTION OF STORAGE RESERVOIRS. By ARTHUR JACOB. With Illustrations.

VII. SURCHARGED AND DIFFERENT FORMS OF RETAINING WALLS. By JAMES S. TATE, C.E.

VIII. A TREATISE ON THE COMPOUND ENGINE. By JOHN TURNBULL. With Illustrations.

IX. FUEL. By C. WILLIAM SIEMENS, to which is appended the value of ARTIFICIAL FUELS AS COMPARED WITH COAL. By JOHN WORMALD, C.E.

X. COMPOUND ENGINES. Translated from the French of A. MALLET. Illustrated.

XI. THEORY OF ARCHES. By Prof. W. ALLAN, of the Washington and Lee College. Illustrated.

XII A PRACTICAL THEORY OF VOUSSOIR ARCHES. By WILLIAM CAIN, C.E. Illustrated.

XIII. A PRACTICAL TREATISE ON THE GASES MET WITH IN COAL MINES. By the late J. J. ATKINSON, Government Inspector of Mines for the County of Durham, England.

XIV. FRICTION OF AIR IN MINES. By J. J. ATKINSON, author of "A Practical Treatise on the Gases met with in Coal Mines."

XV. SKEW ARCHES. By Prof. E. W. HYDE, C.E. Illustrated with numerous engravings and three folded plates.

XVI. A GRAPHIC METHOD FOR SOLVING CERTAIN ALGEBRAIC EQUATIONS. By Prof. GEORGE L. VOSE. With Illustrations.

XVII. WATER AND WATER SUPPLY. By Prof. W. H. CORFIELD, M.A., of the University College, London.

XVIII. SEWERAGE AND SEWAGE UTILIZATION. By Prof. W. H. CORFIELD, M.A., of the University College, London.

XIX. STRENGTH OF BEAMS UNDER TRANSVERSE LOADS. By Prof. W. ALLAN, author of "Theory of Arches." With Illustrations

XX. BRIDGE AND TUNNEL CENTRES. By JOHN B. MCMASTERS, C.E. With Illustrations.

XXI. SAFETY VALVES. By RICHARD H. BUEL, C.E. With Illustrations.

XXII. HIGH MASONRY DAMS. By JOHN B. MCMASTERS, C.E. With Illustrations.

XXIII. THE FATIGUE OF METALS under Repeated Strains, with various Tables of Results of Experiments. From the German of Prof. LUDWIG SPANGENBERG. With a Preface by S. H. SHREVE, A.M. With Illustrations.

XXIV. A PRACTICAL TREATISE ON THE TEETH OF WHEELS, with the theory of the use of Robinson's Odontograph. By S. W. ROBINSON, Prof. of Mechanical Engineering, Illinois Industrial University.

XXV. THEORY AND CALCULATIONS OF CONTINUOUS BRIDGES. By MANSFIELD MERRIMAN, C.E. With Illustrations.

The University Series.

No. 1.—On the Physical Basis of Life. By Prof. T. H. Huxley, LL.D., F.R.S. With an introduction by a Professor in Yale College. 12mo, pp. 36. Paper cover, 25 cents.

No. 2.—The Corelation of Vital and Physical Forces. By Prof. George F. Barker, M.D., of Yale College. 36 pp. Paper covers, 25 cents.

No. 3.—As Regards Protoplasm, in relation to Prof. Huxley's Physical Basis of Life. By J. Hutchinson Stirling, F.R.C.S. 72 pp., 25 cents.

No. 4.—On the Hypothesis of Evolution, Physical and Metaphysical. By Prof. Edward D. Cope. 12mo, 72 pp. Paper covers, 25 cents.

No. 5.—Scientific Addresses:—1. On the Methods and Tendencies of Physical Investigation. 2. On Haze and Dust. 3. On the Scientific Use of the Imagination. By Prof. John Tyndall, F.R.S. 12mo, 74 pp. Paper covers, 25 cents. Flex. cloth, 50 cents.

No. 6.—Natural Selection as Applied to Man. By Alfred Russell Wallace. This pamphlet treats (1) of the Developement of Human Races under the Law of Selection; (2) the Limits of Natural Selection as applied to Man. 54 pp. 25 cents.

No. 7.—Spectrum Analysis. Three Lectures by Profs. Roscoe, Huggins and Lockyer. Finely Illustrated. 88 pp. Paper covers, 25 cents.

No. 8.—The Sun. A sketch of the present state of scientific opinion as regards this body. By Prof. C. A. Young, Ph. D. of Dartmouth College. 58 pp. Paper covers, 25 cents.

No. 9.—The Earth a Great Magnet. By A. M. Mayer, Ph. D., of Stevens' Institute. 72 pp. Paper covers, 25 cents. Flexible cloth, 50 cents.

No. 10.—Mysteries of the Voice and Ear. By Prof. O. N. Rood, Columbia College, New York. Beautifully Illustrated. 38 pp. Paper covers, 25 cents.

www.ingramcontent.com/pod-product-compliance
Lightning Source LLC
LaVergne TN
LVHW010227110826
845151LV00004B/1214

* 9 7 8 1 4 2 5 5 2 6 0 2 3 *